This latest coaching manual by Carl Wild is an excellent working tool for use in the practical side of player development. Each practice with adaptations is clearly structured and its contents provide the football coach with comprehensive information on the most ideal way to model coaching sessions in an objective, interesting, varied and practical fashion.

The simplicity of the practice design saves time on session planning and allows the modern coach to focus on creating an environment conducive to player development. This book gives valuable guidance and constitutes an ideal working tool for every ambitious youth coach.

–Jack Trainer, UEFA 'A' Licence Coach, FA Advanced Coaching Licence, Coach Educator, Former FA Tutor, Former Bolton Wanderers Coach Education Manager

---

Essential Practices for Player Development is a must-have book for all coaches aiming to offer their players a progressive pathway of development across a season. The concept of the book, which details 10 fundamental practices with multiple adaptations, offers coaches a wonderful opportunity and insight to scaffold player challenge through carefully considered practice designs and progressions. Reading this book allows coaches to get comfortable with a format of practice design they feel meets their players' needs, then have the opportunity to progress it when they feel the time is right.

This book not only supports coaches' own coaching progress, but offers a resource they can revisit throughout the season (season after season!). A must-read to offer insight, detail, and progression to your coaching practice and player development.

–Noel Dempsey, UEFA 'A' Licence Coach, Coach Educator, University Lecturer and Former FA Tutor and Coach Mentor

CARL WILD

ESSENTIAL PRACTICES FOR PLAYER DEVELOPMENT

THE ULTIMATE PROGRAM FOR AN ENTIRE SEASON OF TRAINING

Meyer & Meyer Sport

British Library of Cataloguing in Publication Data
A catalogue record for this book is available from the British Library

Essential Practices for Player Development
Maidenhead: Meyer & Meyer Sport (UK) Ltd., 2022
ISBN: 978-1-78255-243-7

© 2022 by Meyer & Meyer Sport (UK) Ltd.
Aachen, Auckland, Beirut, Cairo, Cape Town, Dubai, Hägendorf, Hong Kong, Indianapolis,
Maidenhead, Manila, New Delhi, Singapore, Sydney, Tehran, Vienna
Member of the World Sport Publishers' Association (WSPA), www.w-s-p-a.org

Printed by Print Consult GmbH, Munich, Germany
Printed in Slovakia

ISBN: 978-1-78255-243-7
E-Mail: info@m-m-sports.com
www.thesportspublisher.com

Contents

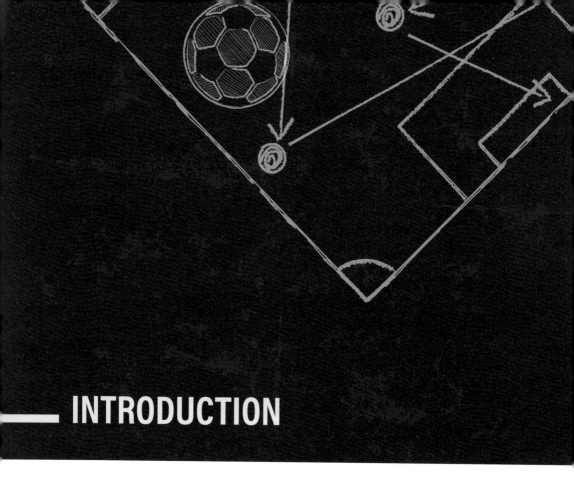

INTRODUCTION

As coaches, we often find ourselves scrambling around at the last minute to put together a session plan for training that is taking place later on that day. This could lead us to search for a session from the internet or in books, such as this one. And there is nothing wrong with doing this; as coaches, we are all magpies, we all look to take practice ideas from other coaches, and why not? If a practice design looks as if it would be something that the players would enjoy and would produce an effective environment for the players to learn and develop a particular aspect of the game, then, obviously, we would want to use it with our own players. Particularly if the practice was produced by someone we see as a more experienced or qualified coach; someone we see as a more 'advanced' coach. We do, of course, have to be mindful that just because a practice looks good and may well have been effective for other players, it may not be a suitable practice for the group of players we are working with. There is a possibility it could be either too challenging or not challenging enough or that it may not be relevant for the players' development at that particular moment in time.

A further challenge that we face as coaches when producing a session plan is that we habitually look to produce or find something we have never done before. We put ourselves under pressure to create something new, as we believe that is what everyone expects, including the players, parents and other coaches. There is a suggestion that players only learn and develop if they participate in a practice they have not done before; if they take part in a practice they have previously completed, they will not progress as a player or a team because they have already learned how to do whatever it is the practice teaches them. However, we do not see this approach within schools as teachers often use the same strategy or task, especially when teaching something new. If something has proven to be an effective strategy for learning to take place, why would you not use the same strategy again? Especially if the people taking part in this activity not only develop and improve but enjoy it as well?

Probably the most relevant examples to demonstrate that we do not need to create a new practice for every training session – out of fear that the players will complain that 'we have done this before' or they will find it too easy – are computer games and the game of soccer itself. The first thing we need to identify and recognise is what these two things have in common, and that is that they are both 'games', which would straight away indicate that they are both fun to do. In addition, the environments in which these games take place are constantly changing and evolving. Although the players return to the same activity time and time again, they are not actually repeating the same action over and over again or doing the exact same thing they did the last time they played it. They also find these experiences challenging, and they enjoy the competitive nature they both provide. Therefore, if we are able to replicate these key components in the practices we use in our training sessions, there is no reason why we cannot use the same practices on a regular basis.

Another reason we should consider moving away from producing different practices for every single training session is the need to maximise the time we have with the players. The amount of time we spend with the players is very limited, and one of the biggest complaints we receive as coaches is that we do not get to spend enough time working with them. Therefore, during a training session, we obviously want to provide the players with as much time as possible to practise, whatever the topic for the session is that night. What we would prefer not to have to do is spend time explaining to them how the practice works, what they can and cannot do and what the rules and scoring systems are. In addition, no matter how well we explain it to them, they still need to spend some time working it out for themselves. Plus, inevitably, some players will work it out quicker than others and, therefore, these players will get the opportunity to practise the topic of the session for longer while other players are still working out how the practice works. During which, as coaches, we may have to spend our time supporting those players who need help to work out the practice, instead of observing all the players to determine if the practice is actually working or not and, if it is, what specific support the players need going forward and, if it isn't, what changes need to be made to it. Although this may seem that it will not take up much time, even if we say 5 minutes to do this for one practice, then that is nearly 10 per cent of an hour's session. If we consider this is likely to occur more than once during a session – and sometimes it may take much longer when we have to make changes to the practice or the players just do not understand what it is they are meant to be doing – then it would be reasonable to say that over eight to 10 sessions, we would lose a complete hour or a full session.

One of the main arguments against repeatedly using the same practice or practices, is that the players will only keep learning the same things and there is no flexibility for them to learn something new. However, this is not necessarily true. First of all, it depends on what specific aspect of the practice the coach concentrates on. In most game-based practices, there is a range of different elements of soccer happening within them. The most obvious example of this is that there is a player or players in possession of the ball, and the opposition is therefore out of possession, and of course, when there is a change in who is in possession, then for a short period of time, transition has taken place. So, there is no reason why the practice cannot be used one week to work on an element of 'in possession' – such as passing or dribbling – and then used again the following week with the focus switched to out of possession, and provide support and guidance to the players when they do not have the ball. In addition to this, there are also ways in which the practice can be used for a range of topics for the same principles of the game, whether this is in possession, out of possession or one of the transitions (from out to in possession or from out to in possession).

If we consider a practice that focuses on in possession and specifically passing, the basic set-up of the practice could be that the players are split into two teams and within the area, there are a number of gates, and the teams simply win a point every time they successfully pass the ball through a gate. At the following training session, the same practice could be set up, and the players told they just need to do the same thing again, but this time, instead of passing the ball through a gate to win a point, a player has to drive through the gate with the ball. Therefore, the focus of the session has switched from passing or support play to driving with the ball, just by making one small change to the point-scoring system within the game.

This book will present to the reader 10 core practices and, with each one of these practices a further nine adaptions will be provided, giving a total of 100 practices that can be used throughout the season. Each of the practices put forward have a focus that is taken from the 13 key session topics that can be found in chapter 1, with each topic selected as a key area of development for all players. An outline of why these topics have been selected is provided and why, specifically, they play an important part in a player's development. The practices can be used completely on their own to form all of the content for every session throughout the season, or they can be used to create the basis of each session, which then allows further practices to be added. In whichever way they are used, they will provide the coach with a bank of practices that they can refer to throughout a season.

The core practices are designed to be really simple for the players to understand and to get them active almost immediately. Therefore, it is suggested that whichever adaption of the practice is used for the session, the original version of the practice is used first of all, as this is the practice the players recognise. Then after a small period of time (i.e. a couple of minutes), the necessary changes to the practice are made so that it becomes the selected adaption. Quite often these can be made while the players continue to play. Adding these while the players are active in the original version of the practice makes it much easier for the players to understand the adapted version – we are basically just adding a 'progression', as we would with any other practice. If we start with the adaption version from the start, some players may just see it as a completely different practice and, therefore, they are more likely to approach it with less confidence, as they will not be totally clear about what they have to do. Therefore, by using the original set-up first, before introducing the adaption, we are removing the possibility of the players not understanding what they have to do and allowing them to start playing almost immediately.

Another recommendation to get the full use out of these core practices, is to give each practice a name so they are easily recognised by the players. So, when the players arrive to training or after they have just had a drink break, they could simply be told to go and play the 'Connor' practice or the 'Sammy' practice, and the players will know which specific practice this is and can go straight over to the area and begin the practice immediately. To help with this, a number of different strategies could be used to decide the names of the different practices. First of all, the practices could be named after professional soccer players that the players recognise and aspire to be, or the actual players' names could be used. If this second option is chosen, it can also have an impact on their social development, in particular developing leadership, ownership and taking responsibility. Whichever player the practice is named after, they will be expected to lead the practice and get the players active within it as soon as possible. In addition to this, clear links can be made to the main characteristics of the practice and the player it is named after. For example, if the practice is based around individual possession or one versus one situations, it could be named after a particular player who is renowned for being really good in this area of the game. Again, this could be a professional player or a player from the group the coach is working with. Finally, a copy of each core practice can be sent to all the players so they can learn and memorise them. And if you have a group chat with the parents/guardians of the players, then before training a quick message could be sent confirming which of the core practices will be used, giving the players an opportunity to double-check the practice if they need to, just so they can reconfirm the rules of the practice and how you play it. Introducing all these strategies will help engage the players with the concept of using these core practices within the training environment. It should also ensure that the strategy of getting the players active quickly and concentrating on playing in the practice, rather than trying to work out what to do, is fully achieved.

These practices do not need to be restricted to just the training environment either, they can be used on a match day as a warm-up activity. Again, it allows the players to become active really quickly, and it also provides the coach with an opportunity to complete the many tasks they have to do, ahead of the game. A core practice used in the last training session before the game could be used, and the same adaption could then be introduced after a short amount of time, which will then allow the players to continue to practise whatever the topic of the session is. Or, the same core practice could be used each week to provide continuity for the players if this is what they need or prefer. This will provide structure to the time leading up to the match and allow the players to fully concentrate on the forthcoming game.

As coaches, we do not need to keep producing new practice designs – there is no need to provide something new for the players every week. The important thing we need to remember is that the practice we deliver is: fun, engaging, challenging, relevant to the game and provides lots of opportunities for the players to practise, whatever we have chosen to be the topic of the session. Therefore, if we can create a small number of practices that achieve all of this, why would we not use them? Especially when it allows us to maximise the time we have with the players and covers all the key areas for their development as a player as well.

The practice table at the end of this section provides an instant guide where practices for each of the 13 key session topics discussed in chapter 1 can be found throughout the book. This will then allow you to easily locate practices that have the same topic and can, therefore, be put together to produce a full session. Alternatively, if you do not want to use the practices to create a full session, then whatever is needed to complete the session can also be located easily and quickly. To help further, the 10 core practices have been categorised into four different types of practices, which, again, can be put together to form a complete session. These are: starter practices, small number practices, squad practices and games practices. Not all four practice types are needed in every session, but it would be recommended that a starter practice and a game practice are always used.

These can then be complemented with a small number practice and squad practice, or just one of them or two of the same type, e.g. two squad practices. So, for instance, if you are delivering a session on 'turning', a starter practice, a squad practice and a game practice, all with turning as the topic, can be easily found and selected to provide the players with a clear learning focus.

The starter practice, commonly known as an arrival activity or warm-up, should allow the players to go straight into the session as soon as they reach training. It is seen as an introduction to the session and helps to grab the players immediately so that they are both engaged and active from the start. Both Practice A and Practice B achieve this, as they can begin with just two players and then, as other players arrive to training, they can join in, as and when they arrive. Therefore, the initial set-up of the practices can be used while we are waiting for the full complement of players to arrive. Then, once all the players have arrived, the required changes can be made, so that it now provides them with an opportunity to develop around the topic of the session. Once they have then spent a short time within the starter practice, where they will develop an initial understanding of what they are going to learn in the session, they can then transfer over to the next practice.

The small number of players and squad practices are the 'main' practice or practices of the session, and they are where the players will get lots of opportunities to practise the topic of the session while receiving support from the coach. Within these practices, the players are given the opportunity to practise in an environment that replicates the game of soccer or a part of it. This then allows the players to transfer what they have learned during training into the actual game more easily, and when they come across a situation within a game, they can use their experiences from training to help solve the problem that they are facing. The small number practices (practices with a small number of players within them) provide the players with more opportunity to develop around the focus of the session compared with squad practices. Due to the smaller numbers within the practice, they will get more touches of the ball and further chances to practise the topic of the session. The small number of players within the practice also reduces the number of decisions that the players have to make, thus allowing them to concentrate mainly on improving the aspect of performance that is the session topic. These practices are definitely more suitable for younger and less experienced players rather than squad practices, however, this does not mean they cannot be used with any type of player. Not only do they allow the players to perfect their performance of a particular aspect of the game they can also make it easier for the coach to provide support. As there is less going on within the practice, it can be less challenging to identify what went wrong and where and when a player needs support. Therefore, it is likely the players will receive the support they need more often within a small number practice.

Squad practices will provide an environment closer to the game due to the increased numbers and, subsequently, the greater number of decisions that will need to be made because of these extra players. Therefore, these practices focus more on the players' ability to use the element of the performance at the correct time and to execute it correctly within an environment that will be more variable, compared with the smaller number practices. These squad practices provide the next step in the process before they move on to attempt to apply their new-found skills in an environment even closer to the game of soccer. And although we might reduce the number of opportunities that the players have to practise the session topic, they gain the chance to start developing more of the decision making that goes with it, such as when they should apply it.

The final practice type is a game practice, where the players have an opportunity to practise everything they have learned previously in the session in a game situation. The game needs to be a conditioned game where the condition or conditions are linked back to the focus of the session. However, certain aspects of it should remain in place: two teams (could still use support players), direction, a perimeter and goals. Then, as the session enters its final moments, the conditions can be removed from the game and it can move into free play where the players can experience just playing the game and, subconsciously, they will be applying everything they have learned previously in this and previous sessions. At this stage, it is important the players are just given the opportunity to enjoy actually playing the game, without any stoppages or interruptions.

Practice Table

PRACTICES	INITIAL PRACTICES		SMALL NUMBER PRACTICES			SQUAD PRACTICES			GAME PRACTICES	
	A	B	C	D	E	F	G	H	I	J
Individual Possession	44			131		183	205	237		284
One v One Attacking	50	70		125			215		260	
One v One Defending	*	*	103	127	163			231		288
Team Possession	56		***	***	***	181	203	235	266	278
Forward Passing		74	117	135	151	187		233	256	
Receiving to Play Forward		68	115			185	207			286
Receiving Under Pressure		66		129	153	189		239	264	
Finishing		78	111	137	157	191	211		258	290
Driving With the Ball	54	72	109	133	161	193	209			292
Turning	52	76			159			241	268	
Shielding	46		113			195	213		262	
Pass or Dribble?	58	80	119		155		217		270	280
Counter-Press	60	82		139		197	219	229		294
Recovery Runs	48		107		147			227	272	
Cover and Support	**	**	105	141	149			225		282

* Although there are not any specific starter practices that have a focus on one versus one defending, the practices for one versus one attacking can be used instead. The focus just switches to the player defending.

** As these practices are essentially one player working with a partner, it is not possible to incorporate the role of the second defender (cover and support). Therefore, any out of possession adaptions from Practice A or Practice B, can be used as a starter practice, when the session topic is cover and support.

*** The topic (team possession) does not lend itself to small number practices and therefore squad practices should be used instead.

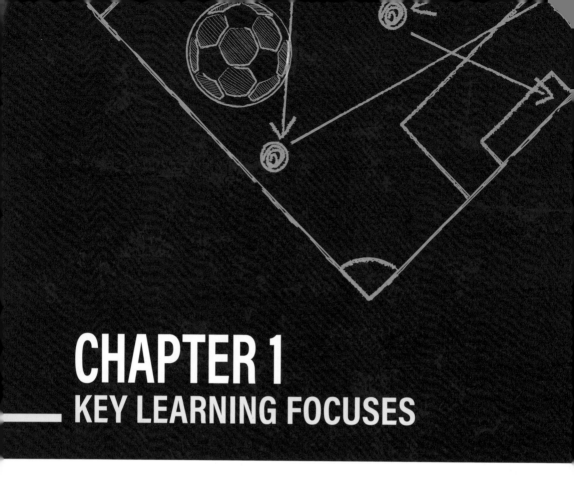

CHAPTER 1
KEY LEARNING FOCUSES

When it comes to choosing what we want the players to work on in training, we often look back on the game just played and identify areas within it that we believe, as a team, we did not do very well and need to improve on. However, this approach is extremely short term and only considers the players as they are now, when, ideally, we should be planning for how we want them to turn out at the end of the development process, in other words, when they are no longer 'youth' players. We can also be guilty of trying to cover aspects of the game that they do not currently require or do not need to learn yet. From the time most children start playing the game, at six or seven years of age, they will have approximately 10 years of training in which to learn all aspects of the game. Therefore, there is no need to rush through everything straight away; we have the opportunity to take our time and be patient with the process. This then allows us to concentrate on the key aspects of the game that are crucial to their development, and will provide the essential foundations to everything they will need as a player.

We need to remember that whatever we teach them in these developmental years, especially the very early years, will have the greatest impact on the player they will become. For instance, if we never encourage a player to take a risk and we always tell them to pass the ball or 'get rid' of it in dangerous situations, then this will be their experience of the game for as long as they play. We have a duty as a coach to provide the players with the opportunity and the support to help them reach their full potential as a player. Our role is not to try and win games but to develop them as players. Therefore, the rest of this chapter will put forward the main aspects of the game, which it is recommended are covered throughout the season, through a carefully planned curriculum. This guarantees that there is a pre-planned schedule to ensure there is a focus on all these key areas of the game throughout the season, rather than just choosing a topic each week, which we believe the players need to work on. Greater focus can be put on the areas the coach believes are more important, or where the players need to spend a bit more time developing. But the essential part is that it is all pre-planned at the start of the season to ensure that the players get time to practise and develop all key aspects of the game. There is also no reason why the schedule cannot be reviewed and, if needed, amended at predetermined times, during the season.

Each of these areas are identified in the rest of this chapter and an outline of their importance is also provided, as well as a number of key points that we need to take into consideration when we are delivering the topic. These key areas then appear regularly throughout the rest of the book, as every adaption of the 10 core practices has a focus around one of these areas. Therefore, whichever area of the performance is due to be the focus for training, a number of the practices can be selected to create the whole session, or just one or two can be used, leaving room for an additional practice.

Individual Possession

Arguably the most important skill we should help the players develop is the ability to retain possession of the ball on their own. In the modern game of soccer, players are often under instant and constant pressure from an opposition player or players. The solution to escaping this pressure is not always immediately available to the player on the ball, for instance, they may have to wait for a teammate to change their position on the pitch, before they become a viable option to pass the ball onto. Or it could be that they have to create their own solution by keeping hold of the ball until they have worked an opening where they can travel with the ball themselves or are now able to share it with a teammate, or possibly even shoot. What is important to understand is that quite often in a game, a player will need to select and then execute a number of the other skills that are key requirements to the game of soccer, such as passing or driving with the ball while under pressure. Therefore, they need to be comfortable and have confidence in their ability to be able to retain possession of the ball, which will then allow them to concentrate on getting the ball away from the pressure, whether this is individually or with the help of a teammate.

There are a number of key requirements that a player needs to be able to do, for them to be successful in maintaining possession of the ball. The main requirement is that they need to be able to manipulate the ball quickly and confidently. They need to make it difficult for the defender to predict which direction they are going to travel in and when they are going to do it. Feints and disguise should be used to shift the body weight of the defender to create opportunities to move the ball in an opposite direction. It also requires a number of physical attributes – strength is probably the most obvious one as it allow a player to hold off the defender, but other physical characteristics are just as important. Balance may not be seen as being vitally important to a player when they are attempting to keep hold of the ball, but due to the pressure and contact from the defender, it is quite easy for a player to lose their balance, which makes any task much more difficult. In addition to this, other key physical attributes needed include agility, coordination, power and speed. The other main requirement is awareness of where they are on the pitch, where exactly is the defender in relationship to them? Where other players are on the pitch and where there is space?

The most effective way in which the players will develop all of these different parts, which are needed to be able to keep possession of the ball, is by being put into a situation where they have no choice but to keep hold of the ball. Constantly changing the environment in which they have to keep the ball – for example, against different opponents, in a range of areas, shapes, sizes, etc. – and by giving them a variety of tasks to complete while keeping the ball, allows them to discover a wide range of strategies and solutions they can use when they are playing in a game. This will take a significant amount of time, and they will obviously make countless mistakes, and it is therefore important we provide constant support and encouragement, but the end result will be invaluable for the players.

One Versus One Attacking

Although a lot of emphasis is put on passing, as it is seen as the most effective way of progressing up the pitch, disrupting the opposition and penetrating defensive lines, if a player is able to do it on their own, it can often be a lot more effective. A player going past an opposition player with the ball will often result in one of two things occurring. First of all, the player may find themselves in the position to do what they wanted to do next. For example, if we picture a player in a wide area just outside of the penalty box, it is likely that their main aim is to provide a cross, but they are unable to do so because of a defender preventing them. Therefore, to be in a position to be able to cross the ball, they are going to have to get past the defender or at least create enough space to attempt the cross. The other likely outcome is that once they go past one defender they attract a second defender, which again makes it difficult to do what they may have wanted to do next. However, by forcing the second defender to leave their original position, it produces a gap in the defensive organisation of the opposition, which can be exploited in a number of ways.

Similar to developing a player's ability to retain the ball individually, supporting players to improve their one versus one skills is mainly about increasing their confidence and providing them with lots of different environments where they cannot keep using the same solution each time. When a player is at the beginning of their journey and developing their one versus one skills, a coach may often see that they are hesitant and revert to protecting the ball instead, which involves turning away from the defender and facing the opposite way to which they want to travel. The main reason for this is that they are concerned about losing possession of the ball and the possible consequences. Hopefully, we already recognise that players will make mistakes and that it is part of the learning process and, therefore, they know if they do lose the ball, it does not matter, and they are praised for trying. What they might not realise, however, is that the reason we encourage them so much is the risk of them losing the ball is more than balanced by the rewards it brings if they are successful. Therefore, we just need to replicate this 'reward' within the practices we place them in. For instance, we may award bonus points if a player manages to complete the task without passing the ball. The option to pass is therefore available, but the players know that if they do pass, they will not win as many points. As well as giving them praise and encouragement, we also need to provide the players with an incentive, so they have a reason to stay on the ball and attempt to go past defenders.

One Versus One Defending

When we look at the phase of the game when the team is out of possession, a lot of emphasis is placed on 'pressing' and winning the ball back quickly, either high up the pitch trying to prevent the opposition from playing out from the back or trying to win the ball back immediately after losing the ball (counter-pressing). And although these have become a common part of the modern game, it is important we do not forget the basic art of defending and, specifically, one versus one battles. The benefits of a player being able to go past a defender with the ball have just been highlighted and, therefore, we also need to support the players in preventing this from happening. They need to have the required knowledge of what they need to do, to stop the player on the ball from going past them.

The important element of a practice when the focus is on one versus one defending, is that the defending player needs to have something to defend. The main principle of defending within soccer is to protect the goal, and to help achieve this players need to protect spaces on the pitch, such as the space near to the goal or the space 'in behind', in other words, we do not want the opposition players and the ball to get past the last line of defence. The other key element we need to consider about the game of soccer and how it relates to the principles of defending is 'direction'. A key component of soccer is the need to progress forwards and get close to the opposition goal, so as well as giving the defenders something to protect, we also need to ensure that the practice is directional so the defenders are not just protecting something, they are also trying to force the attacking player away from it. Therefore, though there are numerous benefits to a 'rondo' practice, they are probably not that suitable for a session that has a focus on defending. The attacking players are basically just retaining possession without any purpose, so it is difficult for the defending player to force the ball away from danger and into a safer part of the area because there is no safe part to the area as there is no direction to the practice.

Another key consideration that we sometimes overlook when planning a session around defending is what happens next? What happens if the defender wins the ball? Quite often, once the defender wins the ball, the practice just stops, as they have completed their task. There is definitely an argument here that because the focus is on defending, there is no need to work on what they do when they have the ball. But we just need to remember that we will not actually provide any support when they reach this part of the practice, we are just motivating them to win the ball and then rewarding them as well. It is also about getting them into the right habits. Once they have won the ball in a game, the last thing we want them to do is give possession straight back to the opposition, whether this is through putting the ball out of play or by not taking any care where they play the ball, in other words, they just clear the ball. Therefore, providing the players with a simple task after they have won the ball, such as passing the ball into a small goal or driving with the ball under control out of the area, will not only give them an incentive to win the ball but also plants a seed to remind the players that even though they may have won the ball, there is still work to be done.

Team Possession

Retaining possession of the ball as a team or passing and receiving is obviously a key element of the game. As touched upon earlier in the chapter, it can be an effective way of disrupting the opposition, and it can also be a good strategy of preventing the other team from scoring – if they do not have the ball then they cannot score. A key element of this is knowing when a player should pass the ball, but this will be looked at later on in the chapter within the 'Pass or Dribble?' section. Therefore, this part of the chapter concentrates on the actual pass and receiving of the ball.

We will often tell players to pass the ball or inform them that they should have passed the ball, but what we rarely do is support them with the actual details around the pass, specifically the weight of the pass and the exact area to pass to. If we look at the area of pass to start with, the first decision the player passing the ball has to make is whether to pass the ball to the player or into space. If the ball is being passed to the player, the decision then has to be made about where they want to receive the ball? Consideration needs to be given to the positioning of the player marking the teammate that the player is passing to. If the defender is to the right of the player receiving the ball, then they will probably want to receive it on their left foot as it makes it easier to protect it from the defender. Or if the teammate is in space, do they want to receive it on their back foot so that they can receive to play forward? Or do they want the ball to played into space? If the player is making a run, they will want the ball played in front of them so that they can move onto the ball, and the player passing the ball will then need to predict where the player will be by the time the pass arrives, and also exactly how far in front of them they want/need the ball to be? It might be that the player is not on the move, but the correct decision is still to play the ball into the space ahead of the player. For instance, a central defender passing to the other central defender may play the pass in front of their teammate. This will not only encourage them to play forward as it forces them to move forward onto the ball, but it will also encourage them to do it quicker. There are numerous factors that players have to take into consideration when deciding exactly where to play the pass, which will take a long time to develop and will only do so as they start to understand the game more and the impact that all these small details can have on what happens next after the pass has been made.

With regard to the weight of the pass, it is very similar to the area of pass, in that there are a number of factors that the player passing the ball has to take into consideration. The most obvious aspect of the pass that they need to identify is the distance that the ball has to travel and also the proximity of opposition players to the path that the ball has to travel. The ball needs to be able to reach the intended target, while also ensuring it is not over hit, making it difficult for the player receiving the ball to control it. The player making the pass also needs to try and predict what the player receiving the ball wants to do next, so that the amount of weight that they put on the pass, is the correct amount to make the execution of the next action as simple as it can possibly be. Finally, the player passing the ball needs to understand that the weight of the pass can also have a significant impact on the tempo of the game. Just because the ball they are playing is a relatively short pass with no real risk from opposition players does not mean that it should not be played with a good amount of weight. Putting pace on a pass can allow a team to play with a high tempo and with purpose, which can make it more challenging to defend against as there is less time to adjust and react to the ball changing position on the pitch.

If we switch our attention to the player now receiving the ball, the first thing they have to do is to make sure they are an actual option for the player currently in possession of the ball. There needs to be a clear pathway between them and their teammate so that the ball can travel safely to them. If there is not a clear pathway, as there is a player in the way – this could be a teammate or an opposition player – then can they adjust their position so that they can now be seen by the player with the ball. They will need to continuously reassess their position to ensure they continue to be available to their teammate as other players from both teams will be moving and the player in possession could be shifting the ball while under pressure from a defender. Obviously, it is not feasible for all players to be an option for their teammate, so here we can challenge the players to either make it easier for a teammate who is looking to receive the ball, for example by making a movement that will create space and time by dragging defenders away from them, or we might ask them to predict where the pass is likely to go if it cannot go to them and then can they think about getting into a position so that they are an immediate option for that player.

If a player is a possible option for their teammate on the ball, they need to consider their exact position to ensure that they are a suitable choice. This often depends on the distance and angle between the two players. Although sometimes the players need to be separated by just a short distance, for example when players are looking to combine quickly and in tight areas, such as in and around the penalty box, often a greater distance is needed as it makes it more difficult to defend against. We therefore need to ensure that the environment allows the players to practise being a suitable distance apart. Sometimes we prevent the players from being able to create enough distance between themselves and the player on the ball because of the area size that we set up. We often want a small, tight area because we want the practice to be played at a quick tempo. But then when we move into a game, we expect the players to make the pitch big when their team has possession of the ball. So, it is important that we produce an area size that represents the distances that they will pass the ball over during a game. Similarly, if the player wanting the ball creates an angle between themselves and their teammate on the ball, it is harder for the opposition players to defend against. Passes that are flat or straight are easier to intercept and are also easier for the defender pressing the ball to cut off the passing line as well. Producing an angle also usually means the player receiving the ball is in an advanced position and can see more of the pitch, due to the body shape that they will adopt (this will be looked at further, later on in this chapter). Quite often, we will ask players to find space or to move when we want them to help support the player on the ball, but we rarely look at the specifics in terms of where exactly we want them to be.

The final aspect of receiving the ball is to help the players recognise the importance of knowing what they are going to do with it when they actually receive it. Young players usually get so fixated on just wanting the ball that they do not think about what they are going to do when they have it, and understandably so, they just want to have the ball – it is why they play the game. But if we can get them to think ahead and decide earlier what they are going to do next, it makes it much easier for them to retain the ball, and it will also allow them to play much quicker. To make the decision on what they are going to do once they have received the pass, they will first need to be aware of what is around them and also what options they have available – this could be to drive into space or to pass it to a teammate. Making a decision, or at least having an idea of what they would like to do, before they have even got the ball will allow them to take a first touch that enables them to execute their next action more easily. If they want to drive into space, then their first touch needs to be out of their feet and towards the space that they have identified. This, in turn, also enables them to play quicker; if they do not make a decision to drive into the space before they get the ball, then they will just control the ball first, then identify the space and, finally, take a second touch into the space, all of which takes time. Because of this, not only does it slow down their play but it also gives the opposition players more time to close them down and attempt to win the ball. The main way in which we can support players to do this is through the questions that we ask the players during individual interventions, which will be discussed in greater detail in chapter 7. By asking players the right questions at the right time, we can start to guide them to make decisions, either before the pass has been made or as the ball is travelling.

Forward Passing

Although we may have just discussed passing in the previous section, there is a significant difference between passing the ball and playing a forward pass. As already touched on, because soccer is an invasion game there is a requirement for teams to progress forwards into the opposition's territory. For this reason, the team out of possession will try to prevent their opponents from advancing towards their goal, so, inevitably it is more difficult to pass the ball forwards compared with any other direction. Unsurprisingly, players will quite often look to pass the ball sideways or backwards, as this a safer option when compared with playing the ball forwards. This becomes more apparent as the players progress through the different formats of the game and the number of players on each team increases. When this happens, there are more opposition players trying to prevent the ball from being played forwards, and not just because there are more players on the pitch but because players are starting to understand the game better and they have an advanced understanding of their positional responsibilities and the teams are more organised. This reinforces the need for players to practise this particular element of the game from an early stage so that they have lots of opportunities to develop an essential part of the game.

When we play the ball forward, it often involves splitting two opposition players, which means the pass will have penetrated one of their units. By doing this, there will be fewer opposition players between the player on the ball and the goal and, if it is the last unit, in other words, their defensive unit, it could mean that they have no players at all in a position to get between the ball and the goal. Therefore, forward passing not only allows a team to progress up the pitch but it can also be used to create goal-scoring opportunities. As with some of the other aspects of soccer that we have already looked at, forward passing is a lot about being confident and brave on the ball. The pass also needs to be played with 'purpose' because it is likely that it will need to travel through small gaps, which can disappear suddenly and, therefore, the pass needs to be early and quick.

With any type of pass there needs to be a player at the end of it to receive the ball. Therefore, if we want a player to play a forward pass, they need to have options ahead of the ball. This again is an area of the game that we have to encourage the players to develop. In the same way that a player making the pass feels more confident passing the ball backwards or sideways, a player receiving the ball may often prefer to stay behind the player on the ball because it is the safer option. They will likely have more time and space to receive the ball if they stay behind the ball rather than getting ahead of it. Therefore, usually, the only options that the player on the ball has to play the forward pass are to the players that were already ahead of them when they received the ball. These players are often more difficult to find as it is easier for the opposition to see them and defend against them. These players will need to find a way to receive the ball more securely or they need to make a run from behind the ball to get ahead of it. We need players to recognise the body shape of the player on the ball and identify that they want to pass forward and, in order to do this, they need to have options ahead of them.

Receiving to Play Forward

The importance of being able to receive the ball to play forward is now widely recognised across the game. Receiving the ball on the 'half turn' or on the 'back foot' gives the player an opportunity to see more of the pitch as the ball is travelling to them, and it also allows them to play forward much quicker. Receiving the ball to play forward allows the individual player and the whole team to be more aggressive and purposeful in their play. When receiving on the back foot, the first touch can either provide the player with an opportunity to pass forward or to travel forward with the ball, without any delay, therefore ensuring the momentum of an attack is not slowed down or even lost. Receiving the ball 'square-on' or directly facing the player passing the ball takes a number of touches and also a certain amount of time to face forward, which delays the attack.

It is important that we recognise what is needed to produce the correct environment for players to practise this particular skill. If we look at the most common picture of a player receiving to play forward in a game, it is probably a midfielder collecting a pass from a defender. Therefore, in this picture, the player we are concentrating on (the midfielder) is receiving a pass that has been played forward by the defender, and they then receive it to play forward themselves, making them the middle link in the chain of the ball being played in a forward direction. So, it is important that if we want to replicate this within the training environment, we ensure the player receiving the ball receives it from a player who is passing forwards. Then, once they have received the ball, their next task needs to be 'ahead' of them. This does not necessarily have to be a pass; it could be to dribble or to drive with the ball. The essential part is that they need to be encouraged or motivated to play forward. The purpose of a player receiving the ball to play forward is so that they do play forward and that they do it quickly. After taking a touch forward, there is no point if they then turn back and lose the momentum that they had just created for themselves.

Receiving Under Pressure

As much as we would like players to receive the ball in space and be able to receive a pass on the back foot so that they can play forward, it is not always possible to do so, as an opposition player maybe preventing them. It can also be advantageous if they actually receive the ball under pressure from one or more opposition players if the player on the ball is attracting the attention of at least one player from the other team; it means that there is probably more space for their teammates. We are often fixated on players receiving the ball in space and telling players not to pass to a teammate unless they are in space as we are concerned that a player receiving the ball while under pressure is likely to lose the ball. This, of course, probably will happen if we have not provided the players with an opportunity to practise receiving while under pressure. Like everything else, the players will make mistakes while they are learning, and they most definitely will lose the ball on countless occasions, but we just need to remember that we are focusing on the end product: the player they become.

When a player receives the ball while under pressure, their key focus is to keep the ball away from danger. This might be achieved by the player immediately sharing the ball with a teammate. This is often seen in the shape of a 'bounce pass' where the player recognises they cannot receive to play forward due to the close attentions of a defender and, therefore, they play a one-touch pass to another player, who may be in a position to go forward with the ball. To achieve this, the player needs to be aware of the options they have around them, which goes back to knowing what you are going to do with the ball before you receive it. The slight difference here is that they need to do it while under pressure from a defender who is either attempting to win the ball or making it much harder to complete the selected technique, which in this scenario is the pass. If the player decides not to pass it on but instead keep the ball themselves, then once they have received the pass, it moves from receiving under pressure to individual possession. Here, there is a requirement for the player to be able to control the ball in a way that will protect it from the defender and, at the same time, keep it close to themselves so that it can be manipulated quickly and easily if required.

A coach will often tell the players to be brave on the ball, but it takes bravery from the coach to actually allow the players to fully commit to this. We need to let them take risks and recognise that they will make mistakes and lose the ball. There will be lots of times when they do lose the ball and they had the opportunity to play safe but chose instead to be brave and take responsibility of the situation and we must continue to support them and praise them in these situations, for being courageous on the ball. And there is no greater example of this than demanding the ball from a teammate, even though they are being closely marked by a defender. So instead of encouraging players to find space before they want the ball or telling players to only pass to a teammate if they are in space, can we support them to become confident enough to receive the ball at any time, no matter whether they are in space or not.

Finishing

The overall objective of soccer is to score more goals than the opposition. Therefore, unsurprisingly, being able to score or finish is an essential part of the game. But it is also possibly the element that has the most variants. There are numerous different ways in which a player can score, so it can be quite a difficult topic to coach. A common practice that we often see is the coach or a server, who is positioned quite central to the goal, setting a ball back for a player to run onto and attempt to finish, quite often with a first time shot. Although this will definitely help the players practice finishing with power and accuracy, how often do players actually shoot at goal in this way in a game of soccer? How many times do they shoot from a position straight in front of the goal from a ball that has been played back to them? During a game of soccer, it is highly unlikely that any one shot is repeated. Therefore, repeating the exact same shot over and over again is probably not the most effective way of preparing the players for what they will need to do during a game.

A finishing practice should provide the players with lots of opportunities to have a shot at goal in lots of different ways. The first thing we need to look to avoid is queueing, which is something that we should avoid in any practice. To increase the number of opportunities that they have, we can either reduce the number of players within the practice by having several mirrored practices or several different practices that the players can rotate around. The difficulty with this can be the number of goals that are available during the practice, but this should not deter us from still proceeding with several different areas. It is much better to provide the players with lots of opportunities to have a shot at a makeshift goal than use a 'normal' goal but make them wait their turn. Another way that will increase the number of shots players have at goal is to make it easy to actually have the shot. So, for example, making the practice nondirectional with lots of goals available to shoot at will allow this to happen. Or we can set out an area that basically allows a shot to be taken from anywhere within it, such as an area that is small in dimension.

The other key element is that it provides the players with an opportunity to finish in a number of different ways. This does not mean that we have to set up several different scenarios from which they have to shoot, it just means that the environment within the practice is variable or random; it is not a constant practice where the players continue to repeat the same action. By being involved in a random or variable practice, the players are unlikely to repeat the exact same action, so although the task they have to complete may always be the same, how they complete it will always be different. Therefore, the next shot that they have, will always be different to any of their previous attempts on goal, whether it is the distance they shoot from, the angle of the shot, the positioning of the goalkeeper or all of these, or one of many other possible variants. By providing this type of environment we are allowing the players to practise a range of finishing, that will prepare them better for the situations they will themselves in during a game.

Driving With the Ball

Driving with the ball is possibly one of the most underrated skills that a player can possess and also maybe the one that we spend the least amount of time working on during training. Yet it can change the position of where the game is being played in an instant. It can take you away from your own goal and close to the opposition's in just a small amount of time. It can be difficult to defend against as it will often cause the defender to retreat towards their own goal, and it can also disrupt an organised defence, creating gaps and providing space for teammates. A player running at pace with the ball is an effective way to advance a team up the pitch and also to create goal-scoring opportunities. However, the ability to travel with the ball at speed, keep it under control and adjust the line in which you are travelling through a slight touch on either side of the ball is a difficult skill to master, and players need to be given opportunities and time to practise it.

When we think about a player driving with the ball, we usually think of them running in a straight line and travelling up the pitch. And when we do set up a practice with a focus of driving with the ball, it typically represents this picture of a player travelling in a straight line with space in front of them. This, undoubtedly, is a great starting point and provides players with an opportunity to practise key components of this particular element of the game. However, there are also other areas of this skill that are often missed within a practice design. On receiving the ball, we usually ask the player to take a big touch out of their feet, to allow them to accelerate into the space ahead of them and then get up to full speed, which is absolutely correct when there is space directly in front of them. However, quite often, the space is not immediately there and, therefore, it needs to be found with the player's first touch or touches before the second or third touch can be used to exploit the space in front of them. This often involves taking the touch with one foot and using the other foot to move into the space or using the same foot but different parts, for example, taking a touch to the side with the outside of the foot and then redirecting the ball forwards with the inside of the foot. Therefore, we need to try and introduce this part of driving with the ball into some of the practices that we use.

The other part we do not always cater for when we look at driving with the ball, is the direction or path that a player takes when they do this within a game. In a practice, we will often ask a player to get from point A to point B as quickly as they can, and the pathway that they have to follow to achieve this is usually a straight line. First of all, within a game, when they are travelling with the ball they are usually closed down by opposition players from all directions and in different ways. So, one scenario could be that they are closed down by a defender approaching them from their right-hand side.

In this instance, they might shift the ball to the left to give themselves more time and/ or to protect the ball. Or, if there is an opportunity to do so, they will shift the ball to the right with the intention of getting across the defender so that they are now in front of them. Another scenario could be a defender directly ahead of them in their path who is stationary and holding their position. So here the attacking player may just need to move the ball 'off line' slightly to enable them to glide past the defender at speed. The other consideration we need to make when we think about driving with the ball is that it does not always have to involve the player travelling up the pitch to get them closer to the goal; it can be just as effective for a player to do it across the pitch. Travelling with the ball at speed across the pitch will drag opposition players with them, who will be looking to close the gaps centrally and also in the direction that the player is heading. This then provides an opportunity to exploit space in the part of the pitch that the player started their run from, which can be achieved by a lay off to a teammate who then plays an early pass into that area, allowing another player to take advantage of the space that has been created by the initial run.

Again, this highlights the need to provide the players with a range of different environments and experiences to practise different aspects of a particular technique or skill. It also offers another example of the need to understand how the technique or skill is actually used within the game so that we can match it as close as we can within our practices so that the players are given relevant and realistic situations that they will come across again when they are playing the actual game.

Turning

Changing direction or turning with the ball is used in numerous ways by a player during a game to achieve a range of different outcomes. For instance, they might be travelling with the ball and believe a defender running alongside them is getting closer to being in a position to win the ball, and the player will therefore change direction to protect the ball and to provide them with a bit more time. Or it could be used as part of a predetermined plan to attack a player's piece of space on the pitch; they will move the opposition player away from the space by travelling in a different direction before turning back towards it, allowing the player to get ahead of the defender. Therefore, it is an extremely useful skill for a player to learn as it will enable them to create time and space for themselves. However, it is only effective if it is executed correctly and to a high standard; otherwise the reason for doing it will not be achieved.

Whatever the reason a player chooses to complete a turn and whichever type of turn they select, certain components are needed for all of them. First of all, the player needs to ensure the defender is going in an opposite direction to where they want to go, this does not mean that they have to actually be moving, it is just a matter of shifting the defender's body weight one way. This can be achieved by actually moving the ball in one direction, or by feinting to do so, before moving in an opposite direction. Doing this gives the player on the ball an opportunity to move further away from the defender, even if just for a split second, and it also allows them to move into an area that may not have been available previously as it was being blocked by the defender. However, shifting the defender's body weight will not be enough – if the player does not demonstrate a high level of agility within the turn, they will lose their advantage before they have had time to use it. Therefore, the turn needs to be quick and sharp to ensure that the advantage they are looking to create over the defending player is as big as it can be. In addition to this, the number of touches that the player takes to complete the turn will also affect how quickly the turn is executed; the fewer number of touches taken by the player, the quicker the turn.

The final element needed for a successful turn is that whatever the player does next must be done with speed. If they are turning to create an opportunity to cross the ball, then the cross must be made straight away before the defender recovers and closes the space again. Or if the attacking player completes a turn so that they can drive into a space, once the turn has been executed, they must explode into the space to ensure that they get away from the defender before they have time to recover. Therefore, the areas in which a turning-focused practice takes place is usually quite small and tight. For a player to be successful, they must achieve all these components when they are completing the turn.

Shielding

Although it is similar to receiving the ball while under pressure, shielding is a unique skill that a player should learn and develop. The main difference is that when shielding the ball, the player receiving the ball will have decided to hold their ground and receive the ball where they are situated. In doing so, they will need to prevent the defender from initially getting in front of them and intercepting the ball, and then, once they have received it, they will need to continue to fend off the defender before they carry out their next action. By adopting the correct stance, and through strength and determination, a player should be able to shield the ball successfully from a defender. However, there is one further factor that needs to be perfected to ensure that the ball is shielded successfully, and this is possibly the hardest element of the technique: the first touch to control the ball. Due to the player's stance, the ball needs to be controlled with the outside part of the foot, which players will find challenging because they are more used to using the inside of their foot.

In the context of the game, the most suitable scenario that can be replicated within a practice would probably be a pass into a forward player who will usually be closely marked by a central defender. Here, the forward player will usually look to shield or 'hold up' the ball, while waiting for support from their teammates. In this situation, the forward player is only likely to remain in possession of the ball for a short period of time until they look to lay it off to a supporting player. Once they have achieved this, their next action is to try and get back on the ball, but this time facing the goal instead of having their back to it. Coaches will often refer to this action as 'spinning off'. By doing so, the forward player will usually be able to lose the attention of the defender, either because the defender follows the pass and closes down the player receiving the ball, or due to the speed of the movement, they can get ahead of the defender and into a position to receive the ball back – either in front of them as they are making a forward run or onto the back foot as they can open up their body to receive to play forward as they are now in a pocket of space. Therefore, we should not only provide the players with the opportunity to practise shielding the ball, but they also need to be given a chance to rehearse the actions that take place afterwards.

Pass or Dribble?

Although we have already looked at both passing and dribbling (one versus one attacking), there is a real need to support the players with their understanding of when they should keep the ball themselves and when is the right time to share it with a teammate. Of course, we should encourage the players to stay on the ball themselves and have the confidence to try and go past players. As we discussed earlier within the chapter, it can have a real impact on the game in terms of creating space and gaps to move opposition players out of position or, even better, allow a player to get beyond the last line of defence. But at some stage, they are going to have to pass the ball onto a teammate; it is just about them recognising when it is the right time to do so.

The easiest thing to say to a player is that they should have passed the ball after they were tackled by a defending player. But just because they lost the ball does not necessarily mean it was the wrong decision to try and go past the defender. And there is probably no definitive answer to when a player should keep the ball or when they should pass it onto a teammate. We could say to pass the ball if a teammate is in a better position but, what is a better position? And if the player on the ball chooses to keep the ball and goes past an opposition player, could they then be in the better position? It is very difficult for us to clearly outline when a player should keep the ball and when they should pass it to a teammate, but what we can do is provide some guidance around what they need to do beforehand, and also what they might need to consider when they are making their choice.

Occasionally, when a player decides to pass the ball onto a teammate, they make the decision and complete the action too early. There are times in a game, particularly when a player is travelling forwards with the ball, that they release the ball too early and, by doing so, make the decision for the player who is attempting to defend the situation. Ideally, the player in possession of the ball should try to delay the decision until the defender has committed to close down them down. This does not mean that the player should then pass the ball, but it does mean that the player now needs to make a decision on whether or not to keep the ball. Similarly, sometimes when a player does make the decision to pass the ball, rather than retain it themselves, they make it too obvious that they are going to pass the ball. Just before playing the pass, they open their bodies out and face the number way in which they are going to pass the ball, making it easy for the defender to read the situation and intercept the pass. By delaying the pass and making the defender commit to the ball, it is then easier for the player to play a disguised pass with the outside of their foot, making it much more difficult to read.

A number of factors will influence whether or not the player should retain possession, for instance, has the defender closed off the passing line to their teammate, thereby making the pass difficult or even impossible? Which other players are in the picture and where exactly are they? Is the risk (keeping the ball) worth it (because of the possible reward they will get if they are successful)? Each situation will be different, and our main role as coaches is to support the player and help them believe in themselves to make the right decision when the time comes. By putting the players in an environment where they have a choice to keep the ball or to pass it onto a teammate, we are giving them a chance to practise a wide range of situations where they have to make this decision. And by doing so, they will find it easier to make the correct decision when they have to make it during a game.

Counter-Press

So far, the only out-of-possession topic that we have looked at is one versus one defending. And this does not necessarily mean that we should concentrate more on in-possession topics, it is just because there are more in-possession topics to cover. In addition, in-possession topics are more difficult for the players to master, basically because they involve the actual ball. The other main factor that makes us concentrate more on when the team has the ball is that the players enjoy this more, and, quite often, we, as coaches, do as well, after all, the main thing we all love about the game is to have the ball. But this, of course, does not mean that defending within the game is not as important as attacking and, just as there are key fundamental skills players need to learn when they have the ball, they need to do the same, for when they do not have the ball.

Pressing within the game has become extremely popular, and it could also be said that it is almost 'trendy'; coaches feel that it is almost expected that they should tell their players to press the player on the ball. But if we look closely at pressing within the professional game, it is a highly organised tactical strategy that requires the players to have a thorough understanding of what they have to do as individuals and as a team. It would be unrealistic to expect a lot of young players to be able to do this, and it is probably something that we should leave until later on in their journey. But what we can do, is start getting them into the habit of closing players down and having a real desire to win the ball back, and we can introduce this through the concept of counter-pressing.

A natural reaction of a young player when they lose the ball is to be disappointed, and understandably so; they love having the ball, and there is a possibility that they have only just got possession of it. But while they are going through these emotions of frustration and disappointment, the ball has moved away from them and the transition phase of going from in possession to out of possession, is already over. Therefore, we have to guide and educate the players to understand that one of the best opportunities to win the ball back is immediately after they have lost it. So instead of watching as the opposition player moves away with the ball, can they react instantly and look to win back possession of the ball?

When doing this, the player basically just needs to make one main decision: do they have an opportunity to actually win back the ball or not? The preferred option always would be to try and win the ball, however in some situations, winning the ball off the opposition player may not be possible. For instance, they may have managed to get their body between the player and the ball or they may have already managed to gain enough of an advantage over the player counter-pressing them. When this happens, chasing the ball may well be in vain, and therefore, a different approach should be taken and instead of trying to gain back possession, the main aim is to stop the player on the ball from progressing forward, either by running with the ball or with a pass. Preventing this from happening will allow the team to get defensively organised and to go from being vulnerable to the counter-attack. Whichever decision the counter-pressing player makes, both actions require the player to act immediately and with controlled aggression and determination. It is these traits that we should look to build into the players.

Recovery Runs

This might not be an area of the game that immediately springs to mind when choosing key areas for a player's development but it is a skill that helps develop players' understanding of many key principles of defending. When chasing an opposition player in possession of the ball, players will often fixate on the ball and just concentrate on trying to win the ball, even when there is little chance of actually being able to make a tackle. Similar to counter-pressing, players need to have the ability to identify when they are in a position to actually win the ball and when their priority is to protect the goal.

When a player is making a recovery run, their first aim should be to get between the ball and the goal. Quite often, the player will try to make a tackle from behind the player on the ball or when they are on the wrong side of them. This will result in them either failing to win the ball or committing a foul. The line that they should take when making their recovery run should not be direct to the ball but to an area on the pitch where they can position themselves between the ball and the goal. Once they have achieved this, they can actually engage the player on the ball and attempt the tackle. Helping the players understand the need to get into the right position first will help develop their understanding of the concept: to protect the goal is the first and main priority when they are out of possession.

This can be extended to when they are making a recovery run but they are not the closest player to the ball — in other words, they are not the first defender. This theme of being the second or covering defender will be looked at in more detail in the next section of this chapter, but there is an element of recovery runs that needs to be covered within this section, as when a player is making a recovery run, they will not always need to go towards the player on the ball. A good example of this is when a defender has left their position to engage the player on the ball, and a player running back to help their defence may need to fill the gap that their defender previously occupied. As an approximate guideline, we can inform the players to imagine a direct line between themselves and the goalpost nearest to where the ball is situated. Obviously, we do not want them to carry on running all the way to the post, but following this line will allow them to reach the point where they should position themselves to protect the goal to support the defender who has engaged the player on the ball and to help the team to be compact. This point will, of course, be different on each occasion that they do this and will depend on the positioning of the ball, their teammates and the opposition players.

To help the players develop an understanding around recovery runs, whether they are going to be the first defender or a supporting defender, the practices that we put them in just need to have a few key elements to ensure that they are experiencing realistic situations. First of all, the practice must have direction so that the player is actually having to recover to somewhere. Then, there must also be something for them to defend, a goal, a gate etc. This not only gives them something to actually protect but also provides them with a guide so that they know where their recovery run should be taking them. Finally, they need to actually make a recovery run, so their original start position needs to be behind the ball, in other words, they need to be farther away from whatever they are defending, in relationship to the person on the ball, while also ensuring that they have a realistic chance to recover in time. The practice needs to be challenging but, at the same time, it needs to be achievable.

Cover and Support

The final topic that a player should develop is their role as the 'second defender' or 'supporting defender'. When a player is not required to engage the player on the ball because a teammate is already doing this, they will naturally think they should go and mark another player instead. They do this, as they think this player might receive the ball next, when the danger is actually still the player on the ball. The reason, of course, is that there is a possibility this player may be able to go past the defender who has closed them down and, if they do so, they are then in an advantageous situation.

The ideal position of a second defender – so they can provide cover and support to the first defender – is to be in a position to engage the player on the ball in case they go past the first defender, while also being in a position to get across to another attacking player, should the ball be passed onto them. The angle and the distance between the two defenders are key; the supporting defender cannot get too close or too flat to the first defender because, if they do, it might be possible for the player on the ball to beat both defenders in the same movement. At the same time, if they are too far away, it will leave the first defender isolated and it will actually just create a one versus one situation.

As with anything, it takes time and practice for the players to gain a good understanding of where they should be positioned as the second defender. But it is something that they can usually pick up reasonably quickly, especially at the start of a practice, when their roles are clear and easy to identify, for instance, the player nearest to the ball becomes the first defender and the other defender provides cover and support. The difficulties usually arise once the practice is up and running and the picture within it is ever-changing. It becomes especially challenging when the ball is transferred from one attacker to another, which should result in the defenders reversing their roles. This can also happen if the first defender is beaten by the player with the ball. It is not usually too much of an issue for the player who becomes the first defender, as they have a clear and easily identifiable objective: close down the player on the ball. It is however more challenging for the player who should now provide the cover and support, as they can easily get caught chasing the ball or searching for the area on the pitch where they now need to go to provide their teammate with cover and support (this links back to recovery runs, which were discussed in the previous section). By allowing the players to repeatedly see these types of scenarios, they will be able to develop their understanding and, as a result, will be able to make quicker decisions and, more likely correct decisions as well.

Summary

It is highly unlikely that any other coach will agree exactly with this list of areas that young players should prioritise in their development. Soccer, after all, is a game of opinions. These have only been put forward for consideration, and it is entirely down to the coach which ones are used in their training curriculum. However, if a decision is made to exclude some of them or even add additional areas that have not been discussed, then the coach should, first of all, ask themselves the question whether or not the element that they are removing or adding to the curriculum is an integral part of the game that the players need to master from a young age? If the answer is yes, and you firmly believe that it is essential in their development and will support them in reaching their full potential, then it should definitely be included. Once the topics have been confirmed, there needs to be a commitment to concentrating on these areas of the game in a schedule created and shared at the start of the season. This schedule should then only be changed after a careful review at predetermined times throughout the season, and the topic of the week should not be altered just because something happened within a game.

The practices outlined in the rest of the book are designed to replicate situations and actions that occur within the game and provide the players with a realistic situation to develop these key skills. And by using the same practices, the players will not need to worry about working out what they need to do and, instead, can focus on the topic of the session. This also means that we can use an adaption of the main practice more than once during the season as well. If a particular practice was highly affective for developing a specific skill, then why would we not use it again? It is likely that during a session that the players will only spend approximately 20 to 30 minutes within a practice, so how could they possibly be in a situation within that time where it is no longer challenging for them? So, whether it is used as a warm-up activity on match day or whether it is used again later in the season, we should absolutely revisit it so that the players get further opportunities to master all the actions that take place within it.

The key element to all this is that the players have a long journey in their development, which is discussed further in chapter 4. Therefore, there should be no expectations from the coach for the players to master everything straight away. They need time and patience from the coach to give them the opportunity to develop around the key areas of the game. Providing them with the familiar surroundings of the core practices will help to accelerate the learning process by allowing them to spend more time practising and focusing on the topic of the session.

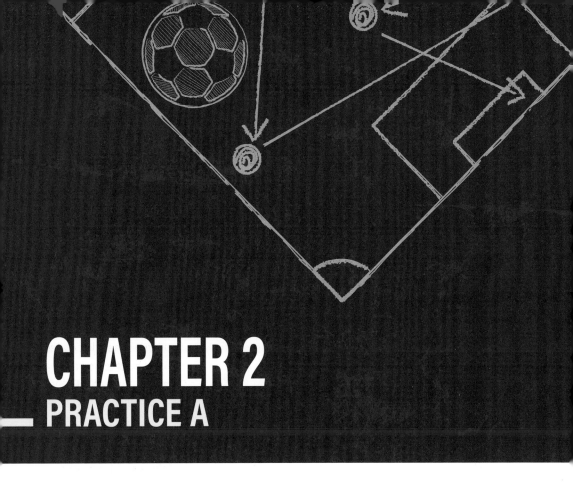

CHAPTER 2
PRACTICE A

A game of tag might be a surprise choice for the first of the core practices, but when we break it down and analyse exactly what is happening within the game, it is clear numerous transferable skills are being performed that are essential to many aspects of soccer, specifically, the physical demands of the game. When we refer to these physical demands, quite often our first thoughts are directed towards strength, speed and endurance, and these are, without doubt, extremely important. However, strength and endurance are elements of physical fitness that can be affected mainly later on in a child's journey, which is why we should not spend time trying to improve these areas of the player's development solely, when it will have little impact. Instead, we should focus on the elements of physical performance that are not as easily identifiable at first and that only have a small window of opportunity where they can be developed, and that are, in fact, crucial to the game of soccer.

Agility, balance and coordination are used across all elements of the game. They play an important role in the execution of all techniques within the game and, therefore, they will help determine the level of ability that a player will achieve at the end of their development years. If we take finishing as an example, for a player to be able to execute a half volley strike, first of all, they will need to have a stable stance while standing on one leg (balance), they will also need to connect with the ball at the exact right time to ensure that the shot is hit with power as well as accuracy (coordination). Finally, to get their body in the correct position to strike the ball correctly, they will require an element of agility as well. Another example would be dribbling; to be able to dribble with the ball at speed, the key physical requirements are agility and balance. To be able to change direction quickly, a player will obviously need a high level of agility, but with their centre of gravity constantly changing, they also need to remain balanced so that it is easier for them to keep control of the ball, as well as start, stop and accelerate.

Agility, balance and coordination are the foundations of all athletic development and physical literacy and are essential in all sports and, in particular, soccer. In addition to these, we can add speed as an aspect of physical performance that we can and should develop while the players are still of a young age. Speed has become increasingly important within the game of soccer and is a valuable asset for all playing positions, including the goalkeeper. There is a point of view that someone who is slow will always be slow and someone who is fast will always be fast because how fast you can run depends a lot upon body size, body composition and muscle fibre type. There is clearly some truth to this as each individual person has their own top speed that they can achieve and, once they reach this, they will not be able to run any quicker. What we can do, though, is help each individual player to achieve their full potential so that they can become as quick as their bodies will allow them, and to do this, we need to put the players in situations where they need to run as quickly as they can to either avoid or achieve something. They need to be able to practise their running patterns so that their body understands the movements it needs to make to reach its top speed. Then, later on in their development, when their bodies are ready, we can start to focus on muscle development.

All four of these key fundamental physical attributes can be developed within a simple game of tag due to the simple make-up of the game, which is that the players are either chasing or being chased. It is this simple structure of the game that makes it so effective; children basically love to be chased. The thrill that children get from playing the game is provided by the simulation of 'predator-prey'. This behaviour can be seen in all youngsters across all species of mammals. If we look at dogs as an example, most dogs love to be chased by other dogs, they will often initiate being chased through playfully nudging or mouthing another dog before running off in the hope that they will be chased. If it does result in the other dog pursuing them, then once they have caught up, it usually responds with a similar nudge or playful bite, and then the tables turn, and the former pursuer flees with the other dog in pursuit. Basically, the dogs are playing tag and, as with young children, the greatest pleasure that they get from the game is being chased. So, we are able to use this desire to be chased and determination to avoid being caught to develop the core physical foundations of agility, balance, coordination and speed.

Tag games can be a great introduction to a session as they can be set up very quickly with a small amount of equipment, and the game can begin with just two players, with other players joining in as and when they arrive at training. The other significant advantage of the game is that, with a few simple adjustments, the returns from it can easily be enhanced. If we look at the size of the area first, if we want to concentrate on the players' ability to twist and turn (agility) to avoid being tagged, we make the area smaller. Doing the opposite (i.e. increasing the size) will reduce the likelihood of the players having to escape the taggers by twisting and turning, and instead, there are likely to be more straight-line chases, where the players rely more on speed to avoid being tagged. Changing the shape of the area can have a similar impact on what occurs during the game. If we look at the traditional shape of a square or rectangle, these naturally provide areas where the players can become trapped: the corners, and if they find themselves in one of these, they will need to rely on their agility to escape. If we change the shape to a triangle, then we decrease the number of corners but possibly increase the level of difficulty to escape, while a circle provides an area with no corners, and the game then becomes less about agility and more about speed. Additional areas can also be added to the main area and used in a number of ways including safe zones for the players being chased. It is recommended that players can only pass through them and not wait in them, with the taggers having to run around them, or they could be areas in which none of the participants involved in the game can enter.

A game of tag is a fun and high-energy game that is enjoyed by all ages, and it provides the coach with a fast start to their sessions that can be easily altered to meet the needs of the players and the outcomes of the session. The physical outcomes that it develops are crucial to the game of soccer and need to be prioritised in the early years of the players' development, as once these years have gone, it is extremely difficult for the players to be able to improve these key physical fundamentals. Instead of making the players complete physical activities that have no relevance to the game or the needs of the players, such as doing laps of the pitch, we need to provide them with activities that will develop key physical requirements for soccer, which will have a direct impact on their ability to play the game.

Practice A: Original Set-Up

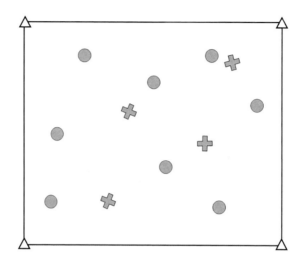

Set-Up

- Area size appropriate for the group of players.
- A number of players are selected to be the taggers. There should be more players trying to avoid being tagged than there are taggers.
- The taggers hold a bib in their hands so that they can be identified as a tagger.
- If a player is tagged, the tagger passes the bib to them and they become the tagger.
- Practice lasts for a set period of time and the players who are not taggers at the end win a point.

Focus

- Awareness of space and where the taggers are positioned within the area.
- Acceleration to initially move away from the tagger.
- Speed to remain away from the tagger.
- Agility to avoid being tagged.

Possible Progressions/Regressions

- Alter the size and/or shape of the area.
- Change the number of players who are taggers – increase or decrease.
- Add safety areas that the players who are avoiding being tagged can run through but the taggers are not allowed in.

Practice A: Individual Possession

This first adaption involves just two minor changes to the original game of tag. First of all, each player is given a bib that they tuck into their shorts and must protect from every other player. They are not allowed to hold onto their bib, and they can only protect it by keeping it out of reach from everyone else. The other main difference is that there are no longer different roles within the game; every player is now a tagger, so while protecting their own bib, they are also attempting to grab the bibs from the other players. This allows all of the players to remain active throughout the practice while also having two tasks to complete. It also means that the players will need to be aware of all the players around them as they may have to defend their bib from players approaching from a range of different angles and more than one player at once. This provides the players with a similar environment to the one that they will experience when they have to retain the ball within the game. They could have an opposition player approach them from any angle, and there is also the possibility that they could be closed down by more than one player, therefore, it allows the players to practise having to protect and retain something from a number of players who want to take it away from them.

In this game, the positioning of the bib is key to the developmental returns that the players gain from participation. Usually, the bibs will be positioned at the back of the player, which links back to the concept of why children enjoy playing the game so much: chasing and being chased. Because the bib is at the back, the players will usually decide that the most effective way to protect it is by fleeing from anyone who is trying to take it. They will only revert to trying to shield the bib if they believe they are about to get caught, and they will do this by facing the player who is chasing them. By doing this, they are using their body to protect the bib by hiding it from the player trying to take it. This is similar to the tactics that they will adopt when trying to protect the ball and retain individual possession. The key difference is the position of the object that they are trying to protect – the bib is at the back of the player, but the ball would be at the front. Therefore, we need to create the same scenario within this particular practice, which is achieved by simply placing the bib at the front of the player. By doing so, the players will start to use the same movements that they will employ when attempting to keep possession of the ball. Though there might only be slight differences in the actions that the players use to protect the bib, depending on its location, these will have a significant impact on their learning. We need to remember it is important that within any practice we allow or even force the players to rehearse a specific element of the game.

Practice A: Individual Possession

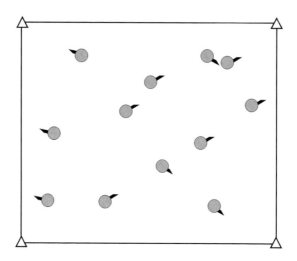

Alteration to Original Set-Up

- All players are now taggers.
- Each player is given a bib that they tuck into their shorts with as much of the bib showing as possible.
- Every player has to protect their own bib (they are not allowed to hold onto it) while also trying to take the other players' bibs at the same time.
- If a player loses their bib they still continue to try and take the other players' bibs.
- The game continues until just one player still has their bib; this player earns two points.
- For each bib they collect a player earns one point.

Focus

- Protect the bib, keep your body between the defender and the ball.
- Use feints/disguise to move away from the defender.
- Accelerate away into space.

Possible Progressions/Regressions

- Each player is given two bibs to protect.
- A number of small areas are added inside the main area, which no player can enter.
- Players take it in turns to have the 'golden' bib, which is worth extra points.

Practice A: Shielding

The positioning of the bib is again key to this particular practice and, once again, it is positioned at the front of the player. By doing so, we are replicating the position of the ball and asking the players to protect the bib in a similar way to which they would protect the ball. There are obviously some key differences; they would usually be protecting a ball located at their feet, but by getting them to participate in this practice, we are helping them develop an understanding of what they need to do/can do, to keep the opposing player far enough away from the ball that they cannot attempt to make the tackle.

An essential element of this adaption is that the players try to keep the bib away from their partner through shielding it rather than fleeing. Therefore, if it is needed, the area should be split into smaller areas with the pairs allocated and locked into one of these reduced spaces. So, for instance, it could be split into quarters or sixths, with one or two pairs allocated to each area. Significantly reducing the area reduces the amount of space that the players have to escape from their partner and forces them to protect the bib in a different way, and the only other real option that they have is to shield it. The size of the area should meet the needs of the players and it should be determined by the coach, who needs to make sure that it allows the topic to be practised.

When shielding the ball (or bib), the most effective tool the player can use is their own body, using it as an actual shield to hide and protect the bib. The key element to this is ensuring that their body is always between the opponent and the ball, which ensures that the opponent is unable to reach the ball. The player can then make it even more difficult by making the body as big as possible so that it is even harder for the defender to reach the ball. This is achieved by the player standing more side-on rather than flat and using their stance to increase the amount of ground that they can cover, thus increasing the distance between the ball and the defender. This part of shielding will not be developed within this specific practice because if the player does this, they will open up a route to the bib and will therefore no longer be able to protect it as well. The main focus of the practice is for the players to improve their awareness in terms of identifying where exactly the defender is positioned and then altering their own position to ensure that the bib remains protected. It is essential that they do not allow their partner to get past and in front of them where they are then in a position to grab the bib.

Practice A: Shielding

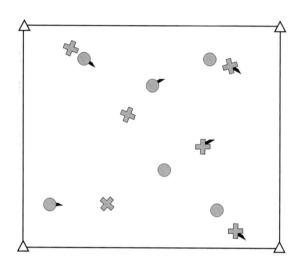

Alteration to Original Set-Up

- Players now work in pairs.
- One player is given a bib that they tuck into their shorts with as much of the bib showing as possible.
- The player with the bib has to protect it (they are not allowed to hold onto it) from their partner.
- If the player grabs the bib, the roles of the two players swaps and the game continues.
- The player in possession of the bib at the end of a set period of time wins a point.

Focus

- Use your body to hide the bib from the other player.
- Awareness of the other players' positioning; which side are they on?
- Change position to keep the bib hidden.

Possible Progressions/Regressions

- Add a central area that if the player with the bib runs through, they win a point (this encourages the player to shield and then turn).
- Players stay in pairs but work as part of a team. The team with the most bibs at the end wins the point.

Practice A: Recovery Runs

Bibs are used again in this adaption of the practice, but this time, the players are working in a team and not as individuals. The concept of the practice is similar to the previous one, where the players tried to grab the bibs from other players, but this time, the focus is on how the players react to losing their bib rather than trying not to lose it at all. It may well take a little time for the players to get used to this concept, as their natural instincts will be to concentrate on not losing the bib, and rightly so. But as with counter-pressing, it is about how they respond to losing the ball, or in this instance, their bib.

When a player has just been tagged in a game of tag, or if they have just lost the ball in a game of soccer, they will instinctively chase the person who just tagged or tackled them, which is what we encourage and develop further within counter-pressing. However, we also need the players to understand that it is not always about working hard; it is also about being smart in their play and they will need to identify that sometimes it is not the right decision to chase and instead they should recover. When a player can see that they will not be able to win the ball – either because the player has managed to get away quickly and has an unassailable advantage or the ball has been moved on through a pass before they even get an opportunity to win it back – they should forget about the ball and focus on helping the team get compact and organised instead.

This scenario of ignoring the player and concentrating on getting back to the right position is perfectly replicated by the set-up in this practice. Once a player has lost their bib, their focus needs to switch immediately to getting through the gate before their opponent. To help achieve this, firstly, the player needs to be aware of exactly where they are within the area. Similarly, in a game, they need to be aware of where they are on the pitch at all times. In the previous chapter it was discussed that when making a recovery run we provide the players with a target to aim for, for example, one of the goalposts, to allow them to get into an area where they are likely to be in the right position to protect the goal and help the team remain compact. The gates in this practice replicate the area on the pitch where the player needs to be to help their team defend. Therefore, once they have lost their bib, they do not need to worry directly about the player who has just grabbed it; instead, their primary focus is to get through the gate as quickly as possible and before their opponent. And if they achieve this, they are rewarded by being given their bib back.

Practice A: Recovery Runs

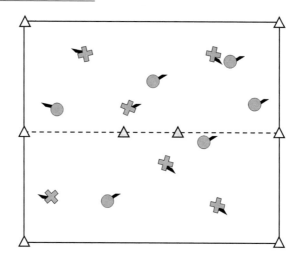

Alteration to Original Set-Up

- Players are split into two teams.
- Each player is given a bib that they tuck into their shorts with as much of the bib showing as possible.
- Area is split into half with a gate situated on the line that separates the area. Players are allowed to go where they want within the area.
- Players try to take the bib from the players on the opposite team. First team to collect all of the other team's bibs wins.
- When a player takes a bib, they must run through the central gate before the player from whom they took the bib off. If they are unsuccessful, the player gets their bib back.

Focus

- Awareness of where you are within the area and where you are in relation to the gate.
- Identify the quickest route to the gate.
- Focus on the gate and not the player.

Possible Progressions/Regressions

- If the player who lost their bib gets to the gate first, they not only get their bib back but they also win the other player's bib as well (if they still have their bib).
- Gates are positioned at two opposite ends of the area. Players have to run through the gate in the opposite half to which the bib was grabbed.

Practice A: One Versus One Attacking

The use of feints and disguises are a key requirement when a player finds themselves in a one versus one situation and they need to go past the defender. To achieve this, the attacking player needs more than quick feet and the ability to perform specific skills; they also need to display a number of physical abilities. The player dropping their shoulder and making a movement to one side can be enough to trick the defender into thinking that this is the way in which they want to go with the ball. Doing so shifts the defender's body weight to that side, giving the attacker a window of opportunity to go past on the opposite side.

Adding two gates to each side of the area guarded by a defender replicates the picture of an attacking player approaching a defender and having the option to go past either to the left- or right-hand side of them. Therefore, to achieve success, the players will need to 'open up' the pathway to one of the gates, which can only be achieved by shifting the tagger to the other gate. The need to do this is emphasised further by the defenders being restricted to sideways movements only (the younger players usually enjoy being referred to as crabs). As the taggers start to work out the tactics the players use to go through a gate, the players need to alter their approach to be less predictable. This will involve slowing down sometimes and almost stopping or stopping completely before attempting to explode through a selected gate. Another option they are likely to use is a double movement, where the player ends up going through the original gate that they moved the defender towards. All these are strategies that they will also use when facing a defender in a one versus one situation

There is the likelihood that some players will travel through a gate by waiting until the tagger is occupied with another player allowing them to travel through a gate without the need to produce any form of disguise. Basically, they are identifying space and attempting to travel through it quickly, before it disappears. There is an argument that this is relevant to the focus of the practice and that it also introduces differentiation into the practice, as some players will adopt this tactic more than others because they will see it as an easier option to gain points. There is, however, an alternative side to the argument, which is that this is not relevant, as it involves players moving quickly into space, for example, driving with the ball. To reduce the likelihood of players adopting this tactic, further gates and taggers should be added to the practice. Having the same number of taggers as there are players avoiding being tagged and adding a rule that only one player can attempt to go through a set of gates at a time will prevent players from using this tactic.

Practice A: One Versus One Attacking

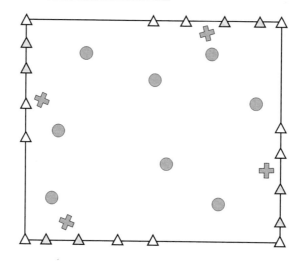

Alteration to Original Set-Up

- Two gates are added to each side of the area.
- A tagger is allocated to each set of gates to guard them.
- The taggers are only allowed to move side to side.
- Players win a point every time they travel through a gate. Taggers win a point for every player they tag.
- After travelling through a gate, the player returns to the area and attempts to travel through a different set of gates.

Focus

- Use of feints and disguise.
- Agility to change direction quickly.
- Acceleration to get through the gate before the defender recovers.

Possible Progressions/Regressions

- The players are given a ball (not the taggers).
- Add an additional tagger who is allowed to move freely inside the area. If a player is tagged by them, they must exit the area from any place and they can then return immediately.
- The distance between the gates is changed.

Practice A: Turning

Similar to one versus one attacking, players need to master physical movements that will support them when they are producing a turn with the ball and, without these, the turn is likely to be ineffective. As discussed in chapter 1, the purpose of a turn is to either allow a player to get away from a defender or to give them the opportunity to use space on the pitch that was previously blocked off by the opposing player. Whatever reason the turn is used for, the common theme in place each and every time is that once the turn has been completed, the space or time that it created for the player will only last for a short period of time. Therefore, unless the turn is performed effectively (i.e. quickly), it will not do the job that it was selected for, and the quicker it is performed, the greater the advantage the player will have over their opponent. The need to maximise the player's potential to change direction quickly and accelerate away is therefore paramount when it comes to supporting their development in turning with the ball.

Another area that players will need help with when it comes to turning is when and where to turn. A common mistake that players often make is turning into an opposing player and subsequently losing possession of the ball. A phrase that is often used by coaches when they get frustrated by a player losing the ball is 'you are turning into trouble', which is basically because the player is unaware of what is around them before they have turned; they have not scanned the area that they wish to go into before they turn into it. It is, therefore, imperative that while they are travelling with the ball and/or just before they complete the turn, they have their head up and are aware of what exactly is around them so that they can ensure they are turning into space and not into danger.

Positioning the two gates next to each other and making the players travel through the first gate in one direction and the second gate in the opposite direction will help the players get used to changing direction quickly. The additional rule of then having to get out of the area to secure the point will also help the players understand the importance of accelerating away afterwards. The longer that they take to complete either of the two actions, the greater the chance they have of getting tagged. The practice set-up also allows the taggers to employ the tactic of waiting by the exit of the second gate, and this means they know which way the players have to travel as part of the task that they have to complete to earn a point. And here is where we can work on the player's awareness – if a tagger is waiting for them, then now is not the time to complete the turn; instead they should just continue in the direction they are travelling and seek out a set of gates where they can perform a turn.

Practice A: Turning

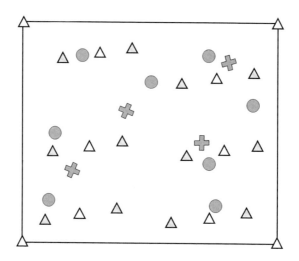

Alteration to Original Set-Up

- A number of paired gates are added to the area.
- To win a point, a player must first travel through a gate and then immediately back through the other gate right next to it.
- After completing the turn, they must then get out of the area without being tagged before they can claim the point.
- If at any time a player is tagged, they lose a point and must exit the area before they can return back again.
- The taggers win a point for each player they tag.

Focus

- A quick change of direction.
- Accelerate away after completing the turn.
- Identify where the taggers are situated; do not turn into a tagger.

Possible Progressions/Regressions

- Add a further gate next to the paired gates so that there are now three gates next to each other, this then allows the player to turn left or right if they travel through the central gate first.
- Give the players a ball each (not including the taggers).

Practice A: Driving With the Ball

Developing the players' straight-line speed, or their maximum speed, will obviously benefit them in most aspects of the game of soccer. Whether defensively, in terms of a recovery run, or in transition, trying to support a teammate situated further up the pitch. The ability to cover the ground quickly, allowing a player to get from a defensive position to an offensive position, or vice versa, within a small amount of time, can change the dynamics of a game almost instantly. This is particularly evident when a player is travelling with the ball, as they have not only changed their positioning on the pitch but also altered the location of the ball as well, with it likely moving further away from their own goal and therefore closer to the oppositions.

A key element of running with the ball is that the player keeps moving forward for as long as they can or need to. As discussed in the previous chapter, this could be in a direct forward action, for example, in a straight line, or it could be across the pitch. However, what we do not want the players to do is to end up facing their own goal. Having driven forward and gained momentum by travelling with the ball with pace and putting the opposition players under pressure, we do not want the team to lose this momentum. This can happen quickly if the player turns back, allowing the opposition to get numbers back behind the ball and organised. By keeping the ball moving forward, it is more likely that the opposition players must revert to emergency defending where they are scrambling to fill gaps and get organised. As with other aspects of the game of soccer, players will look to turn back towards their own goal when they are concerned about losing the ball; by turning back, they can use their bodies to protect the ball. Therefore, we need to change the players' psychological mindset so that when they are travelling forward, the ball continues in this direction, whether it is through the players themselves keeping it and going forward or through a forward pass. But we also need to help them develop physically in terms of maximising their speed.

The key message within this practice is 'commit'. Once the player has identified an area to run to and they have set off to reach it, they need to commit to this decision. Players will often slow down and swerve if they think they are being caught. This often causes the chaser to go past them, which results in them being in a position to defend the area, which essentially turns it into a one versus one situation, and the momentum and advantage have been lost. Players need to focus on powering forward and staying ahead, rather than worrying what is behind them; they need to remain positive, rather than wanting to be safe.

Practice A: Driving With the Ball

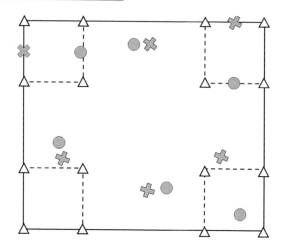

Alteration to Original Set-Up

- Four areas are added to the main area. These are four small squares, with one in each corner of the main area.
- Players now work in pairs.
- The player being chased decides each time which side of a small area they want to start. The tagger then stands on the opposite side.
- When the player is ready, they attempt to get to one of the other small areas before they are tagged by their partner.
- If successful they win a point, if they are tagged their partner wins the point.
- After each go the players swap roles with their partner.

Focus

- Acceleration to get away from their partner.
- Look to take the shortest route, unless they think they will get caught.
- Always travel forward, do not head back.

Possible Progressions/Regressions

- Changing the size of the small areas will not only change the distance the players have to travel but also the advantage they have over their partner.
- Change the size and/or shape of the area; a rectangle can add differentiation.
- Give the players a ball each to travel with (not the chasers).

Practice A: Team Possession

One of the hardest parts of passing for players to understand is where exactly they need to pass the ball and the amount of weight that they need to put on it. On paper, this would seem to be quite a simple task and within a closed environment it usually is; if we ask two players to pass the ball between themselves through a gate, they are usually very successful. The task becomes a lot harder if the environment becomes a variable or random environment where the players have to deal with constantly moving obstacles that impact and alter the spaces available for the ball to travel through. Add to this that the player receiving the ball can also move, and passing the ball becomes a lot more challenging as a number of varying factors have to be taken into consideration to ensure that the pass is executed successfully.

Within this particular adaption of the practice, the focus now turns to the taggers and not just their ability to tag the other players but also the passes they make to their teammates as well. Even though they are using their hands to pass and receive the ball, it will still help the players with their coordination skills and, more importantly, it will support them in 'judging' the pass. The practice allows the players to experience sharing the ball with a teammate, over a range of distances, within a random environment. By participating in this adaption, the players can practice key elements of passing the ball within a game situation, such as when to actually play the pass. So, for instance, they may need to delay a pass because someone moves through the pathway in which the ball needs to travel. Plus, they can develop their receiving skills as well, for example, they may need to adjust their position so that the player passing the ball can actually see them. There are a number of transferable skills that the practice allows the players to develop and then use within the game of soccer.

Possibly the most important skill this practice supports is the players' understanding of where they should play the pass, in particular, not playing the ball to where the player is situated when the pass is about to be made, but to where they will be once it has been completed. This may, of course, be the exact same place because the person receiving the pass may not move, and therefore, it is the correct decision to play the ball into the area where the player was first identified. However, a lot of the time, the teammate receiving the pass is on the move and so when playing the pass, the player needs to calculate where the ball needs to end up. In this practice, a player will either pass the ball to a teammate, who will likely be on the move as they are following an opposition player, or they will try to tag an opposition player who will more than likely be moving to try and avoid the ball. Therefore, it provides the perfect environment for the players to practise this particular skill.

Practice A: Team Possession

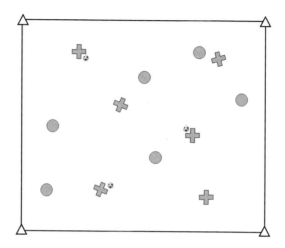

Alteration to Original Set-Up

- The teams are split into two teams.
- One team are the taggers and they are given a number of small balls (these could be tennis balls).
- To tag a player, the taggers must throw a ball underarm and hit a player beneath the knee.
- As soon as one player successfully tags an opposition player, the teams swap roles.
- The team in possession of the balls at the end of a set period time loses the game.

Focus

- Try to identify where the player will be, not where they are.
- Ensure the ball ends up where you want it to go.
- Use the right amount of power to reach the target while maintaining accuracy.
- Identify which teammates are in a better position.

Possible Progressions/Regressions

- Add safety areas that the players can travel through (they cannot wait in these areas).
- Change the type of ball that is used.
- When in possession of the ball, players cannot move.
- Each team is given an even number of balls, if a play is tagged, they have to take the ball. The team with the least number of balls at the end of a set period of time wins.

Practice A: Pass or Dribble?

The key aspect of this particular element of the game is understanding when a player should keep the ball and when they should release it. There are, of course, other aspects that were touched upon in the previous chapter, such as the timing of the release, but before the players learn these particular parts of the process they need to start to learn when they should pass the ball to a teammate. They can only achieve this by being put into situations where they have to make the decision and choose whether or not to pass the ball and, even then, they are not always going to make the correct decision. But by putting them in these environments, they are more likely to make the correct decision, and they will also start to make the decisions much quicker and will start to be more decisive in their actions.

Within this practice, the players who have possession of the ball are trying to identify which of their teammates need the ball and, in this particular game, it is those who are being chased by a tagger. This may well go against what we would prefer the players to do, in other words, we would prefer them to pass to a teammate who is in space, rather than a player who is being closely followed by an opponent. However, as discussed in chapter 1, we should not really be encouraging this anyway; we should try and develop the players so that they are confident and happy to receive the ball under pressure. Plus, that is not the main focus for this particular adaption – the main aim is to support the players in understanding when they should be releasing the ball.

To achieve this, the players should only release the ball when they really need to; they should not pass the ball to a teammate when there is no real need to do so. Passing the ball just for the sake of moving it on to a player who wants it could then slow down the process of passing it onto a teammate who really needs it. Another key point is that when a player does have the ball, they need to be ready to pass it onto a teammate as soon as they need to. To achieve this, the player should be on the move constantly, scanning the area, looking to identify the position of their teammates and the opposition players. From the information that they gather, while scanning the area, they need to identify when they should release the ball and when they should keep hold of it. Passing the ball to someone at the wrong time could result in a teammate or even themselves being tagged. A teammate could also get tagged if the player does not release the ball when they should have. Therefore, when they are in possession of the ball, the players constantly have to decide when they should release the ball, preparing them for when they have to make similar decisions during a game of soccer.

Practice A: Pass or Dribble?

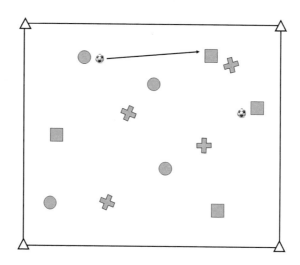

Alteration to Original Set-Up

- The players are split into three teams. One team are the taggers and the other two teams work together to avoid being tagged.
- A number of balls are given to the players who are avoiding the taggers. The number of balls needs to be fewer than the number of taggers.
- While in possession of the ball, a player cannot be tagged.
- Players must carry the ball in their hands and throw the ball to pass it.
- If a player is tagged, then they are 'frozen' until a teammate passes them a ball.
- At the end of a set period of time, the defenders are awarded the same number of points as the number of players that are frozen at the end of the game.

Focus

- Awareness of other players in the area – teammates and taggers.
- Identify which player needs the ball.
- When to keep the ball and when to release it.

Possible Progressions/Regressions

- Use a different type of ball.
- If a ball touches the floor, the player who made the pass becomes frozen.
- Increase or decrease the number of balls within the practice.

Practice A: Counter-Press

A key element to counter-pressing is the player's ability to react quickly to losing possession of the ball. The longer it takes for the player who has just lost the ball to react to the change in circumstances, the greater the opportunity for the player who has just won possession to get away from them, which, in turn, makes it a lot harder to win the ball back. Therefore, the quicker that they react and attempt to win the ball back, the greater the chance they have of being successful. This particular adaption will therefore focus solely on reaction speed and the ability to chase down the player who tagged them, in preparation for when they lose the ball in a game.

The major difference between the situation that this practice produces and the one that the players will experience in a game is not just that there is no ball involved, but the fact that the players are waiting to be tagged. The players know that they cannot do anything until they have actually been tagged, so they will actually allow the player to tag them so that they are in charge of the situation and will therefore have a better opportunity to catch the player before they return back to their half of the area. Obviously, this goes completely against what the player attempts to do within the game. They will do everything they can to retain possession – they will not just wait and allow the defender to win the ball so that they can attempt to win it back. But this is the sacrifice we need to make within this particular practice to allow the players to develop the key physical and psychological requirements of counter-pressing.

Psychologically, we not only want the players to react quickly to being tagged, but we want them to show determination as well. They need to do everything possible to prevent the player from reaching their side of the area and only stop trying when it is no longer possible, which is when the player has made it back to their own half. Physically, they need to demonstrate an initial burst of speed, in other words, they need to have good levels of acceleration. Without this, the player they are chasing will be able to create a large enough distance between the two players that will be impossible to close in the short amount of time it will take for them to reach their side of the area. The levels of physical and psychological demands that we place upon the players can also be increased. We just need to make sure that the changes we make are appropriate and safe for the particular group of players participating within the practice. By simply changing the tag rule to a 'tackle', for example, the chasers have to stop the players completely, we can increase the level of determination needed, while also adding aggression and strength to the outcomes of the practice.

Practice A: Counter-Press

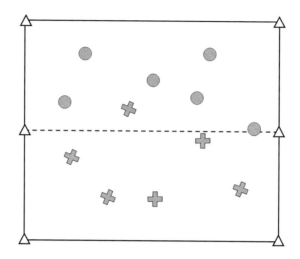

Alteration to Original Set-Up

- The area is split in half.
- The players are put into two teams with each team allocated half of the area.
- Players attempt to enter their opponent's half of the area and tag one of the opposition players. On doing so, they look to get back to their own side of the area without being tagged by the player that they tagged. They gain a point if they are successful.
- The two players must both attempt to tag a different player.
- At the end of a set period of time, the team with the most points wins.

Focus

- Immediate reaction to being tagged; quick reactions and determination.
- Awareness of where in the area they have been tagged.
- Identify when they do not have much time left to tag the player.

Possible Progressions/Regressions

- Players have bibs that the opposition players try to grab and return to their side of the area.
- Cones are placed throughout the area and the players try to take them from the opposition's half of the area back to their own. If they get tagged while holding a cone, they must drop the cone immediately.

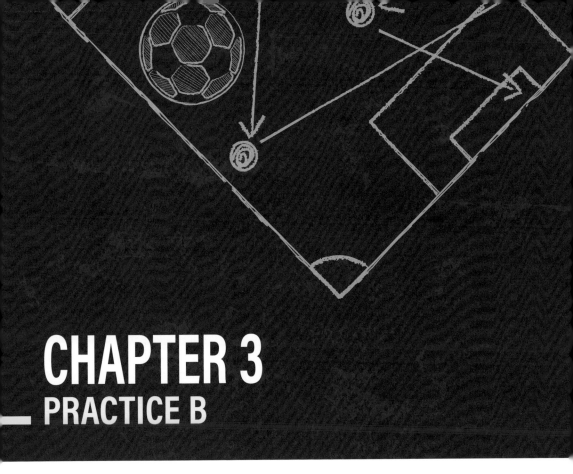

CHAPTER 3
PRACTICE B

The ability to keep possession of the ball without the aid of teammates, as outlined in chapter 1, is an extremely effective tool for a player to possess. Therefore, it is essential that, as coaches, we regularly expose players to situations where they have to retain the ball for as long as possible, giving them little choice but to keep the ball themselves, rather than having the safer option of passing it onto a teammate. This practice concentrates primarily on this ability to retain possession of the ball while under continuous and concentrated pressure from an opposition player. The environment in which it takes place is ever-changing, forcing the players to constantly review their situation and adapt accordingly, working out the solutions for how to keep the ball away from the defender. This is due to all the players using the same area while concentrating on their own task – either retaining their ball or trying to win the ball from their partner. Therefore, the spaces that are available within the grid are constantly changing; a space that a player has identified to travel into could disappear almost immediately due to other players within the practice moving into it.

A further challenge that the players face in this particular practice is that they are constantly involved, with little or no time to rest or recharge. This is therefore not only challenging in terms of the physical demands placed upon them, but it is also extremely testing psychologically because they are always having to think and make decisions. However, this is an integral part of the practice design as it means the players will not only practice retaining individual possession of the ball when they are fully focused and full of energy, but also when they are tired, both mentally and physically. This obviously has clear links to the game itself, as, throughout a match, players levels of tiredness fluctuate, and the players need to be able to retain possession of the ball, despite different energy levels. Basically, we need to expose and challenge the players to be able to keep possession of the ball while they are tired.

The practice design also allows the players to become active almost immediately; as soon as they have selected or given a partner and grabbed a ball, they can go and play, and then as more players arrive, they simply just join in. There is no need to wait for the players or coach to provide any essential information. It is just simply to keep the ball or try and win the ball. The simplicity of the practice means the coach can set it up really quickly, and it can be altered just as quickly if the size needs to be adjusted for any reason.

The practice can also be easily adapted to meet the different needs of the players, such as those who are excelling and those who may need some extra support. There is an argument that this is simply achieved by organising the pairings by ability, putting the 'stronger' players together so that they challenge each other. However, if we continue to put the players who might need some help together all the time, then are we not restricting their development? If, sometimes, we pair them with stronger players, will they then have to find a way to be successful? Will they be pushed to increase their level of performance? This, of course, does not mean that they should not be paired with players of the same ability, just not all the time; they just need to spend time playing against different players with different levels of ability, replicating exactly what will happen during match day. This can be easily achieved by regularly rotating who the players are paired with, but it may need some additional planning on top this.

Although it has just been recommended that we should make it uncomfortable for players by pairing them with players with a higher level of ability, that does not mean we do not need to provide them with some form of support. For instance, some areas can be added to the practice that players without the ball cannot travel through. It is just important that an additional rule is added that the players with the ball can only travel through the area, in other words, they cannot wait in the area. Doing this provides the player on the ball with a small amount of respite from the defender, while also ensuring that they do not hide within this 'safe zone'. Another option available to the coach when there is an odd number of players is to put some of the players into a group of three. By putting the players who are competent at retaining possession of the ball in the group of three, we are then able to challenge these stronger players, as, essentially, it becomes a one versus one versus one situation, where the player on the ball needs to protect it from two defenders.

This practice can also be used at any other time within the session; it does not have to be restricted to the first practice used to get the players active quickly. For example, the importance of the players experiencing the practice when they are physically and mentally tired was raised earlier in the chapter, so would it not make sense for the practice to be introduced at the end of session? Traditionally, we always finish a session with a game and there are numerous reasons why we do this, such as providing the players an opportunity to practise what they have learned previously in the session in an actual game environment. Or because, basically, it is what the players want or expect and, most importantly, it is what they enjoy. So, it is not a question of whether or not we replace the game at the end of the session with this practice, it is whether we finish the game five minutes earlier (there is no reason why we cannot start the game five minutes earlier) and then introduce this practice for the final five minutes of the session, when the players are arguably the most tired. It could also be used within a whole-part-whole session where training begins with a conditioned game and then a practice can be introduced to 'refine' the focus of the session before returning to the conditioned game and then progressing into a normal game.

All the key elements of this practice have important connections to the modern game of soccer. With the current trend for teams to employ a high press, when they are out of possession or set traps within a mid-block, players will find themselves under pressure from opposition players when they are in possession of the ball, no matter what position they play or where they are on the pitch. It could, in fact, be argued that hiding the ball from a pressing defender is now a skill that all soccer players need to be able to execute to prevent the opposition from winning the ball in dangerous areas, and while the team is unorganised, in terms of their defensive shape. Therefore, this practice provides an environment where the player on the ball will be put under pressure in countless different ways and, subsequently, they will need to find a range of solutions for how to keep the ball. Then, with the introduction of the adaptions to the practice, they will also start to develop an understanding of what they can then do as a result of retaining possession of the ball.

Practice B Original Set-Up

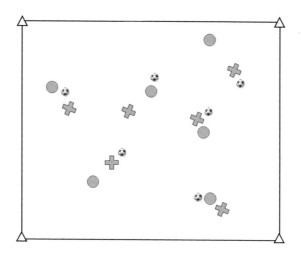

Set-Up

- Area size appropriate for the group of players.
- Players work in pairs with one ball for each pair.
- One player starts with the ball and tries to retain possession of the ball while their partner attempts to win the ball.
- If the other player wins the ball, the players' roles just change around.
- If the ball goes out of play, players restart by dribbling the ball back in.
- Practice lasts for a set period of time; the player in possession of the ball at the end wins a point.

Focus

- Protect the ball, keep your body between the defender and the ball.
- Use the foot furthest away from the defender.
- Use feints/disguise to move away from the defender.
- Accelerate away into space.

Possible Progressions/Regressions

- Alter the size and/or shape of the area.
- And 'safety zones' for the players in possession of the ball.
- Use smaller balls.

Practice B: Receiving Under Pressure

This particular practice focuses on players being able to receive the ball while under pressure, and then being able to play forward. The most suitable picture of this occurring within the game is a midfielder receiving a pass from a defender, while under pressure from an opposition midfielder. In this instance, we quite often encourage the player to pass the ball backwards – play the way you face, mainly because we do not want them to lose the ball in what could be a dangerous area of the pitch. However, the impact that a player can have on a game if they can receive the ball under pressure and still be able to play forward can be significant. By doing so, they are likely to not only take the player that is pressurising them out of the equation, but also several of that player's teammates as well, especially those positioned as far up the pitch as the player applying the pressure.

Using servers and adding an area in the centre of the main area allows the scenario of a midfielder receiving the ball under pressure and then playing forward to be replicated. Making the player receiving the ball travel through the central area before they can pass it to another server forces them to play forward. The positioning of the defender when they receive the ball will almost always be closely behind the player receiving the ball, as he/she will choose which server they want to receive from as they exit the central area. Therefore, the defending player will always be playing 'catch up', but they will make ground while their partner is waiting for the pass to come into them from the server. This enables the defender to apply pressure as they receive the ball. And by not allowing the player receiving the ball to play it back to the server who passed it to them, we are forcing them to deal with it themselves and protect the ball while finding a way to progress forward with it.

Through participating in this practice, players will start to understand and recognise the importance of knowing exactly where the opposing player is and, specifically, which side they are on. They will also start to judge how close they are as they receive the ball and also once they are in possession of the ball. Once they have collected all this information, they can start to use it, to work out how, first of all, they can retain the ball, before finding the solution to how they can start to travel forward with it. But for us to truly support them in this area of the game, we have got to allow them to practise it during a match day. What we cannot do is discourage them from doing it because we are worried that they will lose possession in a dangerous area of the pitch. They need to know that if they are unsuccessful, instead of being blamed for losing the ball, they will be praised for being brave and having the confidence to receive the ball while under pressure.

Practice B: Receiving Under Pressure

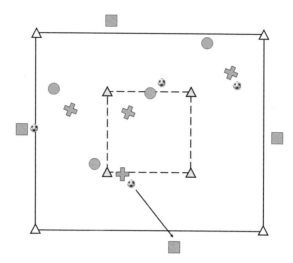

Alteration to Original Set-Up

- Players are split into three groups. One group acts as servers on the outside, and the other two work in pairs in the centre.
- Small area added to the centre of the main area.
- Players receive the ball from a server and must then travel through the centre area (they must exit through a different side to which they entered) before looking to pass to a server without a ball.
- When doing so, they run through the central area and then collect a ball from another server and the practice continues.

Focus

- Awareness of the defending players' positions.
- Body shape as they receive the ball.
- Which foot is chosen to receive the ball?

Possible Progressions/Regressions

- Add an additional area so that there are two central areas, making it more difficult for the defender to anticipate where the player on the ball wants to go.
- Decrease the size of the central area.

Practice B: Receiving to Play Forward

Ideally, we would prefer that a player did not receive a pass while under pressure due to the risk involved and the increased likelihood that they could lose possession of the ball. The preferred option would be for a player to receive the ball in space, such as, a midfield player receiving the ball in space from a defender or another midfielder, so that they are able to execute whatever it is they want to do next, while under very little pressure, giving them more time to do it. It will also allow them to take the ball with an open body so that they are facing forward, which, of course, allows them to play forward quicker and to have a clearer picture of what is around them. Providing a player with the opportunity to practise this can quite often be difficult unless we put them in an unopposed environment because, for a player to be able to do this, they need to have the space to open out otherwise they should not be doing it. To counteract this, the practice allows the player to receive the ball unopposed before the defender becomes active. Therefore, the main aspect of the practice is actually the one versus one dual that takes place between the two players, but we are providing the players with an opportunity to rehearse the action of receiving to play forward before they engage in the opposed element.

As they exit the central area and approach the server, the players are imitating the movement of a midfield player dropping to receive a pass from a centre-back or forward player completing the same movement to receive from a midfielder. The key component to this movement is the area where they position themselves at the end of it, specifically in relation to the player making the pass. It is not uncommon for players to stop directly in front of the server making the pass, which is understandable as it would seem to be the most appropriate place – if you want to receive something from someone, you would stand directly facing them, like when throwing and catching a ball with someone. However, doing so causes two problems for the player; first of all, if there is a defender nearby, they do not really have to make a decision, it is very easy for them to close the player down while also cutting off the passing line to the player looking to receive the ball. The other challenge is that standing directly in front of the player passing the ball makes it more difficult to receive onto the back foot with an open body. The target area that the player passing the ball has to hit is much smaller if the player stands directly in front but with an open body. Creating an angle between themselves and the player making the pass makes it much more difficult for the defender to close down the player on the ball and cut off the pass, and it also provides a bigger target area for the player making the pass. And though the main concern within the practice is the player receiving the ball, we can also provide some help and support to the player passing the ball because a key aspect of whether or not the player can receive to play forward is that the pass is to their back foot.

Practice B: Receiving to Play Forward

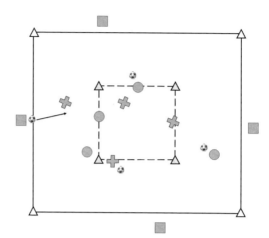

Alteration to Original Set-Up

- Players are split into three groups. One group acts as servers on the outside and the other two work in pairs in the main area.
- Small area added to the centre of the main area.
- Players receive the ball from a server and must then travel through the centre area (they must exit through a different side to which they entered) before looking to pass to a server without a ball. Their partner (the defender) must wait in the centre area until the attacking player takes their first touch.
- On completing the task, they run through the central area and then collect a ball from another server while their partner returns to the central area. The practice then continues.

Focus

- Angle of approach and body shape; side-on.
- Receive pass on the foot furthest away from the player passing the ball.
- First touch to go towards the centre area.
- Pass from the server; play to the foot furthest away from you.

Possible Progressions/Regressions

- Alter when the defender can exit the central area.
- Change the size of the central area (this will affect how far away the defender starts).

Practice B: One Versus One Attacking

The addition of a central area is used once more for this practice; to create a one versus one situation, where the defender engages the player on the ball face to face. As with all the one versus one practices throughout the book, the focus can be on the attacking aspect of the dual or the defensive part. The most important thing to remember is that, as coaches, we only focus on one of them. The players will inevitably get to practise both parts of the situation as they will get to spend time being the attacker and also the defender. But, as coaches, we should have a narrow focus for the session and this will be linked in with one of the principles of the game – in possession, out of possession, transition from in to out of possession, and transition from out to in possession. Therefore, the session focus dictates which player we, as coaches, support within the practice. If it is an in-possession practice, there is no need to spend time working with a player and helping them improve their defending. There is a time and a place to do this, and this is when the topic of the session comes under 'out of possession'. If we try and give players too much information in a practice, there is a real possibility that they will not actually learn anything.

Restricting the defenders to the centre area and then making the attacking players enter this area to win a point produces a scenario where the two players are face to face, with the defender defending the space behind them and the attacking player looking to go past the defender. Due to the size of the area and the space available to the attacking player, the practice is more suited to the player with the ball. There will be plenty of opportunities for the player to practise taking the defender one way, which, subsequently, will shift the defender's body weight in the same direction, enabling him/her to attack the space on the opposite side. The design of the practice also means that there will be other players constantly travelling around both of the two areas, which means the space available within the areas will be constantly changing. Therefore, it is not just a matter of the attacking player choosing the side that they want to drag the defender to before attacking the other side; they will need to be aware of where the space is currently available, but more importantly, they will need to predict where the space will be once they have executed the skill. This ability to read the game and to be able to anticipate what is going to happen next is an important skill for any player and is transferable across many aspects of the game. For instance, if a player is looking to pass to a teammate who is making a run, they need to be able to forecast where the player will be once the pass has been completed; it is no good passing to where they are when they decide to make the pass as they will no longer be there by the time it is completed. Similarly, out of possession, defenders need to predict what the player on the ball is likely to do next.

Practice B: One Versus One Attacking

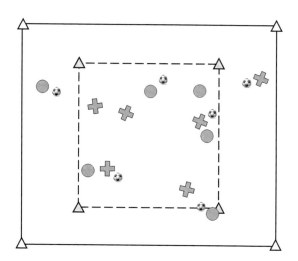

Alteration to Original Set-Up

- A large area added to the centre of the main area.
- Players continue to work in pairs, but the player who does not have possession of the ball is restricted to the centre area.
- Player on the ball wins a point by entering the centre area and then exiting it through a different side.
- If the defender wins the ball, they look to exit the centre area with the ball, and they then become the attacking player, and the practice continues.

Focus

- Awareness of what is around you: the defender and their body shape, other players and space to move into.
- Feint and disguise to shift the defender's body weight in a selected direction.
- Shift the ball quickly in a different direction.
- Explosive acceleration to exploit the space they have created and to move away from the defender.

Possible Progressions/Regressions

- Change the size of the central area.
- Only allow the attacking player to exit through the side of the area that is directly opposite to the side that they entered.

Practice B: Driving With the Ball

In addition to the development of the players' ability to be able to retain individual possession of the ball, there should also be a purpose to it. There are, of course, a number of purposes, all of which will be discussed and covered within this chapter; however, it could be argued that some reasons are more important than others, and one of the most significant is to progress forward, particularly as an individual. The key to this is for the player to retain possession of the ball until they have identified a space that they can travel into, and then, once they have done this, can they get into a position that provides them with an opportunity to attack this space. Doing so will not only help their team progress up the pitch and closer to the opposition's goal, but they will also disrupt their opponent's defensive set-up by forcing players to leave their current position, leaving possible spaces that could be exploited. This version of Practice One aims to mimic this situation of a player retaining the ball against the pressure of an opposition player while scanning the pitch for areas of space that they can drive into.

The areas of space on the pitch are represented simply by a number of gates that are placed throughout the area. Players are awarded a point each time that they successfully travel through a gate. It is important that at this stage that we carefully consider the size of the gates, the number of gates and also the position of the gates. First of all, if we look at the size of the gates, we need to ensure that the practice does not develop into the players dribbling. This could occur if the width of the gates allows the possibility of the player on the ball going through it, even though their partner is guarding it, for example, by travelling through by dribbling past the defender. To prevent this, the gate should be small enough in width so that if a player is guarding it, then there is no possibility of the player on the ball going through it. The purpose of the practice is for the players to identify space and then move into it quickly. Similarly, the number of gates that we add to the area will also have a significant impact on what the players are doing within the practice. If there are too many gates, it will mean that the proximity of a gate to other gates will be really close, which could result in the players travelling through a number of gates in a very short period of time, and having to regularly change the line that they are travelling on. In short, they will be dribbling not driving with the ball. We also need to be mindful that only having a small number of gates will make the practice more challenging, which is not necessarily a bad thing. Finally, positioning the gates too close to the edges of the area will limit the space the players have either before or after they go through the gate. Again, this does not mean that we do not place them here; we just may need to position some of them more centrally to provide different levels of difficulty.

Practice B: Driving With the Ball

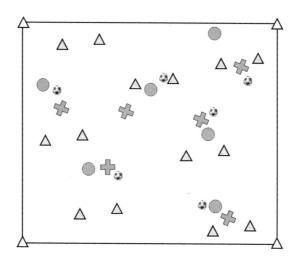

Alteration to Original Set-Up

- A number of small gates are added to the area.
- Players are awarded a point each time they travel through a gate with the ball.
- The player with the most points at the end of the allocated time wins the game.

Focus

- Awareness of the positioning of the gates and those available to travel through.
- Acceleration to explode away from the defender.
- Long strides to cover the ground quicker.
- Ball out of feet to allow long strides.
- Ball to remain under control.

Possible Progressions/Regressions

- Two different coloured gates are used; the different colours are worth different numbers of points.
- Two different coloured gates are used; after travelling through one colour, a player must travel through the other colour next time.
- Reduce the number of gates within the area.
- After travelling through a gate, the player must continue and travel out of the area to win the point. Possession of the ball then transfers to the other player.

Practice B: Forward Passing

In the previous practice, the importance of being able to progress forward as an individual was highlighted, as well as how a player may need to protect the ball and maintain possession until they have been able to identify a space that provides them with an opportunity to drive forward. Once they have done this, it may not always be possible to continue to drive into space, or there could be better options. It could be that the defender is recovering quickly and there is, therefore, a need to move the ball onto a teammate, or it could be that the teammate is in a better position and the pass to them is the better option. This practice will allow players to develop their forward passing while on the move and under pressure from a defender.

The practice produces a situation where players must advance forward against a player applying pressure before attempting a pass into one of two targets. Due to the set-up of the area, the defender will never be too far away from the attacker, even when they have managed to travel into the other half of the area where they are allowed to attempt the pass. The defender will always be close enough to challenge the attacker within a few seconds, should they choose to stop or slow down. This means that the attacking player will not have the affordability of being able to stop to make the pass that wins them the point; the pass will need to be made while the player is travelling with the ball, which requires a completely different type of pass. The positioning of the goals outside the area is also key; there needs to be a significant amount of space from the edge of the area to the actual goal to provide a suitable and realistic distance that the pass has to travel. If we position the goals directly on the edge of the area, it is possible that, sometimes, the pass may only need to travel a few yards, which, it could be said, is not a pass. The final action of the player (i.e. the pass) needs to be completed with purpose, and it needs to replicate the type of pass they will make during a game.

The type of pass this action replicates in a game could be a midfielder travelling forward with the ball and then releasing a forward player with a pass that allows them to run onto it and penetrates the oppositions defensive unit. Or it could be a run from midfield that drags the opposition's players in one direction before releasing a pass the opposite way (reverse pass) to a teammate, who now has some time and space to work in. All these actions need to be done with purpose and speed, which the practice produces as a result of the close attention of the player's partner.

Practice B: Forward Passing

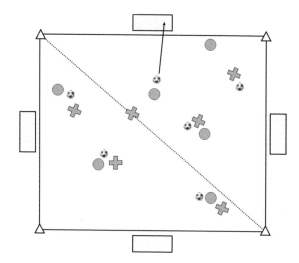

Alteration to Original Set-Up

- Four small goals are added, one to each side of the area. These are situated away from the area so that the players have to make a 'realistic' pass to achieve the point.
- Area is split in half by a line that runs from one corner of the main area to another, creating two triangular areas.
- Whichever half the pair start in, the player on the ball must travel into the other area before they can attempt to pass into one of the two small goals positioned in that half of the area.

Focus

- Head up as travelling with the ball to identify where to make the pass.
- Outside of the foot pass where necessary.
- Inside of the foot can be used for a 'reverse' pass.

Possible Progressions/Regressions

- Move the goals further away or closer to the area. These do not all have to be the same distance; additional points can be awarded for passing into goals further away.
- Have different sized goals/targets. These do not all have to be the same size; additional points can be awarded for passing into smaller goals.

Practice B: Turning

The ability to turn quickly with the ball can be extremely beneficial for players for several reasons. It can provide them with a different option, such as a different teammate to pass to or the possibility to cross or shoot. It can also provide them with more time or space, allowing them to assess their options and, hopefully, select the right one. This particular practice concentrates on turning to allow a player to get out of tight spaces and away from the close attention of a defender.

Four areas are added to the main area, and the players earn a point by successfully travelling into and then out of one of these areas. Using the corners of the main practice area limits the directions that the player can go in after they have entered one of the four areas. They will be restricted to exiting an area either to the left or right (depending on which side of an area they enter) and backwards, in other words, the same side that they entered. But having more than one option is also important. If we only provide the player with one option, then it will be far too easy for their partner to defend. Having two possible options to exit provides the player on the ball with options. It is down to them to select the correct option and then execute it effectively. The harder of these is obviously exiting the same side of the area they entered, as they will be followed into the area by their partner, who will therefore automatically be defending that side of the area. So, players need to be motivated and rewarded for attempting to exit this particular side of the area, which can easily be achieved with a simple alteration to the scoring system. Awarding players additional points if they exit the area through the same side they entered will encourage players to try the more difficult option, with the increased risk being rewarded by earning more points.

Having four additional areas in each corner of the main area provides further opportunities for players to develop and practise their turning skills. They may use a turn first of all when attempting to create space to move away from their partner so that they can travel towards one of the four areas. This could then be followed by the player performing an additional turn as they travel to the chosen area. If the player feels that the defender is gaining ground on them and that there is a possibility that they could catch them before they reach the area or that they are already too tight to them, they may look to give themselves more time and space by changing the choice of destination and, therefore, changing direction. All these types of turning require the key ingredients needed to make a turn effective: disguise, balance and speed.

Practice B: Turning

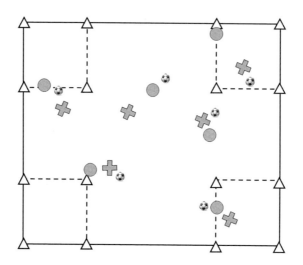

Alteration to Original Set-Up

- Additional areas are added to the main area, one in each corner.
- Players are now awarded a point if they successfully enter and exit any of these new areas.
- Players compete against their partner. The player with the most points at the end of the specified amount of time wins the game.

Focus

- Which direction to turn? Away from danger and into space.
- Choice and execution of turn.
- Touches: use the smallest number of touches needed to execute the turn.
- Speed: sharpness of turn and acceleration away from the defender.

Possible Progressions/Regressions

- Change the size of the areas in the corner, making them either larger or smaller, therefore changing the amount of space the player has to turn.
- Add an additional area in the centre of the main area. Do not allow the player to exit the side of the area directly opposite the side that they entered. Or, if they do, they do not win a point.

Practice B: Finishing

Being able to retain possession of the ball as an individual close to the opponent's goal can be very rewarding; it can result in space being created for an attempt at goal. For example, if you picture a player receiving the ball in or around the penalty box, if they can keep hold of the ball while under pressure from a defender and manipulate just a small amount of space, this could allow them to get a shot on goal. Therefore, the ability to manipulate space while working in a tight space, close to the opponent's goal, can be priceless. The important message that we need to get across to players in a practice to develop this area of the game is to make sure that they make the most of any space they create immediately. Because of their close proximity to the goal, opposition players will try to close any space instantly to ensure the goal is protected, therefore, any space created by the attacking player will disappear almost immediately, so the shot needs to be taken without any delay.

The number of goal-scoring opportunities that players get within the practice will be largely dependent on the rules that we put in place, particularly around which goals the players can attempt to score in. If we allow players to score in any of the four goals within the practice, it will be very easy for them to create a goal-scoring opportunity as their partner will not know which goal to defend. If the topic of the practice is solely focused on finishing, then this is something that we would likely apply to the practice so that players spend most of their time trying to score. One thing we need to consider with this rule is the safety aspect due to the possibility that a goalkeeper could face more than one shot at the same time. To prevent this, gates may need to be added to the area that players need to travel through before they can attempt a shot on goal, thus restricting when a player can shoot. It also provides the goalkeeper with a trigger for when a player is about to shoot, rather than having to try and watch the whole area and observe numerous players at the same time.

The other option is to restrict players to scoring in just one of the four goals. This will mean that players are defending one goal and trying to score in another one, which is essentially the main principle of the game of soccer. This, in turn, will put more emphasis back on the player retaining possession of the ball while trying to create an opportunity to get a strike on goal. The pressure from the defender is to try to force the player away from the goal. Therefore, they will need to try and find a way to protect the ball while also attempting to maintain their position on the pitch or make progress towards the goal.

Practice B: Finishing

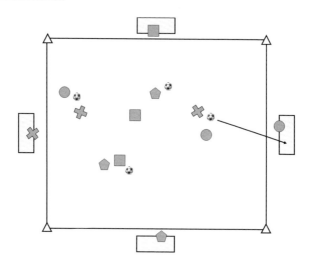

Alteration to Original Set-Up

- Four goals are added to the outside of the area, one to each side. These are situated a distance from the area to ensure that the players have to strike the ball when they are shooting.
- Players continue to work in pairs, and also work with another pair, with one pair working in the area and the other pair acting as the goalkeepers.
- If a player scores or a shot goes wide, the practice restarts with the goalkeeper who plays out to their teammate.

Focus

- Positive and confident in front of goal.
- Having created the opportunity to have a shot on goal; ensure you take it.
- Good balance and a controlled strike.
- Accuracy ahead of power.

Possible Progressions/Regressions

- Move the goals further away or closer to the area.
- Alter the number of goals that the players can score in.
- Add adaptions from other versions of this practice.

Practice B: Pass or Dribble?

Throughout this book, it is stressed that, as coaches, we need to encourage players to keep the ball themselves and provide them with lots of opportunities to practise retaining the ball individually and go past opposition players. But we cannot ignore the fact that passing is an essential part of the game; soccer is, after all, a team game, and so players need to be able to share the ball with their teammates. The design of this practice, however, still encourages, or it could be said 'forces', players to retain the ball individually. The difference now, though, is that sometimes they have the option to pass the ball onto a teammate and need to decide whether or not they need to pass the ball, and if they do, who do they pass to?

There are no actual changes to the practice area; the only difference is that a number of balls have been removed, and the players are now working in teams again. Half the balls are allocated to one team and the other half to the other team. The number of balls used will have a significant impact on what the players actually do within the practice. If too many balls are removed, then the players will spend most of their time passing and receiving. If we do not remove enough balls, then the players will spend a lot of time either trying to keep possession of the ball or win it off another player, meaning there is little difference to the original practice. Therefore, it is important that we get the right balance so that the players retain possession of the ball and only share it with a teammate when they need to or when it is the right time. The main influence on this decision is the group of players in the practice. For instance, it could be that the players have not had much time practising retention of the ball and may need a comfort blanket of a few extra teammates to use when they need to. Equally, more experienced players, or players with higher levels of ability, may need to be challenged further, so fewer options should be available to them.

Because no further alterations are needed, it does not mean that changes cannot be made, and there is no reason why some of the previous adaptions could not be used, alongside the removal of the balls. For instance, the gates that were added to the area for the 'driving with the ball' practice could be included and the same point-scoring system could be used. This allows the players to concentrate on driving with the ball when they have space in front of them, so the focus would be initially on their first touch as they receive the ball from a teammate who is currently unable to drive forward. Or the goals from the finishing practice could be added, with extra goals awarded if a player scores without passing the ball.

Practice B: Pass or Dribble?

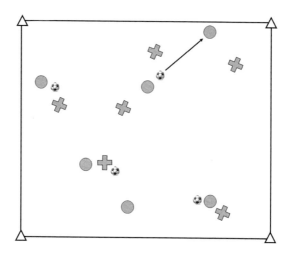

Alteration to Original Set-Up

- Players are put into two teams and are no longer paired up with another player.
- Each team starts with a set number of balls. The total number of balls must be less than the number of players in a team. For instance, if each team has six players, no more than five balls should be used.
- The team in possession of the most balls at the end of a specified time wins the game.

Focus

- Decision making: when to retain the ball and when to pass it?
- Can you use the supporting player to help keep the ball individually?
- If you decide to pass, where exactly does the player receiving the pass want the ball?

Possible Progressions/Regressions

- Add some of the previous adaptions from this chapter.
- The teams do not need to be split equally – challenge the stronger players in the group by putting them on a team with fewer players.
- Have three teams competing against each other (reduces the number of options they have to pass to and also increases the number of opposition players).
- Use a range of different sized balls.
- Change the shape and/or size of the area.

Practice B: Counter-Press

Although this practice still provides the players with an opportunity to develop their ability to maintain individual possession, the focus for the coach now moves on to what the player does immediately after losing possession of the ball. With players and teams often looking to make the most of winning possession of the ball, through exploiting an unorganised and out of shape opposition team, the players should attempt to win the ball back quickly, straight after they have just lost possession. The practice design helps to develop the players' mindset so that they react quickly and either delay the player who has just won the ball, preventing them from progressing forward, or ideally, win back the ball.

Although the players continue to work in pairs, trying to either retain possession or win the ball from their partner, they are now also working as a team, increasing the level of competition within the practice. Each team is allocated half the area and, at the end of the practice, a point is awarded to a team for every ball in their half of the area, and the team with the most balls in their half wins. So, when a team is in possession of the ball, they will try and retain it in their allocated half of the area. This also means that when a player wins possession of the ball, they will try to travel from the opposition's half into their own half, and it is this aspect of the practice that encourages the players to counter-press. On losing possession of the ball, a player's immediate response should be to try and prevent their partner from reaching their half of the area; they need to try and prevent them from travelling forward with the ball.

The initial thought process of the player who has just lost the ball should be to analyse the situation and identify just how dangerous it is, in terms of how quickly and/or easily can their partner get to their designated half of the area with the ball? They will need to take into consideration their partner's positioning in the area, which way they are facing and their own position. So, for instance, if their partner is close to the line that divides the area in half and is facing in the direction they want to travel, while the player who has just lost the ball is positioned alongside their partner, then this is obviously a highly dangerous situation. An opportunity to prevent the player from travelling forward may not be available, so the priority should be to attempt to win the ball back. If, however, the player is in a corner of the area, there is less urgency to win the ball back immediately, instead the priority is to prevent the player from travelling forward and then, once this has been achieved, the focus can then switch to winning the ball. These all involve some form of pressing; it is just a matter of understanding the type of press and the purpose of the press.

Practice B: Counter-Press

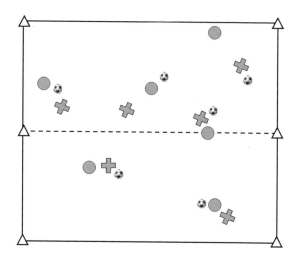

Alteration to Original Set-Up

- Players still work in pairs but are now also put into two teams.
- The area is split into two with one half designated to each team.
- Players try to keep possession of the ball in their team's allocated half. If a player wins possession of the ball, they try to travel with it to their team's half of the area.
- Practice ends after a set amount of time. The team with the most balls in its allocated half of the area wins the game.

Focus

- Immediate reaction to win back the ball: determination and aggression.
- Awareness of the where in the area their partner has won the ball off them.
- What is the purpose of the press?

Possible Progressions/Regressions

- If a team manages to get all the balls into their allocated half, it automatically wins the game.
- A number of gates are added to the line that separates the two halves of the area. Players must travel through one of the gates to get to the other side of the area.
- The area does not have to be split evenly; one area can be larger than the other. This may be an option if one team is having a lot more success than the other.

CHAPTER 4
THE DEVELOPMENT OF YOUNG PLAYERS

The key notion behind these 10 core practices is to provide players with familiar environments that they immediately recognise so that they can concentrate on learning and developing, rather than trying to work out what they are meant to be doing. However, it is pointless placing them within these practices if what they are learning is not important to their development as a player. Key areas of players' performance were discussed within chapter 1 and introduced as topics that a coach should concentrate on as they are the essential foundations needed to play the game of soccer. By concentrating on these fundamental elements of the game, the coach is taking a step towards committing to long-term player development rather than trying to achieve short-term success. However, there are a number of other strategies that need to be put in place and steps that need to be followed if we are going to truly support players in developing over a long period of time, which, in turn, will help them reach their individual potential. As coaches, it is really important that we understand and recognise that the impact we have on the players in the early years of their developmental journey will leave a lasting impression on them for remainder of their soccer career. This is not just regarding the level of ability they reach but also the amount of enjoyment they get from playing the game.

Long-Term Player Development

Before we look at how to implement a long-term approach for the development of the players, we need to fully understand what long-term player development is and why, as coaches, we should adopt this approach. Firstly, we need to understand that it is a systematic and progressive model, which provides an outline of what is needed at each particular stage of the player's journey, regardless of the sport they select to play. It is widely recognised that following this model will provide the players with the best possible chance of reaching their full potential in their chosen sport. In addition to this, they are also more likely to engage in some form of lifelong physical activity. As well as the benefits to the players, it also gives coaches a point of reference to measure the players' progress, and they can monitor what particular areas need less or further development.

At this stage, it is important to highlight that players focusing on just one sport or dedicating their time just to soccer is not being promoted or recommended. In the same way, it is impossible to truly predict what position a young player will be most suited to in the future at the end of their developmental journey (this is why we should never restrict players to just one position at a young age). We cannot forecast for certain that soccer is the sport that they will always enjoy and excel in. Young children sampling a range of different sports should definitely be promoted and encouraged, and hopefully, they will follow a long-term development model in each one, specific to that particular sport. Within the early years of their development, players should experience similar environments in whichever sport they participate in, as a lot of the early fundamental skills and physical attributes they need to develop are applicable to most sports. This is particularly evident in invasion games, such as hockey, rugby, basketball, netball and, of course, soccer. Therefore, experiencing and participating in other sports is actually beneficial to their development as a soccer player. For instance, the skills that players will develop in sports such as rugby or American Football to get past an opponent are very transferable into the game of soccer. The speed, agility and balance, as well as the feint and disguise to shift the opponent's body weight are needed in all three of these sports. Therefore, while getting the opportunity to experience a range of sports, the players are also developing skills that they will use in whatever sport they choose to focus on in the future.

If we look at long-term athlete development models, there are clear guidelines for what we should be doing at each particular stage of training in terms of what is appropriate for their age. And we should definitely use these guidelines to understand the type of experiences that we should provide the players during training sessions. This can, however, get complicated; the guidelines are quite broad and not always suitable or appropriate for the players we are working with. This does not mean that we should not use them; they are definitely an excellent resource with the sole aim of providing children with the best possible opportunity to remain physically active and achieve their full potential in their chosen sport or sports. However, we can simplify them and make them less complicated by following a few simple rules.

The first rule that should always be followed with a long-term player development approach is that at whatever stage the players are at in terms of their journey, they are always children. Even as they enter the final stages of their developmental journey, they are still children and, therefore, we need to treat them as children. There are numerous factors that we need to take into consideration when we are working with children, including the terminology that we use, the need for praise and encouragement, how they enjoy playing games and competition and understanding how they learn. For further information about all of these factors and more, please refer to my previous book, *The Intelligent Soccer Coach*. We are usually quite good at recognising this when we work with really young children, however, as they grow older, we have a tendency to start treating them more like adults, especially in terms of the type of practices that we use in training sessions. This is more than understandable as they are heading towards adulthood and the full version of the game, but the fact remains that they are still children. So, although the practices that we use undoubtedly need to evolve to meet the needs of the players and to ensure that they continue to develop, what needs to remain at the heart of everything that we do, is an awareness that we are working with children.

Another key factor that we need to recognise about the process is that it is a 'long-term' process, therefore, the next rule that we need to adopt is patience. If we recognise that the process needs to take place over a long period of time, we cannot expect to see immediate results or improvements in the players' performance. The reason that it is a long-term process, is because it takes a lot of time for the players to learn and develop the different elements of the game. And when you add into the equation the small period of time that we are actually with the players, surely we cannot expect them to pick up a new skill or make the right decisions after just one training session. There is clearly a need to repeat session topics and give the players plenty of time to understand and learn each particular element of the game and, specifically those outlined in chapter 1.

An important part of this need to be patient is the format of the game they play and not to accelerate this aspect of their pathway. Coaches can sometimes be keen to move players on to the next format of the game and, quite often, this can be before it is time to do so. How often do we hear a coach saying that they need to prepare the players for next season? So, the next important rule we need to follow is that there is no need to rush. It is not uncommon for a coach to put the players in an environment that prepares them for what they will experience the following season. So, for instance, if the players are moving to a format that now introduces offsides to the game, it is often recommended that they should start playing games where the offside rule is used, or that they should start using it in training during the season before they are going to use it so they are ready for next season. And it is not limited just to the rules changing; there are a number of other elements of soccer that change as well as the players get older, such as the number of players, which impacts how teams keep possession. There is also less emphasis on individual possession and more emphasis on team possession or the size of the pitch increasing, thus tactics such as switching play are introduced, as well as techniques like long passing.

Introducing these new factors before the players need to be exposed to them takes away some of the time they should spend practising and playing in the current format. One reason that they are playing this particular format of the game is that it is deemed to be the most suitable version for the players at this particular stage of their journey, taking into account key factors such as physical development and the players' level of understanding of the game. The other main reason they are playing in a certain format is that it provides the players with an opportunity to concentrate on learning and improving specific elements of the game, which they will then use in other versions of the game in the future. Each format is a building block to the next step in the process, with each block as important as all the others. Therefore, we should not be looking to move out of a format prematurely; the players can practise whatever new elements of the game are introduced when they are playing that particular version of the game.

The final rule that we should try and follow with long-term player development is to try and replicate scenarios found in the game into the practices that are used during training. This means not only providing realistic and relevant situations for the players to practise but also scenarios that are specific to the format of the game that they are playing. So, just as we should not rush ahead and allow them to develop and improve in the format of the game that they are playing, we should also ensure that the practices we provide during training replicate the version of the game that they currently play. So, if we take the really young players as an example, when we watch them play a game a common picture is the players retaining the ball themselves – there is not as much evidence that the players share the ball or are in good positions to receive the ball. Therefore, the practices within chapter 3 are ideal for younger children, as they represent what the players will spend most of their time doing in the game. Training should, therefore, be made up mainly of one versus one practices. Of course, team possession should also be introduced and developed, but the principal focus should be on the individual battles that the players will come across during a game. Another example of the pictures we see during a game with younger children is that the ball is usually situated where there are only a small number of players within close proximity to the player on the ball. From this we can infer that there are only a small number of players involved in the actual action at any one time and, therefore, the practices that we provide should represent this.

When we look at the different core practices provided throughout this book, they should not be used exactly how they are shown within the diagrams. Measurements have purposefully not been provided, as the size of the area should be suitable for the players participating within it, and a number of factors should be taken into consideration, such as age, playing experience, ability and the number of players. Similarly, the exact number of players is also not stipulated for the same reasons. In particular, where the practices have more of a team focus rather than an individual focus, such as Practices F and H, the numbers in these type of practices should be reduced when working with younger players and, if needed, two separate areas should be set up to allow for smaller numbers to participate. Just like the different formats of the games they play, the practices should have small numbers to begin with and then, as the players get older, the numbers can increase, which, in turn, increases the complexity.

The overall purpose of adopting a long-term approach to player development is the person and the player they become at the end of the process. Therefore, the only goals that we should look to achieve along the way are enjoyment and progression. If players are going to make it to the end of the developmental pathway, they need to have fun during the whole of the journey. If they do not enjoy themselves, why would they continue with the process? We need to keep the players engaged and motivated, and this will only be achieved if they enjoy the environment we create for them. Our other main aim should be to support them in their development so that they improve and progress continuously throughout their journey. To do this, we need to follow a step-by-step process, concentrating on one step of their development journey at a time, so that they are fully prepared for the next step, which they will move on to, when it is the right time.

Individual Needs

When planning a session or considering the development needs of players, we usually view the players as one group. This is quite understandable with soccer being a team game and all the players needing to practise the same core topics, particularly within the early years of their development. So why would you plan a range of different activities for individual players or small groups of players? However, at the same time, we also need to recognise that the group of the players we are working with is made up of a number of individuals and that no one player is the same. So, although it would not be expected for a coach to plan a range of practices to meet the individual needs of each player, or that we even would if we could, they would not represent the game of soccer. What we can and should try to do, is to meet some of these individual needs within the practices that we provide for the group.

Most coaches will work with a group of players who are all within the same age band, whether this is through their school year or the year that they were born. However, this can be different for some coaches, where they work with 'dual' age bands and the age of the players is spread across two years rather than one, or they may just have one or two players who are playing up an age group. The differences between these players can be quite significant, but the differences between players of the same age group can be just as big, if not bigger. There are no set rules or guidelines that children follow in their growth and we all change in different ways and at varying rates across all elements of human development, including physically, mentally and socially. And even as individuals, our development does not follow a stable and consistent pathway; there will be natural stages throughout our lives where we experience accelerated periods of growth around certain aspects of our development. For instance, physically we go through growth spurts while mentally and/or socially, we can start to mature quite quickly. And then in addition to this, there will be constant changes to our lives that will have either a direct or indirect impact on one or more of our areas of development, for instance, moving house, changing schools, friendship groups or even trying a new sport. So as coaches, not only will we have a group of individual players, the make-up of that group will constantly be changing and evolving, and therefore the needs of each specific player will change throughout the time that we spend with them and, sometimes, this could be as sudden as the time between the last training session and the next one.

We cannot expect players to learn or to progress at the same rate. For starters, they will all enter the developmental pathway at different levels across all the different aspects of the game. They will then create and follow their own personal pathway; they will start at their own point A and arrive at point B at different times to everyone else, and they will need to face and overcome their own personal challenges along the way. Therefore, although the basis of the practice can be the same for every player, the actual support we provide the players during the practice will need to be individualised and specific. This can be achieved in a number of ways, such as individual interventions, which is covered in chapter 8, and individual challenges, which are discussed within chapter 12. One of the other strategies that can be used is to give different options within the practices that provide an assortment of challenges with varying levels of difficulty. Having these different options allows the practice to meet the needs of most or all of the players.

These different options can be achieved in a number of ways, such as through scoring systems, so players are rewarded if they complete more difficult tasks with extra points. So, if we look back at Practice B from chapter 3 and particularly the practice with a focus on driving with the ball, one of the progressions within this practice is to introduce different coloured gates worth different amounts of points. To achieve higher points, the players have to earn them, so the task they have to complete must be more challenging than the one needed for fewer points. In this particular instance, the gates where players can win more points could be smaller in size or located in more difficult parts of the area, such as the corners. Similarly, when the focus is switched to turning and the four areas (one in each corner of the main area) are introduced to the practice, these also do not have to be the same size, and the players score more points by completing a turn in the smaller areas. Another option is to provide a further task that players can attempt if they want to. By completing this additional task, they can they achieve bonus points. If we stay with Practice B and, specifically, the one versus one attacking practice where the attacking player must travel through the central area to gain a point, a further area could be added within it, or gates could be added to each side of the area, or both could be introduced to the practice. Players could then win bonus points by travelling through these additional targets while completing the main task of dribbling through the central area. Adding further ways in which the players can pick up points gives the players 'options' so that they can choose the level of difficulty they face in the practice. By attempting to win the bonus points, they also risk not winning any points at all. Therefore, it is likely that the stronger players in the group, will attempt the bonus points more often, compared with everyone else. By providing the players with these choices, we start to meet their individual needs.

Another option when providing the players with an environment to support their individual needs is to give them the option of making the practice easier so that when they feel they need to they can reduce the level of difficulty. This can be seen within the original set-up for Practice B, where a possible regression is to introduce 'safety areas' where the players on the ball can travel through these areas (they are not allowed to stop) but their partners are not allowed. Additional rules can be added to these areas, such as limiting the number of times the players are allowed to use them, and this can be linked to how well the players are performing within the practice. So, for example, the players who lost the previous round (i.e. did not have possession of the ball at the end of a set period of time) are allowed in the 'safety areas' more times than the players who won. Additional areas such as these can be used in most practices; the rules that we use alongside them just need to be adapted to meet the needs of the focus of the practice.

When incorporating anything into a practice that supports individual development, we need to ensure that whatever we have added is linked to the actual topic of the practice.

Looking back on the one versus one topic for Practice B, a further area and/or gates were added for the players to gain extra points. Both of these possible additions are directly linked to the focus of the session and give the players an opportunity to practise the topic at an increased level of difficulty. If the options are not linked to the focus of the session, say, for instance it was connected to finishing or forward passing, we will not be supporting or challenging the players that need stretching in this particular area of the game. Instead, we will just be adding an additional task to the practice, which can be absolutely fine, as it provides more realism to the practice, by adding an 'after' part to the topic of the session. For example, if the focus is dribbling, in a game when a player dribbles, they would eventually do something 'after' the dribble, such as take a shot or pass to a teammate. So, in a practice we can include one of these for the players to attempt once they have completed the main task of dribbling. But we need to be careful that we do not lose focus of the topic and so all of the support we give to the players is aimed at the topic of the session, including any additional challenges that we provide, which might help stretch and develop the 'stronger' players within the group. At this point, it is worth noting that these additional challenges are not exclusive for the stronger players within the group; all players should be encouraged to attempt them. But because the players have a choice whether or not to try them, and since they will be more difficult to achieve compared with the original task just on its own, it should be expected that the 'stronger' players are more likely to attempt them more often.

Meeting the individual needs of every single player during a session is a near impossible task, and we should never put pressure on ourselves by thinking that is achievable and that we should accomplish it in every session. However, what we should be trying to do, as well as supporting the group as a whole, is to try to support as many players individually as possible. This may be only two or three players, but the benefits that those particular players will gain from this individual support will be significant, as it will act as an accelerant in their development. If we can then switch our focus to a different set of players the following week, we can work towards providing all the players with individual support over just a small number of training sessions. By doing so, we will be able to offer each player specific support that is personal to them, on a regular basis, which can only be beneficial for their development.

Freedom

One of the common themes that runs through all of the core practices in this book is that the players are given freedom in all of them. None of the practices require the players to stand on a cone and pass a ball to a player stood on another cone, nor are they required to dribble the ball along a certain pathway. Yes, the players are asked to complete certain tasks, such as receive a pass and then pass it onto another player, but who they receive the ball from, when they do this and where they position themselves to receive it, is decided by the player and not by the coach, and it is the same when they pass the ball on afterwards. Similarly, the players may be asked to dribble through a gate to win a point, but the path they take to get to the gate and the skills that they use to go past a defender to get through the gate are selected by the player, it has not been predetermined by the coach.

When playing in a game, we want players to be able to make quick decisions and, more importantly, the right decisions. However, when making a decision in a game of soccer, there is not always a definitive answer to the question being asked. For instance, should a player retain the ball themselves or pass it to a teammate? Most of the time, the answer to this question will not be known until later on when the passage of play has been completed and, even then, we will never really know what would have happened if the player had made a different decision. The other important thing to remember is that what might be the right decision for one player is not necessarily the right decision for another player. For example, there could be a situation where a player has the option either to have a shot on goal themselves or share it with a teammate who is in arguably a better position. In certain instances, the right decision for some players would be to have a shot themselves whereas, for other players, it could be that their strengths are more suited to passing and, so, they believe the better decision would be to create a goal-scoring opportunity for their teammate.

Therefore, if we are truly going to help the players get as close as they can to achieving their full potential, a key area that we need to help them develop is decision making. And the only way in which we can do this is to provide them with environments where they have to keep making decisions. By doing so, we are first of all allowing them to come across situations that they will experience in a game, where they will need to make a decision. This could be going past an opponent with the ball – which skill will they use? Which side will they go past the defender? When exactly will they attempt to do this? And, in addition to this, they will learn from the outcome of the decision that they made whether it was successful or not. They will learn what works and what does not work, what they need to do to be successful, what are the likely outcomes of the different decisions that they can make, as well as numerous other pieces of information that will help them make the correct decision when they are in a similar situation within a game.

Quite often, it may not be completely obvious to somebody watching a practice that the players are purposefully placed in an environment that is helping them with their decision making. Instead, what they see is a practice that looks messy, with little learning taking place because the coach is not telling them what to do. Similarly, it can be difficult for coaches to stand back and watch when a practice is not going how we envisaged it would. As coaches, we can be highly self-critical in that we want everything to be perfect, and therefore, we put added pressure on ourselves when we feel something is not working. Because of this, sometimes, we can focus all our attention on ensuring the players are performing how we want them to and making sure the practice looks aesthetically pleasing. Quite often, we mistake this 'correction' for player development, when, in fact, we have either stopped the learning process in its tracks or prevented it from even beginning. When working with young children in particular, we need to be brave as coaches and 'embrace chaos', which can often provide the perfect environment for player development.

Where there is chaos you will usually find problem solving, creativity and decision making. By making a practice too structured, particularly when working with really young players, we take away the opportunity for players to develop these key aspects of the game. We must, therefore, be brave as coaches, by being comfortable with our practices looking 'messy', and see through what might seem chaotic to see the learning that is taking place. The most effective way we can embrace chaos and use it in the development of the players is to actually plan for it so that it becomes 'organised chaos'. To do this, we need to ensure that the practices contain some of the key ingredients – traffic, multiple directions, constant involvement and of course freedom. An example of how this can be achieved can be seen in Practice B, which focuses on driving with the ball. Because all the players share the same area and then, more importantly, try to go through the same small number of spaces (i.e. the gates), players will inevitably get in the way of each other. For some, this may be a concern as it does not allow the players to concentrate on driving with the ball. But we need to remember that when they play in a game, they will be in a very similar environment with the available spaces constantly changing due to the other players on the pitch moving and altering their position. Therefore, players need to practise identifying where the space is within the area/pitch and adapting how they are travelling with the ball. So, for instance, if another player moves into the space where the player on the ball wants to travel to, they may need to slow down and then accelerate, or they might have to change the direction in which they are travelling. By providing a chaotic environment, we allow the players to experience similar situations that they will face in a game and practise lots of different elements of the session topic that they would not be able to do in a structured, 'drill'-like practice.

The Need for Progression

It may seem obvious to say that during their developmental journey, the level of the practices and sessions that the players participate in need to increase in difficulty as the only way they will improve is if they are continuously challenged so they can progress as a player. But this does not just relate to the long-term process but also in the short term, specifically within individual practices. If we do not increase the level of difficulty within a practice, not only do we restrict how much players can improve, but it is also likely that we will fail to keep them motivated and engaged in the activity.

One of the main purposes of the core practices is for the players to recognise and become familiar with them so that they are active immediately. It also allows them to focus solely on playing and learning, rather than trying to figure out what it is they are supposed to be doing. To achieve this, the core practices need to be quite simple in their design so they are easy for the players to understand. Because the practices are opposed, the opposition players will always create some form of challenge and the level of difficulty will constantly change depending on a range of factors, such as the players and how many they are up against, where exactly in the area the dual is taking place and what they are specifically trying to achieve. But despite this level of difficulty naturally occurring within the practice, it still needs to steadily increase if we are to support the players in their development.

The first progression that we introduce are the adaptions that are made to give the practice a specific focus. So, immediately, we increase the level of difficulty by introducing an additional task for the players to complete. So, in Practice B, the initial task is for the players to retain individual possession of the ball, then a further task is added when we introduce the topic of the session. So, for forward passing, the player has to keep possession of the ball while trying to advance into the other side of the area, before passing the ball into a small goal and, to finish, they have to retain the ball while trying to create an opportunity to have a shot on goal. Therefore, we increased the level of engagement and motivation for the players straight away by introducing something new for them to attempt. The next step is to increase the level of difficulty so that there is an impact on their development.

The first important thing to recognise is when to actually introduce the progression. Quite often a progression is introduced because we have planned for one and therefore feel that we should use it, or because it is seen as something that should happen in every practice. But before we do this, we need to make sure that the players are actually ready for the progression to be introduced, there is no point making the practice more difficult if they are struggling to find success in the current format of the practice. If it is the case that they are finding limited success, then there are a number of strategies that we can use to support the players to help them improve. The main two that involve some form of intervention will be covered in chapter 8, and then the other option is to regress the practice rather than progress it. Regressing a practice or making it easier is not something we often do as a coach, whether it is because we do not like to think that the players are not able to do the practice, or that if we do regress it, it means that we have made a mistake in that the practice is too hard for them. Neither of these should be a concern, if regressing a practice is the right decision, in terms of the needs of the players, then that should be the priority. If it is too difficult for the players and they are finding very little or even no success, then just continuing or possibly making it harder by actually progressing it, could have a significant impact on their enjoyment and confidence. The only difficulty we should have is choosing or identifying when we should regress it because if we step in too soon, we might stop the players from solving the issue themselves and therefore we would have taken away an opportunity for them to learn and also develop. No manual can tell us specifically when the time is right to make adjustments to a practice, it takes time and experience on the pitch and, eventually, small 'triggers' will become evident, which tells the coach that the players need support and that the practice needs to be regressed. And this exactly the same for progressions within the practice.

Just because players are finding success within a practice does not mean that a progression needs to be introduced to make it more difficult. First of all, we need to look at how much success they are achieving and the reason why they are achieving it. If players continuously achieve success and find the practice too easy, then something needs to be done to make it more challenging. If, however, they are finding success, but only occasionally, we should not be too hasty in making the practice more difficult. Moving it on too quickly may impact their confidence and motivation. Going from being able to complete a task to then not being able to do it at all can be quite frustrating and demoralising. There is an argument that we need to put the players into what is known as the 'ugly zone', where they find themselves within an environment that pushes their performance until it becomes 'unstable', in other words, just beyond their current levels of ability. And this absolutely needs to be done if we are going to challenge them, which is an essential part of their development. However, what we need to ensure is that while they are within this 'ugly zone' they can see at least small elements of improvement within their performance so that they remain motivated and encouraged to keep trying. Therefore, we need to ensure that the players are ready to move on to the next step and that it is not too big of a step for them to make. We also need to be careful that they are not achieving success because of the practice set-up or design rather than their ability. For instance, if we look ahead to Practice C in chapter 5 and, in particular, the adaption that focuses on driving with the ball, the main reason players find success within this specific practice is because of the starting position of the player who will be driving with the ball. If they are too far ahead of the defender, it could be an almost impossible task to catch the attacking player. Therefore, before we look at increasing the difficulty of the practice, through adding an extra task or making the current one harder, we may just need to adjust the existing practice to ensure it is achieving the aims of the session.

Another factor to consider when we introduce a progression to a practice is whether it is linked to the focus of the session. We can make a practice more difficult in numerous ways, but unless it is linked to the session topic, there is no point in introducing it, as it can either send the players mixed messages in terms of what they are trying to learn or it could even be counterproductive to the learning process. If we use the pass or dribble practice from chapter 3 as an example, if we introduce a progression of a maximum number of touches, then we take away the decision-making element from the players; they will no longer make the decision of when they should pass the ball, instead they will just look to pass it before they run out of touches. So, we need to ensure that the progression that we introduce is directly linked to the session topic. For instance, one of the progressions suggested for Practice B (pass or dribble) is to split the players into three teams. Doing this reduces the number of options that a player has in terms of teammates they can pass to, while also increasing the number of opposition players trying to win the ball from them. Therefore, when they have the ball, it is more difficult to retain possession and also harder to pass it on to a teammate, as there are less options available. We just need to remember that we should only support them in one element of the game at a time (the session topic), so that all of their learning and development can focus on this one particular aspect. Therefore, everything found within the practice – the coaching points, the support provided by the coach, any possible regressions or progressions, etc. – needs to be linked to the session topic.

The final part of introducing a progression is that we should not always know which progression we are going to introduce before the session has started. Sometimes there is a logical order in which progressions can be introduced to a practice, and therefore, they can be pre-planned to be introduced if or when they are needed. However, it can also be beneficial to have a number of progressions to choose from and then select the one that is appropriate in terms of the needs of the players. For Practice B, where the focus is on forward passing, two of the possible progressions are to either move the goals/targets further away from the area or to reduce the size of the goals/targets they are passing into. Moving the goals/targets further away from the area will mainly challenge the players' weight of pass, and by reducing the size of them, we focus more on the accuracy of the pass. If we introduce both progressions, we will impact both of these elements of forward passing. Therefore, instead of already planning which progression we will introduce first, it would be more beneficial for the development of the players if we attempt to identify which one would be more appropriate, from observing the practice and the performance of the players within it. It is, therefore, recommended that a number of progressions are pre-planned beforehand and that the coach then selects one or more of these during the practice to meet the needs of the players at that specific moment in time.

Knowing Your Players

The final part of young player development is the need to get to know the players as a group as a whole and also as individuals. We can put forward a number of ways to support players both in their development and also in their enjoyment of the game, but not everything will work for the group of players that we are working with. As already discussed, players enter the developmental process with different levels of ability across all elements of the game – technical, psychological, physical, etc., and they will then develop across these areas at different rates. In the same way, players differ in terms of how they like to receive support, the way information is given to them, how they like the session to be structured, etc. Therefore, some of the advice given in this book, and all other books and resources, will not be appropriate or work, with every group of players. However, most of them will, it is just a matter of working out which ones do and then using these within the delivery of the sessions.

When trying to work out what the players enjoy or react well to, one thing we should never do is make the assumption that they would not like something. Quite often when a coach does this, it is not because they know the players would not enjoy a particular idea or strategy, but because they think it will not work or that it is a good idea. But before we rule anything out as a coach, we should, at least, give the players an opportunity to have a go and experience it. Young children have a habit of surprising us and not reacting how we expect them to when something new is introduced to them; they can be extremely resilient and can adapt well to change. Therefore, we should allow them the opportunity to decide whether they enjoy something or not before deciding whether to include it or not as part of our coaching practice. Of course, not all children will react the same way in terms of being open to something new, some will react as we predict they will, but this should not discourage us from trying different approaches.

We also need to consider that something the players may like at one particular moment in time can, and probably will, change over time. This is to be expected, as this is the case with most aspects of their lives as they grow older and have new experiences: starting high school, new friendship groups, new interests and needs. Therefore, we need to continue to monitor and evaluate what works with the players and what no longer has the impact that we would like it to have. A good example of this are individual interventions, which we will look at in greater detail in chapter 8. In the early stages of the players' development, players are usually quite happy to be given individual support and information by the coach. The only challenge that we may face is how to keep the players focused. They can be easily distracted by the other players who are continuing to play, because, understandably, they want to get back to playing themselves. However, as they get older, players can sometimes become less receptive to individual support, as they can see it as being singled out or they might feel that they are not doing as well as the other players if they are the only ones who need support. So instead of taking the information on board and being part of the process, they will distance themselves from the coach and attempt to rejoin the practice. Using individual interventions from the start of their development will definitely help reduce this, as it just becomes something that they are used to and see as a normal part of the session, but this still does not guarantee that they will always be receptive to it and, therefore, we may need to approach it differently sometimes.

There are definitely things we should and should not do when it comes to coaching and, in particular, coaching young soccer players. For instance, the environment that we place them in has to be fun and safe, and we need to put them in practices where they have lots of freedom to express themselves with the opportunity to make their own decisions. But just as importantly, there are different ways that we can achieve these 'coaching essentials', which is important, not only to meet the needs of the players that the coach is working with but also to give the coach the opportunity to get their own personality across in their coaching – which is an absolute must. It is important for the coach to be themselves, otherwise they will not enjoy it and they will either stop coaching or the players will pick up on the fact they are not happy. In addition to this, we do not want to produce 'robotic' players or players that have the exact same qualities and characteristics as every other player. So, alongside the strategies that are non-negotiable when working with young players, there also needs to be an individual approach that will help meet the needs of each single player, while they make their way along the development pathway.

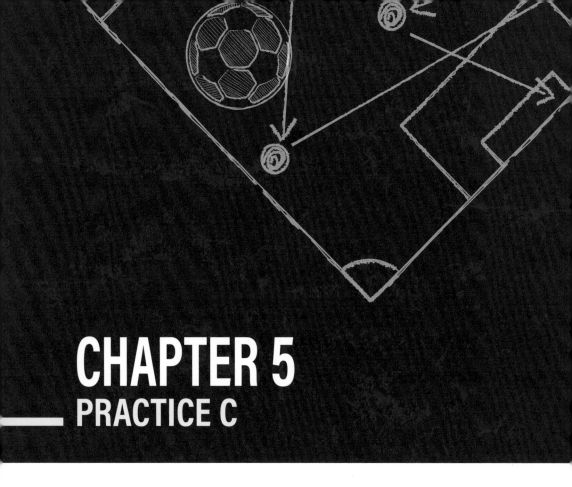

CHAPTER 5
PRACTICE C

Continuing the theme of players keeping possession of the ball, the basis of Practice C is an attacking player attempting to go past a defender. The practice allows the players and the coach to concentrate on both the defensive and attacking aspects of this part of the game. However, while the players will naturally be able to work on both of these parts of the game as they regularly change their role within the practice, it is important to remember that the session should have just one focus and, therefore, the only support that the coach should give to the players is information directly linked to the topic. So, if the session is focusing on one versus one attacking, the coach should only support the attacking players even if the defenders are making mistakes and we can identify what they need help with, we need to remain focused on the players who are in possession of the ball. What we can do, is manage the defending players by ensuring the practice design and set-up allows and encourages them to defend correctly. We will look at this in more detail shortly, but we can just give them small reminders, such as 'think about how we want you to defend'. We can also deliver the same practice the following week and just flip the focus of the session so that all the support we provide is now aimed at the players who do not have the ball, in other words, the defenders. By making sure we only concentrate on the session topic, we ensure that the players have a clear focus in terms of their learning, and we do not overload them with too much information.

When we first think about an attacker coming up against a defender in a game of soccer, our thoughts usually turn to a wide player up against a full back, and this is definitely a suitable example of when this situation would occur. However, in the modern game, these pictures now occur a lot more often, for instance, with a number of teams now applying a high press, defenders attempting to play out from the back will, at some point, find themselves up against an opposition player in a one versus one situation. Similarly, midfielders will try to go past an opponent as a strategy to break a line, to create space and progress forward. Therefore, it is really important that we give all young players the opportunity to practise this specific element of the game, both as the attacking player and also the defender. Obviously, a lot more time should be spent on the attacking side, especially as this will be particularly hard for players to master if they do not start to practise it from an early age. This practice puts them in a situation where they have no choice but to go attempt to go past the defender in a one versus one situation.

As with other practices of this type, such as one player up against another player, it is important that we regularly change who the players work with. Quite often we are tempted to group players of similar ability together, as we believe it is beneficial for their development, as well as their enjoyment of the session and levels of self-esteem. If we pair them with who we perceive to be a stronger player, we think it will be too easy for the stronger player and too hard for the other player, and therefore, it will not benefit either of them in terms of their development. However, what we need to remember is that different players will provide different challenges. For instance, a strategy that is used successfully to go past one player will not necessarily work against another player. Therefore, the players need to build a library of possible solutions that they can use to solve the problem they are faced with, and then they can select the one that they think will most likely to lead to their success. This is really important for their preparation to play soccer because when they come to play in a match, they will not just come up against players of similar ability but will, of course, face a wide range of players with different areas of strength and areas that need developing. So, within our training sessions, we cannot always place them with the same players because we think that they are of a similar level of ability. If we do this, then we are not providing them with the support that they need to be successful within a game.

This particular practice also provides a really good opportunity to discuss the importance of what happens before and after the actual action that is being focused on during the practice. So, in this particular practice, the main focus or action, is on the attacking player attempting to go past the defender. As coaches, we usually only look at this aspect of the performance and sometimes neglect what happens just before the action and straight after. This is shown in the traditional set-up for this type of practice where the defender and the attacker start directly in front of each other and the defender starts by passing the ball to the attacker. The attacker then has to stop the ball on the line where the defender started to win a point. When an attacking player finds themselves in a one versus one situation against a defender during a game, they would not have received the ball from an opposition player standing directly in front of them. Instead, it is a lot more likely they would have received a pass from a teammate playing an angled pass, which is replicated within the practice by the activity that starts with the server playing the pass to the attacker. This allows the attacker to practise receiving the pass and taking their first touch in a more realistic situation, which they are likely to come across during a game. Also, the position of the server can be regularly changed to allow the attacker to practise receiving the ball from different angles. The positioning of the defender is also key. When the attacker initially receives the ball in the game, the defender they are up against is unlikely to be standing directly in front of them. Instead they are likely to approach them at an angle, as beforehand they would have been providing cover and support, and/or helping their team remain compact. Therefore, the starting position of the defender within the practice provides a more realistic situation and enables both of the players to practise in an environment that they will find themselves in during a game. Finally, within a game, once a player has gone past a defender, they will then do something else: pass, shoot, drive with the ball, etc. They will not just stop the ball. Therefore, the extra element of passing the ball into the small goal adds further realism to the practice.

This practice also presents a good opportunity to reinforce one of the key contributors that provides the best possible environment for player development, which was outlined in the previous chapter. In this practice, it is tempting to try and work on a specific skill and restrict the attacking players to use this particular skill to attempt to go past the defender. But it is really important that we provide the players with the freedom to come up with their own solutions and strategies to get past the defender. Restricting them to a specific skill not only makes it easier for the defender – as they will know what the attacker is attempting to do – but more importantly, we prevent the attacking player from being creative and able to make a decision about where there is space to exploit, as well as the positioning and actions of the defender. Being given the freedom to experiment and discover what does and does not work is critical in the development of players.

Practice C: Original Set-Up

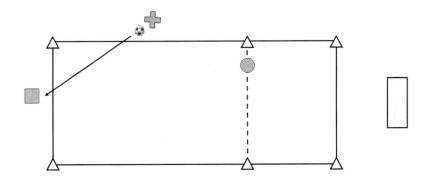

Set-Up

- Three players are allocated to each pitch. One player acts as a server, with the other two players taking on the roles of defender and attacker.
- The server passes into the attacker, and the defender then becomes active and tries to win the ball.
- Once the server has played the ball, they move to where the attacker started the practice.
- The attacker tries to cross the line and get into the second area where they can attempt to pass into the small goal/gates.
- If the defender wins the ball, they win a point by passing it back to the server.

Focus (Attacker)

- Positive in their play: always travel forward and do not turn back.
- Skill: choice, timing, execution, etc.
- Try to shift the defender's body weight one way and take the ball the other way.
- Acceleration into the space once it has been created.
- Completion of the pass into the small goal/gates.

Possible Progressions/Regressions

- Alter the size and/or shape of the area.
- Change the start position of any of the players.
- The server plays the pass once the defender starts to close down the attacker.
- After playing the ball in, the server enters the practice as an extra defender.
- Use a smaller ball.

Practice C: One Versus One Defending

The first number of adaptions to this particular practice will concentrate on the defender, with this specific adaption focusing on the defending aspect of a one versus one. With small adjustments to the original set-up of the practice, the coach could switch their attention to the defender rather than the attacking player. This also allows the players to see that there is now more of a focus on the player defending. The nature of the practice obviously allows the players to practise the attacking element of a one versus one, and this adds to the development of the player who is defending because the attacker will be trying new ideas and learning from previous experiences, thus making the environment unpredictable for the defender.

The switch of focus from attacker to defender is achieved by providing an incentive for the defender and making more points available to them than the attacker. The additional point awarded if the defender can pass the ball back to the server is particularly important as it sends the players a positive message that we do not want them just to try and win the ball, we want them to try and win it and also gain possession, if possible. Although this is not always possible, and the priority should be to prevent the opposition player from advancing and getting closer to the goal, there is obviously a major advantage that can be gained if, while attempting to win the ball, a player can actually win possession of the ball and then move it on to a teammate. By doing so, there is an opportunity for the team to counter-attack; with the opposition not set up defensively, there will be spaces available to exploit.

Rewarding the defender with a point if they prevent the attacker from entering the second zone will encourage the defender to engage the player on the ball quicker and closer to where they receive it from the server. This gives them an opportunity and the time to recover, should the attacker manage to get past them. If they allow the attacker to take control of the situation and come onto them, it leaves them with little or no chance to recover. Therefore, it helps the players develop one of the basic principles of defending – to force the attacking player away from the goal. Forcing the opposition away from the goal in a game of soccer obviously makes it more difficult for them to score while, at the same time, making it easier to score, should you win possession of the ball. The same principle is achieved within this practice through the set-up and the scoring system.

Practice C: One Versus One Defending

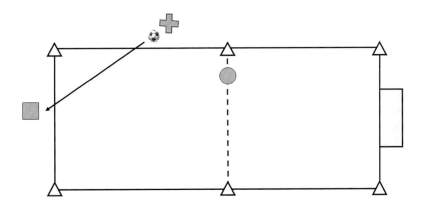

Alteration to Original Set-Up

- The area is extended to where the small goal/gates are situated.
- The attacker needs to enter the second zone before they can attempt to pass the ball into the small goal/gates.
- The defender wins one point if they prevent the attacker entering the second zone and two points if they also manage to pass the ball back to the server.

Focus

- Aggressive and explosive approach to close down the attacker.
- Angle and line of approach.
- Slow down as you get closer to the attacker.
- Body position to be side-on and knees bent.
- Patience – wait for the right time to try and win the ball.

Possible Progressions/Regressions

- Alter the size and/or shape of the area.
- Increase or decrease the size of the goal/gates.
- Change the start position of any of the players.
- Allow the attacker to pass back to the server.
- Use two small goals/gates instead of just one.
- Attacker can attempt to make the pass into the small goal/gates at any time. They receive an extra point (two points) if they do so from inside the second zone.

Practice C: Cover and Support

The theme of defending continues in this next adaption of the practice, but the focus is on the second defender. As outlined in chapter 1, it takes time for players to gain a good understanding of where they should be positioned as the second defender and, therefore, this practice starts to provide them with guidelines of where they should be to engage the opposition player, should they be successful in getting past the 'first defender'. It also allows them to work on switching their role from first defender to second defender and vice versa. The nature of any practice that concentrates on cover and support will also give players a chance to work on their one versus one defending. The focus for the coach, however, needs to stay with the second defender.

The two key aspects of providing cover and support identified earlier in the book are the angle and the distance between the two defenders. It is important that the supporting defender does not get too close or too flat to the first defender, while also ensuring that they are not too far away. Because the practice begins with the two defenders locked into the two separate halves of the area, this almost forces the second defender to be the correct distance from their partner. When the ball is in the opposite half of the area, the player acting as second defender will usually move over as far as they can to their partner's side. In other words, they will position themselves close to the line that splits the area in half. Therefore, the set-up of the area helps the players to position themselves the correct distance away from their teammate, this then allows them to concentrate on ensuring that the angle is correct. If the second defender positions themselves too high up within the area (i.e. level or ahead of the first defender), it could be possible for the attacker to go past both defenders in one action. And if they are too far behind their teammate, the attacker might be able to go past the first defender by entering the other half and then cutting back in before the second defender has an opportunity to engage. Then, as the attacker switches into the other half of the area, the defenders also get to practise, changing their role from second to first defender or from first to second defender.

When the players are ready to be challenged further, we can unlock them from the areas. At first, this may look as if it will make it easier for the defenders, but unlocking them removes their guidelines, putting more ownership on the second defender to position themselves correctly. If needed, the actual line separating the two halves can be left in to provide the players with some form of guide for where they should be in relation to the first defender.

Practice C: Cover and Support

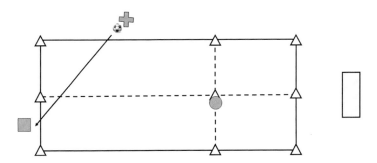

Alteration to Original Set-Up

- The area is split in half, as shown within the diagram.
- The server plays the pass as usual to the attacking player positioned to enter the furthest half of the area.
- Once the server has played the pass to the attacker, they enter the nearest half of the area and become an additional defender. The other defender enters the furthest area.
- The two defenders are locked into their designated halves of the area while the attacker is free to go anywhere as normal.
- If a defender wins the ball, they look to pass to their teammate to win a point.

Focus

- Positioning of the defender in the area where the attacker is not situated (second defender).
- The second defender should be situated further back than the first defender to be in a position to provide cover and support.
- If the attacker enters the other half of the area, the second defender needs to engage the attacker and the other defender becomes the second defender.

Possible Progressions/Regressions

- Alter the size and/or shape of the area.
- The defenders can change the half of the pitch they are situated, but the balance of one defender in each half of the area must remain in place.
- The defenders are completely unlocked.
- Allow the attacker to enter the area in either of the two halves.

Practice C: Recovery Runs

The final adaption for this practice with the focus on the defender rather than the player on the ball looks at recovery runs and getting into the correct position before engaging the attacking player. The set-up of the practice should make it near enough impossible for the defender to win the ball if they decide to go directly to their opponent, as they will not have enough time to get to them before they reach the second zone, which the defender cannot enter. This may be a situation where we have to manage the players carrying out the task not linked to the topic of the practice, in other words, the server and the attacker. It will only be impossible for the defender to catch their opponent if the pass from the server is played into the right area and the attacker is direct in their play. To help ensure this happens, we may need to set the attacker the challenge of 'getting to the second area as fast as possible' (by being direct) and ask the server how they can help them to do this (the pass should be played in front of the attacker or to their back foot). We cannot, of course, expect the server and the attacker to get this right every single time, but encouraging them to play in this way will help create a situation where the defender cannot get to the player on the ball in time.

By creating a scenario where the defender is unable to catch the attacker, it helps the player to understand that if it is not possible to win the ball back immediately, their next priority should be to protect the goal. Even if we want them to press the ball after they have just lost possession (i.e. counter-press), this is not always the correct decision or might not even be feasible due to their positioning on the pitch. In these circumstances, we want the players to help protect the goal by getting themselves goalside and in a position where they help the team remain compact. Although this practice takes away the decision-making process of whether they should counter-press or recover, it allows them to practise making the correct run that enables them to get between the ball and the goal or, in this instance, the second area. Once they have achieved this, they can then engage the attacker using the key coaching points outlined in one versus one defending. Once the players are ready, a number of the progressions can be used to introduce decision of whether to press or make a recovery run. For example, by positioning the defender closer to the attacker so that there is a 'possibility' they could catch them before they reach the second area introduces decision making to the practice. The defender needs to judge whether or not to risk engaging the attacker immediately or to recover first. They need to take a number of factors into consideration such as the weight and area of pass from the server and the attacker's first touch, before deciding whether to go to the attacker or towards the small goal's furthest post.

Practice C: Recovery Runs

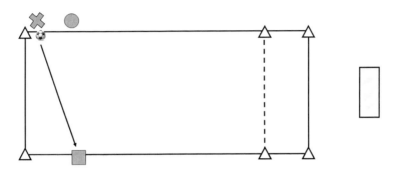

Alteration to Original Set-Up

- The first area is extended in length, which, in turn, reduces the size of the second area.
- The positioning of the three players is altered, as shown in the diagram.
- The practice starts by the defender approaching the server and tapping them on the shoulder. As soon as this happens, the server can pass to the attacker and the defender can enter the area.
- The attacker tries to get to the second area where they must pass the ball into the small goal/gates with their first touch.
- The defender is not allowed to enter the final area.

Focus

- Ignore the ball to begin with.
- Angle of run: head towards the furthest post of the small goal.
- Do not engage the attacker too early; try not to win the ball from behind.

Possible Progressions/Regressions

- Alter the size and/or shape of the area.
- The defender is allowed to enter the second area.
- Move the defender closer to the attacker. The trigger to start the practice could be that the defender starts in their original position and runs to a cone positioned closer to the attacker with the server passing the ball as they travel.
- The server enters the area after they have made the pass. The attacker is allowed to pass to the server but must do so within three touches. On receiving the ball, the server cannot pass it.

Practice C: Driving With the Ball

The first adaption that focuses on the player with the ball has a similar set-up to the previous practice, where the topic was recovery runs. There is no reason why the same set-up could not be used for both topics, but this particular version allows the attacking player to work on a specific aspect of driving with the ball, rather than just concentrating on the actual technique of the drive. This part of driving with the ball has yet to be covered and focuses on the time when they have the ball and are being chased by a defender. If we use the example of a striker receiving a pass and driving towards the goal, they may well have a clear pathway to the goal, but behind them will be defenders trying to catch up. This situation of a player driving with the ball and an opposition player chasing them from behind can occur anywhere on the pitch, and it will happen a lot when a player is travelling forward with the ball, as there will often be defenders tracking back. Therefore, it is important that the player on the ball protects it from the defender situated behind them.

When protecting the ball from an opponent positioned behind them, the attacking player can use a tactic similar to one used when players try to retain 'individual possession' that protects the ball by getting their body between it and the defender. Therefore, when driving with the ball, it is not always the right decision for a player to take a strong touch in front or away from a defender closing them down. If the player does take this option, they give the defender an opportunity to get alongside them and make a tackle, or recover past them and get in a position to defend one versus one or to provide cover and support for a teammate. So instead of taking a touch away from the opposition player or directly towards where they want to go, a better option can be to take a touch across the pathway that the defender is travelling. This allows the attacker to get themselves between the ball and their opponent. Once the attacking player has achieved this, it is extremely difficult for the defender to get in a position where they have a chance of winning the ball. The practice therefore concentrates on the players' first touch and getting across the defender before they start to drive with the ball. This initial action can be quite difficult to master as it involves taking a small number of touches quickly using different parts of the foot while also changing direction at speed. This adaption of Practice C also allows the players to develop their driving with the ball to stay away from the defender, and then they also get the opportunity to complete the 'after' part as well, which, in this case, is a pass. And with the defender now allowed in the area, the transition from driving with the ball to passing needs to be completed in one simultaneous action, as slowing down to make the pass will give the defender a chance to get between the ball and the goal/gates and block the pass.

Practice C: Driving With the Ball

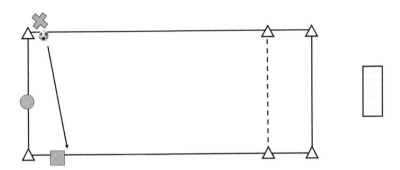

Alteration to Original Set-Up

- The first area is extended in length, which reduces the size of the second area.
- The positioning of the three players is altered, as shown in the diagram.
- The practice starts as usual with the server passing to the attacker and, on doing so, the defender can enter the area.
- The attacker tries to get to the second area where they must pass the ball into the small goal/gates.
- The defender is allowed to enter the final area to try and prevent the pass into the small goal/area.

Focus

- First touch: strong touch out of your feet and forward.
- Get your body between the ball and the defender.
- Strong controlled touches to allow long strides while running.
- Early pass into the small goal/gates.

Possible Progressions/Regressions

- Alter the size and/or shape of the area.
- Change the start position of the defender – further away or closer to the attacker.
- The server enters the area after they have made the pass to act as a second defender.
- Two small gates are added to the line that separates the two areas; the attacker must drive through one of the gates.
- Two sets of two small gates are added to the main area (four gates in total, two lines of two gates), and the attacker must drive through two of the gates.

Practice C: Finishing

Going past a defender in a one versus one situation can be an effective strategy to create an opportunity to have a shot on goal. There are, however, some differences between beating a player to go past them and advance forward, and a one versus one to produce a goal-scoring opportunity. Usually, when a player finds themselves up against an opponent, the overall objective is to get past them and then advance further away from them, whereas if the main aim is to have a shot at goal, then there is no need to fully get past the player, instead just enough space needs to be created so that the shot can be taken. For instance, if we consider a player just outside or inside the penalty box and they are up against a defender, they will often just try to 'shift' their opponent's body weight to gain themselves enough of an advantage the other way to allow them to have an attempt at goal. Or, they might try and do enough to advance forward or even across the penalty box, while holding off the opponent, again with the aim of having a shot at goal. Therefore, with this in mind, this particular adaption aims to replicate this type of scenario.

The key to producing this type of picture is providing an area where the player on the ball is able to have a shot on goal and the only thing preventing them is a defender. Therefore, to begin with, the first area is significantly reduced in size, which, in turn, increases the area where the player is allowed to have a shot on goal. This then allows the attacking player to get a shot in quite quickly, and it does not result in them having to travel with the ball over a long distance before they get to shoot; the practice needs to be quick and sharp, replicating the actions that take place when the player is in or around the penalty box. One of the progressions to this practice allows the attacking player to shoot from anywhere with different points awarded, depending on which area they shoot from. There is an argument that this should not be a progression, and, instead, should be how this adaption actually starts, and there is no reason why it cannot be used at the beginning. The reason it has been included as a progression is that it is likely that if players are able to shoot at any time, they are unlikely to take the option of going past the defender first, even if it provides them with more of a chance of scoring, as they will be closer to the goal. Therefore, by starting the practice that forces them to go past the defender before they can have a shot, they will learn and develop the more difficult choice first of all. So when they do have an option, they will be more comfortable selecting either of the two possibilities available. This means that when they take part in the progression, they will start to select the option that is the correct choice, depending on what they are facing at that moment in time, rather than just choosing their preferred method of creating a goal-scoring opportunity.

Practice C: Finishing

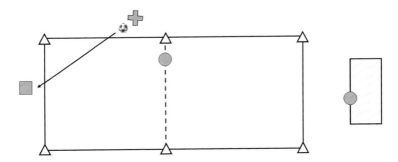

Alteration to Original Set-Up

- The small goal is replaced by a larger goal.
- A further player is added as a goalkeeper.
- The second area is extended in length, which reduces the size of the first area.
- The attacking player can have a shot at goal once they have entered the second area.

Focus

- Positive in your play; always travel forward and do not turn back.
- Skill: choice, timing, execution, etc.
- Look to shift the defender's body weight one way and take the ball the other way.
- Once the space has been created, try to take the shot at the earliest possible opportunity.
- Selection of shot: take into consideration where you are within the area and the positioning of the goalkeeper.
- Ensure that the shot is on target and struck with power.

Possibe Progressions/Regressions

- Alter the size and/or shape of the area.
- Change the start position of any of the players.
- Move the goal closer or further away from the area.
- Change the angle/positioning of the goal so that the players are not just practising finishing when the goal is directly in front of them.
- The attacker can shoot anywhere within the area. They get two points if they score from the first area and one point if it is from the second area.
- After playing the ball in, the server enters the practice as an extra defender.

Practice C: Shielding

In chapter 1, the picture of a striker facing their own goal and holding up the ball protecting it from a defender while awaiting support from a teammate was provided to give an example of when a player might need to shield the ball. And although it is possibly one we do not see as often as we used to in the game of soccer – with modern day strikers more likely to 'drop-in' to receive the ball in the pocket of space between the defensive and midfield units, or running in behind to stretch and turn the opposition defenders – this does not mean it is not an important skill for players to learn, especially when we consider that this is not the only scenario in which this particular technique is used. A more common picture where players now use this particular part of the game is a midfielder trying to get the ball off a centre-back and being tightly marked by an opposition player preventing them from receiving to play forward. Therefore, receiving and protecting the ball from an opposing player while facing your own goal, is a skill needed across many areas of the pitch.

Not allowing the defender to challenge for the ball until the attacker has had their first touch allows the player who the server plays the ball into, to practise the technique of receiving while being closely marked from behind. This can be quite a difficult to get right due to the part of the foot needed to control the ball and also the need to hold off the opponent who will be attempting to steal the ball. Obviously, some players will find it more challenging than others, so introducing the progression of allowing the defender to challenge for the ball immediately can be done on an individual basis. However, it is suggested that all players are exposed to this extra problem as it will give them an opportunity to practise deciding whether to shield the ball or attempt to turn the defender, possibly through rolling them or with a no-touch turn.

The rule that the attacker is unable to play to the server immediately forces the player to protect the ball for a certain amount of time and the set-up of the practice helps to ensure that they develop their shielding skills rather than it turning into 'individual possession'. Also, allowing the attacker eventually to be able to pass back to the server and receive it back again provides them with an opportunity to practise another aspect of shielding, which was outlined in chapter 1, which is where the player attempts to get back on the ball, but this time they are facing the goal instead of having their back to it. And this is developed further when the progression of allowing the server to enter the area is introduced.

Practice C: Shielding

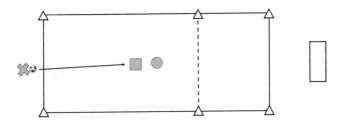

Alteration to Original Set-Up

- Both the striker and the defender are now positioned in the first area. The positioning of the server has also changed, as per the diagram.
- The practice starts as usual with the server playing into the attacker. At this stage, the defender cannot attempt to win the ball until the attacker has had ther first touch.
- On receiving the ball, the attacker is allowed to pass the ball back to the server once and then receive the ball back anywhere in the area. To do this, they must keep the ball for a set amount of seconds (3–5 seconds would be recommended), controlled by the server.
- The practice proceeds as normal with the attacker looking to go directly into the second area or after receiving the pass back from the server.

Focus

- Body shape to receive the ball: wide stance and side-on.
- Knees bent and arm up against the defender.
- Control with the outside of the foot, using the foot closest to the server.
- Use your body to protect and shield the ball.

Possible Progressions/Regressions

- Alter the size and/or shape of the area.
- Allow the defender to try and win the ball immediately.
- Change the amount of time the attacker has to keep the ball before they have the option to pass it back to the server.
- When the ball is played back to the server, they are allowed to enter the area to create a two versus one.
- When the ball is played back to the server, they are allowed to enter the area but the original attacker must replace them outside of the area.

Practice C: Receiving to Play Forward

Another option for the player to receive a pass when they are closely marked by a defender, instead of shielding the ball, is to try and lose the defender, so that it provides them with an opportunity to receive to play forward. This action can be broken down into two stages, the initial movement to lose the defender and then the actual receiving of the pass. The more difficult of these two phases is the movement to lose the defender, because not only does the attacker need to create space between themselves and their opponent, but it needs to be large enough to give them enough time to receive the pass from the server. Therefore, the set-up of this adaption gives the players an opportunity to practise the second stage of the action first; it will be much harder to develop this part of the game, if they are attempting to lose the defender at the same time. Plus, when it comes to completing the full action, they will be more comfortable and confident completing it as they will be able to concentrate on the task of creating the space to receive the pass to play forward.

Having a 'safe zone' provides the attacker with the opportunity to develop the technique of receiving to play forward unopposed in all aspects, and is only exposed to the defender once they have actually completed the action. Usually, we would not promote this as it is more beneficial for the players to practise and develop within an environment that is realistic and close to the game of soccer (i.e. opposed). For this particular action, the players need to find space to complete it, therefore, during a game, they are executing it 'unopposed'. This is also a practice where we do actually need to observe and support two players that have different roles within it; the server and the attacker, as the pass into the players is just as important as how they receive it. Unless the pass is played to the receiving player's back foot, then it is not possible for them to receive to play forward effectively. Therefore, some of our time may need to be spent with the servers, but only after we have supported the attacker and how they receive the ball, as the player passing the ball will, hopefully, recognise where the pass needs to be played.

When it comes to allowing the defender to become active earlier, the players may need some support as the environment that we provide is heavily weighted towards the defender. Because they are aware of the task that the attacker must complete, it is relatively easy to defend against it. Therefore, an option here would be to make a further change and add an additional attacker so the defender is unaware which player will move to receive the ball and, therefore, will not be able to react as quickly, which then makes the environment much closer to the actual game.

Practice C: Receiving to Play Forward

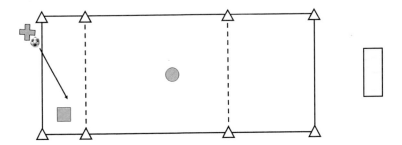

Alteration to Original Set-Up

- An additional area is added at the beginning of the main area.
- The attacker and the defender start the practice in the same position as for the 'shielding' adaption. The server is positioned in the corner as shown on the diagram.
- The practice begins with the attacker dropping into the first area, which starts as a 'safe area' for the attacker (i.e. the defender cannot enter it).
- As soon as the attacker exits the first area, the defender is allowed to engage them. Once they have left the safe area, the attacker cannot return to it.
- Once the attacker leaves this area, the practice continues as per the original set-up.

Focus

- Angle of approach/run into the safe area.
- Body shape to receive the ball from the server is open so that you can see the pass and the defender.
- Pass from the server to the furthest foot of the attacker.
- First touch from the attacker, positive and forward. Exit the safe area immediately.

Possible Progressions/Regressions

- Alter the size and/or shape of the main area and/or the different areas.
- After playing the ball in, the server enters the practice as an extra defender.
- Allow the defender to engage the attacker earlier.
- The first area is no longer a safe area, therefore, the defender can follow the attacker here when they receive the ball from the server (ensure the defender starts further back than the attacker and can only move once the attacker does).

Practice C: Forward Passing

Similar to the finishing practice, this adaption provides the players with the option to make an early pass into one of the targets or attempt to get past the defender first. Both options come with their own particular advantages and challenges, and the players need to come to their own conclusion to which one is the right solution for each particular situation. Should they decide to attempt to make the pass early, they will not have to go past the defender where they risk losing possession of the ball, but the pass will need to be made over a greater distance and there is a possibility that the defender could block the pass. Alternatively, if they get past the defender, they will have a clear pathway for the ball to travel to the selected target. It would also be over a shorter distance, but they do need to get past their opponent in the first place.

A scoring system that offers the players different number of points, depending on which area they attempt the pass, allows the coach to put more emphasis on one of the two options. This gives you the opportunity to tailor the practice to meet the needs of the players, and it also provides different scenarios for the players to practise. Allocating more points to the second area puts more of an emphasis on the attacker making the pass without attempting to go past the defender. The player is therefore likely to receive the ball from the server and then, after their first touch, only take a small number of other touches before attempting to make the pass. This type of action can be seen in numerous situations across the game of soccer, such as a defender receiving the ball and stepping forward before looking to pass to a teammate in the midfield area. Rewarding the players with more points if they are successful from the third area encourages the attackers to try and go past the defender before sliding a pass into one of the small goals/gates. This could represent a midfielder creating their own space by gliding past an opponent before sliding a pass through for a teammate in a forward position. Either way, the players are put in an environment that provides them with a scenario they will come across during a game.

This is another adaption that provides some really good opportunities to introduce differentiation into the practice. With three small goals/gates, we can add a variety of levels of difficulty by having a range of sizes positioned at different distances from the area. The more difficult it is to pass into the target, in other words, the smaller the goals/gates and the further away from the area that they are situated, the higher the number of points that can be awarded to a player for successfully passing the ball into them. This then allows the players to choose to a certain extent, the level of difficulty.

Practice C: Forward Passing

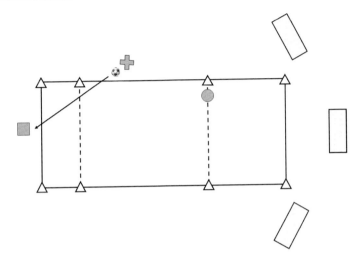

Alteration to Original Set-Up

- The same set-up as per the receiving to play forward adaption but with the players starting in their original positions.
- Two additional small goals/gates are added to the practice, as per the diagram.
- The attacker must travel out of the first area before they can attempt to play into one of the small goals/gates.
- The attacker is awarded a set number of points if they score from the second area and a different number for scoring from the third area.

Focus

- Identifying a clear pathway between the ball and the chosen target.
- Decision making: pass early or go past defender first?
- Type of pass: inside or outside of the foot? Driven, chipped/lofted, etc.
- Weight and accuracy.

Possible Progressions/Regressions

- Alter the size and/or shape of the main area and/or the different areas.
- Change the position of the small goals/gates.
- Different sizes and distances for each small goal/gate, with each one worth a different point.

Practice C: Pass or Dribble?

The final adaption for this particular practice focuses on giving the player on the ball the opportunity to share the ball if they want or need to. As previously discussed, it is really important that we still encourage the players to retain the ball and that they only share it with their teammates if they really need to or if it is the right time to do so. Therefore, the rule that only the attacker is allowed to pass the ball is key to the practice. If we allow the server the opportunity to pass the ball once they have entered the area, there is a danger that the practice turns into two players keeping the ball away from the defender. Having this rule in place encourages the attacker to carefully consider whether or not they should pass the ball to their partner, as they know if they do, their teammate is now on their own and will have to complete the task without any support. The other key element of the practice is the placement of the gates that the server must travel through to enter the area. Having these delays when the server joins in with the practice forces the attacker to keep the ball for a certain amount of time before the option to pass the ball becomes available.

The positioning of the gates also provides an opportunity for the player supporting the attacker to be put in a slightly different situation – they start from behind their teammate who is in possession of the ball and then, ideally, tries to get ahead of them. If they do not get ahead of the attacker, it means that the only way they can receive the ball is if their teammate plays the ball backwards. Not only does this go against one of the main principles of the game – when a team has possession of the ball, the priority is to progress up the pitch to get closer to the opposition's goal – but it also helps the defender. If they do not get ahead of the ball, it also means they will be behind the defender, so if they do receive a pass it is likely that the defender will have enough time to get across and engage the server. However, if they are ahead of the ball and receive a pass, they would be expected to advance to the next area unopposed. Therefore, the coach will need to work with and support both the attacker and the server within this adaption. The server needs to make movements that will take them ahead of the ball and into an area where the defender needs to make a decision about staying with the player on the ball or trying to cover the pass into the supporting player. Attention can then be switched to the attacker and their decision making regarding whether to keep the ball themselves or share it with their teammates. Here, numerous factors need to be taken into consideration including the positioning and the body weight of the defender, the amount of space ahead of the player on the ball and the path that the ball needs to follow if the decision is made to pass it onto their teammate.

Practice C: Pass or Dribble?

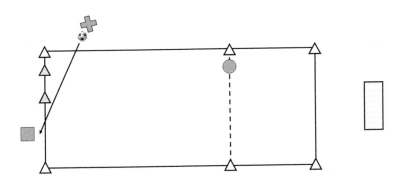

Alteration to Original Set-Up

- The server's starting position is slightly nearer to the corner of the area so they are closer to the attacker.
- A small gate is added to the base line, as shown in the diagram.
- On passing the ball to the attacker, the server can enter the area through the gate.
- The attacker is allowed to keep the ball themselves or pass the ball onto the server. If the server receives the ball, they cannot pass it.
- If the ball is successfully passed into the small goal/gate, the attacker gets fewer points than if they passed it to the server.
- If the defender wins the ball, they try to pass it or drive with it through the same gate that the server entered the area.

Focus

- Decision making: when to retain the ball and when to pass it?
- Can you use the supporting player to help keep the ball individually?
- If you decide to pass, where exactly does the player receiving the pass want the ball?
- For the supporting player, what type of run could you make?

Possible Progressions/Regressions

- Alter the size and/or shape of the area.
- Change the starting position of the server.
- The line dividing the two areas, acts as an offside line so the server cannot wait in this area for the pass (this is only relevant for players using the offside rule).
- Use a smaller ball.

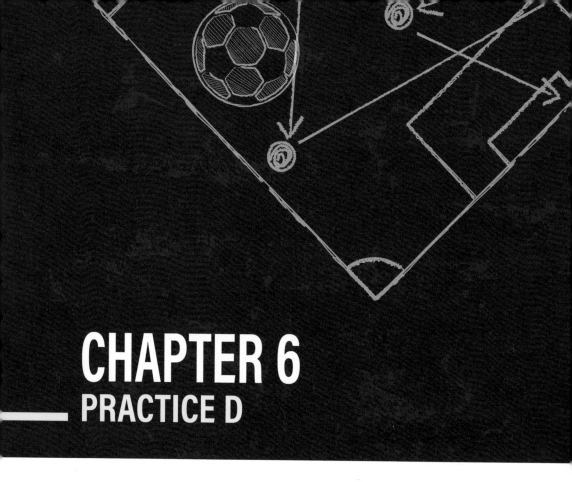

CHAPTER 6
PRACTICE D

Now, the focus of the practices starts to move away from players playing on their own in terms of retaining possession or trying to win the ball back, and there is now more of an emphasis on them playing with a teammate. The key point first of all, is that it is a *teammate* and not *teammates*. Working with just one other player rather than a number of teammates reduces the number of decisions that the player has to make. It also encourages players to retain the ball themselves for longer periods of time, compared with when they play with a number of teammates. These types of practices are particularly important for younger players still learning and developing the core skills needed for the game. Although they will probably play with much larger numbers of players in matches, significantly reducing the numbers in training allows them to concentrate on just the one decision: keep it or share it? This makes the decision-making process a lot easier before we add more players as that then increases the amount of decisions that all players will need to make, not just the player on the ball.

The design of this particular practice allows the players to develop a number of the core skills outlined in chapter 1 without them being a focus of the session. Again, this does not mean we have to provide support for these elements of their performance; our focus needs to remain with whatever is the topic of the session. We can provide some small reminders when needed, but the environment they find themselves in and the task they are asked to complete will naturally encourage the players to complete certain actions. If we look at the start of the practice first of all, the player receiving the ball is likely to be able to receive it on their back foot and try to play forward straight away. Because of the positioning of the server and the direction that the player needs to go to win a point, this allows them to receive the ball from a teammate positioned behind them, and then it encourages them to go forward as quickly as possible. The other aspect of the practice that allows or encourages the players to receive to play forward is that it is a two versus one situation within the first area. Therefore, if the defender decides to mark one particular player, the server will just pass to the other attacker who will be in enough space to receive to play forward. Or, the more likely scenario will be the defender sitting between the two attackers and then possibly pressing whichever player the server decides to pass to. But again, this allows the player to receive to play forward, but they may have less time to complete the action before they come under pressure. Then once they have received the ball, the emphasis is to go forward as quickly as possible. There is likely to be space in front of the player on the ball or their teammate, and to capitalise on this space, the players will carry out one of a number of the key areas of the game: driving with the ball, forward passing or one versus one attacking, and this will then continue once they have entered the second area.

If the players are truly going to perform these particular key aspects of the game, we need to make sure that there is an emphasis of fast play within this practice. We want the attacking players, in particular, to make quick and decisive decisions and to be direct in their actions. What we do not want to see happening, is the attacking players making a number of passes between themselves or spending too long on the ball and not making any progress. As previously mentioned, the first player receiving the ball from the server will often be able to receive it on their back foot, allowing them to play forward immediately. Therefore, we need to encourage them to keep this momentum going in their play. Ideally, from this point in the practice, all their actions should be forward actions, which, in turn, will make it harder for the defenders. As well as these key areas of the game that the players will complete within the practice, there are, of course, a number of other actions that were listed in chapter 1, there are certain actions we do not want them to do, unless they really need to, such as individual possession, shielding or turning. Completing these particular actions means that the impetus has been lost and, instead of playing quickly and directly, they now face the wrong way or spend too much time trying to keep possession of the ball, rather than trying to progress forward.

This practice also provides a good opportunity for the coach to introduce a different type of passing, rather than the more conventional inside- of- the- foot pass. By using the inside of the foot, the player will usually be able to execute a more accurate pass with the right amount of weight due to the size of the contact area this particular part of the foot provides. However, when using this part of the foot, quite often the player will 'transmit' that they are going to pass the ball and also where they want to pass it to. Executing this type of pass usually involves the player opening their body position up, even just slightly, which then provides a clear message to their opponents of what they intend to do. Therefore, in this practice, it often results in the defender reading the attacker's intentions and then blocking or intercepting the pass. The other disadvantage it can have, is that if the player is travelling with the ball, it can be difficult to transfer from dribbling or driving with the ball to executing the pass. This slows the action down and, again, provides the defender with an opportunity to identify what the attacking player intends to do. Therefore, to help prevent this and provide more disguise to their pass, players can be introduced to using the top of their foot or the outside of their foot to push a pass through to their teammate. Not only is this much more difficult for the defender to anticipate and react to, but it also allows the player on the ball to make the transition from dribbling or driving with the ball to making a pass a lot easier. It also allows the player to complete the pass without having to make any changes to their movement patterns, in other words, they can do it while they are still travelling with the ball, allowing the pass to be made early and quickly.

Another option provided by the practice that helps encourage the players to play quickly is allowing the server to enter the game as an extra defender (to the first area only). The coach's initial thought when considering how to support the players might be to allow the server to enter as an extra attacking player. But by doing this, we can actually slow down the play even more, and with the player on the ball having extra options it can make the decision-making process a lot more complicated. The other problem is that the server will probably become an option behind the player, which is a safer option and one that the attacker might be more comfortable selecting, which goes against everything we want from the practice. Therefore, allowing the server to enter as a defender could be seen as making the practice more difficult for the attacking players and can instead have a positive impact as they will try to enter the second area where there is only one defender as quickly as possible, rather than remaining in the first area where it can turn into a two versus two. The attackers will soon identify that if they move the ball quickly to the next area the server will not even get the opportunity to affect the practice as an extra defender. By allowing the server to enter as an extra defender, we are, in fact, just giving the attackers a little nudge or encouragement to play a bit quicker.

Practice D: Original Set-Up

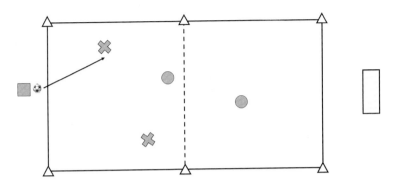

Set-Up

- Five players are allocated to each pitch. One player acts as a server and there are two attackers and two defenders inside the area.
- The area is split in half with a defender allocated and locked to each half. The two attacking players start in the first half but are free to go where they want.
- The server passes to one of the two attackers, who then aim to progress into the second area by any means they choose.
- Once they are in the second area, they can attempt to pass into the small goal/gates.
- If at any time a defender wins the ball, they aim to get it back to the server.

Focus

- Decision making: when to retain the ball and when to pass it?
- Can you use the supporting player to help keep the ball?
- If you decide to pass, where exactly does the player receiving the pass want the ball?
- For the supporting player, can your teammate see your feet?
- Can you play forward as quickly as possible?

Possible Progressions/Regressions

- Alter the size and/or shape of the area.
- The line dividing the two areas acts as an offside line so the server cannot wait in this area for the pass (this is only relevant for players using the offside rule).
- Unlock the defenders once the attackers have received the ball from the server.
- After playing the ball in, the server enters the practice as an extra defender or attacker.
- The attackers cannot play the ball back to the server.

Practice D: One Versus One Attacking

Although the main aim of these practices is to develop the skills needed to understand when and how to share the ball with a teammate, they can still be used for individual focuses, with some element of sharing within them. The first few adaptions will, therefore, look at these individual practices first, before we move onto the sole focus of whether to retain the ball or pass it onto a teammate. To introduce some individual play, we just need to separate the two attacking players for either some or all of the practice.

Introducing an extra area at the start of the practice for an attacker to drop into and receive the ball allows the player to receive the ball and play forward. Although we have already discussed that the set-up of the practice will allow the attackers to do this, there are some key differences that introducing the new area will add to the practice, which will help provide an individual focus. Firstly, allowing the player to collect a pass from the server in the area will definitely ensure the attacker can receive the ball to play forward. Although the practice already encourages this to happen, it cannot guarantee that it will happen each and every time. Secondly, and probably more importantly, the extra area ensures that when the attacker receives the ball, the defender will be positioned behind them and, therefore, they have to get past the defender to progress further. Previously, it was a possibility that the attacker could receive the ball and drive straight into the second area without being engaged by the defender, or they might be in a position where they could pass the ball to their partner. But this is no longer an option, with the attacker receiving the ball now having to be successful in a one versus one situation before they have the option to pass the ball.

How much emphasis is put on the one versus one situation depends on the size of the first area where the attacker receives the ball, the larger the area, the more difficult it becomes because the longer it will be before they have the option to pass the ball. Also, there is more chance of the defender getting further into the area, which makes the task more challenging. As with all of the other practices within this book, no specific dimensions are provided because what is right for one particular group of players will not be suitable for another group; it is something that needs to be decided by the coach. The first thing we need to remember is that whatever size we start with does not have to remain for the whole of the session; if it needs changing, then we should just change it. And secondly, when we have more than one area set-up, they do not need to be identical in dimension; we can have different sizes for different groups of players. It is all about meeting the needs of the players at that particular moment in time.

Practice D: One Versus One Attacking

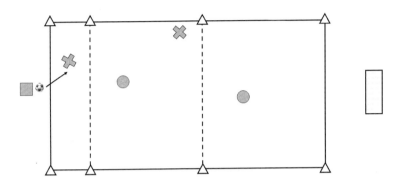

Alteration to Original Set-Up

- An additional area is added to the first area. This is an area where one of the attacking players has to go to receive the ball from the server.
- The defender cannot enter this area until the attacking player has had their first touch.
- The attacker cannot pass it onto their teammate until they have left this area.
- Once the attacker has left the area, the practice continues as normal.

Focus

- Receive the ball to play forward and travel forward with the touch: positive and direct in their play.
- The touch should also shift the ball to the left or the right to make the defender have to move and shift their body weight.
- Feint and disguise to shift the defender's body weight in a selected direction.
- Shift the ball quickly in a different direction.
- Explosive acceleration to exploit the space they have created and to move away from the defender.
- Decision making as you are travelling with the ball: retain or share?

Possible Progressions/Regressions

- Allow the attacker to pass the ball from the first area.
- Do not allow the attacker to pass the ball until they enter the final area.
- Use a smaller ball.
- Allow the first defender to go into the second area once the ball has entered this area.
- Use any of the progressions or regressions from the original set-up.

Practice D: One Versus One Defending

Carrying on the theme of an individual topic, this adaption switches the focus in the one versus one situation to the defender. Again, the previous practice could be used for this by the coach switching their focus to the defender and using the relevant coaching points to provide the necessary support. And of course, this practice can be used within a session that focuses on one versus one attacking. However, each of these two practices are more tailored towards one aspect of this situation. This particular adaption is better suited to the defensive side of the scenario, as once the attacker receives the ball, they do not have any support, so the defender can just concentrate on them, and they do not need to worry about the ball being shared with another player. Whereas the previous practice provides the player with this option to share the ball with a teammate once they have reached a certain place in the area, which allows the attacker to work on their decision making within a one versus one situation

Allowing the server to immediately enter the area once they have made the initial pass creates a two versus one situation in the first area. This helps to ensure that the ball is successfully played into the second attacker. This is important because this is what we want the players to focus on, so they need to spend as much time as possible in this part of the practice. If the first aspect of the practice is too challenging, it could take too long to get the ball to the second attacker or might not get there at all, meaning we might not get to the part of the practice we want to focus on – the attacker in a one versus one against the defender.

On receiving the ball, the second attacker is allowed to take their first touch unopposed and, as with previous practices, they are encouraged to take a touch forward and be positive in their play, dribbling directly at the defender, taking the initiative and attempting to take control of the situation. Another option is not to allow the defender to engage the attacker until they have exited the area and it becomes a safe area for the player on the ball. This replicates a different situation we might find within a game of soccer, which is where the player on the ball slows down the play and does not attempt to progress forward until they have created space in front of them by shifting the defender out of the way. This type of situation usually occurs in a wide area where the attacking player has received a pass and is quickly closed down by a defender to prevent the cross from being made. In this situation, the attacker shifts the ball sideways until there is space ahead of them, which will happen if we allow this space to be a safe area for the attacker.

Practice D: One Versus One Defending

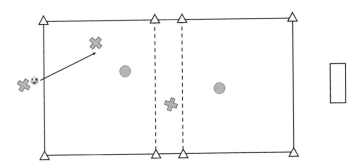

Alteration to Original Set-Up

- An additional area is added in between the two main areas. This is an area where one of the attacking players waits to receive the ball before entering the final area.
- The defender locked into the final area cannot enter this area until the attacking player has had their first touch.
- Once the server plays the pass to the first attacker, they can join in to make a two versus one.
- Once the ball is played into the second attacker, no one can support them – they are left with a one versus one situation.

Focus

- Angle and line of approach.
- Slow down as you get closer to the attacker.
- Body position to be side-on and knees bent.
- Patience: wait for the right time to try and win the ball.
- Force the attacker away from the goal.

Possible Progressions/Regressions

- Add an extra small goal/gate, for the attacker to pass into.
- Allow the first attacker or server to drive into the final area with the ball, bypassing the second attacker.
- Allow the defender to enter the area where the second attacker is waiting for the pass, at any time.
- The defender cannot enter the area at all.
- Use any of the progressions or regressions from the original set-up.

Practice D: Receiving Under Pressure

This next adaption has a very similar set-up to the previous practice; the only slight difference is the size of the middle area that separates the first and last areas. This needs to be slightly bigger as it now has two players occupying it – the second attacker as well as the second defender. It could be asked why is there a need for this area to be added to the practice, why not change the rule that the ball must be passed into the final area by the attacker of the server? Because of the size of the last area, it could be possible for the second attacker to find space in it and get away from the defender. Another option might be that the teammate playing the pass could choose to play the pass into space for them to move onto. Either of these two possibilities results in the player receiving the ball without any direct pressure, therefore, we have moved completely away from the topic. The area in which the second attacker receives the ball needs to be small and tight so that they are under pressure just about every time the ball is played into them.

It can also be argued that the defender should be able to try and win the ball immediately and not have to wait until the attacking player has had their first touch. And the practice can definitely start in this manner, if that is right for your group of players. Or, as mentioned earlier in the chapter, it could be that this particular rule is used on one pitch but not any of the others. As with every other practice within the book, the set-up is extremely flexible, and the starting place should be suitable for the group of players participating. The reason it is suggested that the practice begins with the defender not allowed to compete for the ball until the attacker has had their first touch is to control the level of difficulty and allow the player receiving the ball to have a better chance of being successful. Just because we do not allow the defender to attempt to win the ball does not mean that they cannot put the attacker under pressure as they receive the pass from their teammate. They can still get physically close to the player receiving the pass and put themselves in a position where they can try and win the ball as soon as the attacker has had their first touch. Allowing the defender to try and win the ball straight away gives the attacking player an additional problem to deal with – the defender could actually try and win the ball before it even reaches them. This is something that they will absolutely need to deal with during a game, and it is something that they can learn to take advantage of. If they recognise that their opponent is trying to win the ball, they can get their body in the way and allow the ball to travel across them, meaning they can 'roll' the defender and play forward. However, players often just need to take things one step at a time, therefore, this aspect of receiving the ball while under pressure from an opponent can be introduced whenever it is seen as the right time to do so.

Practice D: Receiving Under Pressure

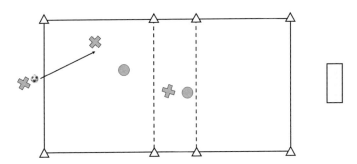

Alteration to Original Set-Up

- An additional area is added in between the two main areas. This is an area where one of the attacking players waits to receive the ball before entering the final area.
- The second defender also waits inside this area and can challenge for the ball as soon as the attacker has had their first touch.
- Once the server plays the pass into the first attacker, they can join in to make a two versus one.
- Once the ball is played to the second attacker, one player can support them by making a run into the final area.
- If the second attacker successfully exits the area, the defender can also leave and enter the final area as well.

Focus

- Awareness of the position of the defending player.
- Body shape as they receive the ball.
- Which foot is chosen to receive the ball?
- Retain or share the ball?

Possible Progressions/Regressions

- Add an extra small goal/gate for the attacker to pass into.
- The second defender does not have to wait until the second attacker has their first touch before they can attempt to win the ball.
- Allow the first defender to enter the area once the ball has been played into the second attacker, creating a one versus two.
- Use any of the progressions or regressions from the original set-up.

Practice D: Individual Possession

The final individual focus looks at individual possession and the attacking players' ability to retain possession of the ball until they are able to complete the task that has been set. There is an immediate concern with this practice: that the first attacker may take a while to complete their particular task, in other words, travel through the gate and then pass the ball onto their teammate. Therefore, both the attacker and the defender in the second area could be waiting a long time before they become active. At the start of the practice, it is even more important that the coach just spends time observing the performance of the players to identify how much success they have and how much time they are standing waiting. And then, from these observations, any required changes that have been identified should be made by the coach.

Having the server pass another ball into the first attacker as soon as the previous ball has been transferred into the second area will ensure that there is no waiting time for this particular player. It can also increase the level of difficulty for the first attacker as well. If they travel through a gate and are ready to make the pass into the second attacker, but their teammate has yet to pass into the small goal/gates, they will need to continue to retain possession of the ball until their partner is ready. Rotating the two attacking players around the two areas after a small amount of time will also ensure that individual players are active for as long as possible. Because the first attacker is always guaranteed to be constantly active, it is important that we allow the two attacking players to take it in turns to be in this position. It goes without saying at this point that all five players need to have a go at all three roles within the practice and that they should all spend, as close as possible, an equal amount of time as the attacker. Also, rotating the two attacking players between the two different areas allows them to play against different players, which, as discussed within chapter 4, is beneficial to their development.

If we find that the first attacker is taking a while to get the ball to the second attacker on their first attempt, another option is to start the practice off slightly differently. Giving the first attacker a ball to play directly into the second player receiving a pass off the server ensures that both attacking players are active from the start. The other option available to the coach on top of this is to allow the server to play a ball into the second attacker after a set period of time or if the first attacker has been unable to get the ball into the second area after a set number of attempts. There are a number of options available; we just need to select the correct one for that specific moment.

Practice D: Individual Possession

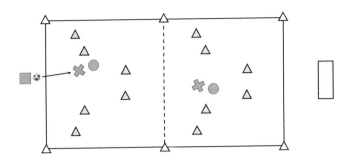

Alteration to Original Set-Up

- One of the attackers has now moved into the second area and both attackers are also locked into their designated area. This creates a one versus one in both areas.
- Three gates are added to each of the areas.
- On receiving the ball, the first attacker tries to transfer the ball to the second attacker only by passing it. Before they do this, they must travel through one of the gates.
- When receiving the pass from their partner, the second attacker must travel through one of the gates before they can attempt to pass the ball into the small goal/gates.
- The defenders cannot attempt to win the ball until the attacker they are paired with takes their first touch.
- As soon as the ball has been transferred to the second area, the server plays another ball to the first attacker.

Focus

- Protect the ball – keep your body between the defender and the ball.
- Use the foot furthest away from the defender.
- Use feints/disguise to move away from the defender.
- Once the space has been created, use it quickly.

Possible Progressions/Regressions

- Add or remove gates.
- The defender does not have to wait until the attacker has their first touch before they can attempt to win the ball.
- Allow the first defender to go into the second area once the ball has entered this area.
- Use any of the progressions or regressions from the original set-up.

Practice D: Driving With the Ball

As we move away from the players working on their own and more towards working as a pair, this adaption looks at players driving with the ball. And though this may seem like it focuses on the player as an individual, the practice concentrates on the decision-making process of the attackers and part of this involves the decisions they make together. The first aspect of this is deciding when they should leave the first area by driving with the ball. To do this, they need to be aware of the positioning of both defenders to see whether the space is available for them to drive into. For this action to be executed with maximum effect, the decision needs to be made by both attackers. For the attacking player to make the decision to drive out of the first area, they need to make sure that neither of the defenders are blocking their route and that they are facing forward. If either of these two key factors is not in place, then the decision to enter the second area should not be taken as they will not be able to do it quickly enough, and there is a risk of losing the ball. A player should only leave the area if they believe they can reach the gates relatively unopposed. To achieve this, the decision to drive into the second area will often need to be made by both players.

The decision-making process to drive into the second area will, quite often, need to start with the attacker who will not actually be doing it. They need to be aware that their teammate is in a position to break out, and then play a pass that almost leaves no option but to drive with the ball. If they are aware their partner has the opportunity to drive into the next area, they should play a pass that encourages them to drive forward. They should do this as their partner may not have identified the opportunity they have, plus by playing this type of pass, it will allow their teammate to drive into the area quickly. Once the pass has been made, the player receiving the ball still has to decide what to do, but hopefully, the actions of their teammate has helped them make the decision to drive into the second area. Playing the ball in front of the player forces them to move towards the next area, which provides them with the momentum to drive forward.

The next decision to be made is more of an individual choice. On entering the second area, the player needs to decide whether to just drive to the gates or get across the defender first to protect the ball. The key factor in this decision-making process is the positioning of the second defender. Ideally, they will be able to drive to a gate without the defender having a chance to catch them in time. They do not want the defender to recover in time and get goalside, which would turn it into a one versus one. Therefore, if needed, they should drive across the defender and get their body between their opponent and the ball.

Practice D: Driving With the Ball

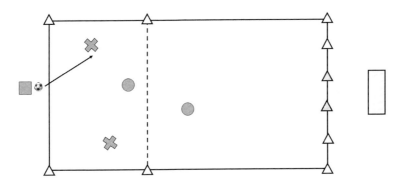

Alteration to Original Set-Up

- The first area is decreased in size, which, in turn, increases the size of the second area.
- Three gates are added to the end line of the second area.
- The two attacking players can use the server to help retain possession of the ball.
- To enter the second area, one of the attacking players must travel into it with the ball. Once they do so, no other player can enter this area.
- Once in the second area, the attacker tries to drive through one of the gates. On doing so, they look to pass into the small goal/gates with their first touch.

Focus

- Identify when to enter the first area: take into consideration how you receive the ball and the positioning of both defenders.
- First touch: Strong touch out of your feet and forward.
- Identify whether or not you need to get your body between the ball and the defender?
- Strong controlled touches to allow long strides while running.
- Controlled pass into the small goal/gates.

Possible Progressions/Regressions

- Allow the first defender to enter the second area once the attacking player has driven into it.
- Remove the central gate.
- The attacking players have a maximum number of passes they can complete before one of them must drive into the second area.
- Use any of the progressions or regressions from the original set-up.

Practice D: Forward Passing

In this adaption of forward passing, there is a real emphasis on playing a pass for someone to move onto, rather than passing the ball where a teammate is already positioned. This type of pass has numerous advantages, one of which is that it is much more difficult to defend against as it is much easier to predict and deal with a pass going to a stationary player. A player on the move has an immediate advantage as will take time, even if it is just for a split second, for the opposition players to react to the movement. In addition, because the player is on the move, it provides an opportunity to continue travelling with the ball once they have received it, giving them momentum and allowing them to be positive and direct. This can be seen in this particular practice. If the attacker can collect the ball and travel into the final area all in one movement, it will be extremely difficult for the second defender to stop them. Whereas, if they are static in the middle area when they receive the pass and then try to move out of it, it is much easier for the defender to stop them. A player on the move has an advantage over a static player because you accelerate quicker from a moving start than a stationary start.

The other key aspect is, of course, the actual pass in terms of the weight and the area it is played to. Obviously, if it is over hit, it will not give the player receiving the pass a chance to collect it. If it is under-hit, it could get intercepted, or the teammate might have to wait for the ball to arrive, thus losing their forward momentum. The pass does need to be played forward into the middle area, but the angle in which it enters will have a major influence on whether or not it is successful. A straight pass will always be difficult for the player receiving the ball to collect, as it will always be running away from them. It will also run out quickly, as it will travel over the shortest distance needed to enter and exit the area. The type of pass that the players should look to play is an angled pass, which provides a much better opportunity for their teammate to receive it. The main reason for this is because the ball will be travelling across the area, meaning that the attacker can 'collect' the ball on their way as they run through into the final area.

Helping the players learn and practice this type of forward pass is extremely important in their development. It is often used within the game of soccer to 'penetrate' or 'break lines', particularly in the final third of the pitch, when the defending teams are compact and there is little room behind them for the ball to be played into. Developing this part of the game provides them with another tool they can use in one of the hardest areas of the game: unlocking an opposition's defence.

Practice D: Forward Passing

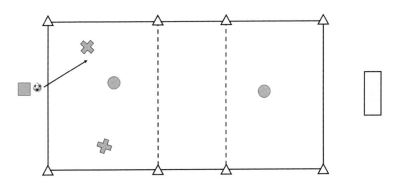

Alteration to Original Set-Up

- An additional area is added in between the two main areas. This is an area where one of the attacking players needs to receive a pass from their teammate.
- The player cannot wait in the middle area when receiving a pass – they can only move into it once the pass has been made.
- Neither of the defenders are allowed in the middle area.
- Once a player has received a pass in the middle area, both attackers can move into the final area, where they try to pass into the small goal/gates.

Focus

- Identifying a clear pathway between the ball and the chosen target.
- Type of pass: inside or outside of the foot? Driven, chipped/lofted, etc.
- Weight and accuracy.
- Pass to where they will be, not where they are.
- Avoid straight passes, look to play an angled pass.

Possible Progressions/Regressions

- Alter the size of the middle area.
- Allow the second defender to enter the middle area, but again, they can only do this once the pass has been made.
- The attackers win additional points if they pass into the small-sided goal/gates from inside the middle area (they must do this within two touches).
- Use any of the progressions or regressions from the original set-up.

Practice D: Finishing

This adaption has a number of similarities to the previous practice; it focuses mainly on the decision-making skills of the two attacking players, rather than the actual technique of finishing. Once more, it looks at both the decision making of both the player on the ball and their teammate waiting to receive a pass. This time, the practice provides an environment where they can learn to create not just a goal-scoring opportunity, but one that allows the attacker attempting to score to execute the shot effectively. It takes both players to make decisions based on their own situation and those of their teammates to achieve this. They need to be able to start to recognise what their partner wants to do and how they can either help them achieve it or use it to their own advantage.

A key element of the practice design that helps the players develop this understanding of their role in the decision-making process when working with a teammate is the scoring system. Quite often, we reward players with extra points if they score with a 'one-touch' finish as it is seen as being more difficult to execute or is a specific type of shot that we want them to work on. However, this particular practice is in place to help the players understand what they need to do beforehand if they want to strike the ball first time and how they can support a teammate to do this as well. Again, it is not particularly about developing players that will be able to shoot first time or who can set up a teammate to do it; it is to help the players understand the game of soccer and how the choices and decisions that they make within it have a significant impact.

So, for instance, if a player wants the opportunity to have a strike on goal with their first touch, one of the more suitable places to position themselves is behind their teammate so that they can step onto the ball. The teammate making the pass needs to ensure that the ball they play back to their partner is slightly to the side; if it is played directly to them, they will need to adjust their position to enable a clean strike of the ball. Or it might be the case that the attacker not in possession of the ball makes a run ahead of their teammate, looking for a ball to be played to them so they can attempt a strike on goal. In this situation, the player making the pass needs to ensure that the right amount of weight is put on the ball. Not enough and it will not get ahead of the player and they will need to adjust their run, too much and they will not catch it or will end up stretching to make the shot, meaning they will be off balance and unable to make the correct contact with the ball. There will be lots of different situations or scenario's occurring in the practice, and the players just need time to learn what is needed for each one.

Practice D: Finishing

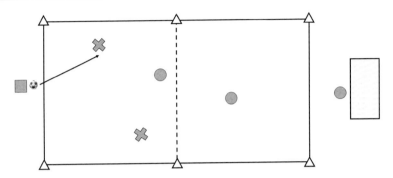

Alteration to Original Set-Up

- The small goal/gates are replaced by a larger goal with a goalkeeper.
- Once the attacking players have entered the second area, they try and score a goal.
- The attackers are awarded more points if they score with a one-touch finish.
- If needed, the server can change their role and become the goalkeeper. The practice then starts with one of the attackers dribbling into the first area. If the defenders win the ball, they earn a point by driving out of the area.

Focus

- Identifying when to have the shot on goal.
- Selection of shot: take into consideration where you are in the area and the positioning of the goalkeeper.
- Ensure that the shot is on target and struck with power.
- If the decision is not to shoot, can you play a pass to your teammate that allows them to shoot quickly/early?
- If not on the ball, can you position yourself so that your teammate can play you a pass that will allow you to shoot quickly/early?

Possible Progressions/Regressions

- Move the goal closer or further away from the area.
- Change the angle/positioning of the goal so the players are not just practising finishing when the goal is directly in front of them.
- Restrict the attackers to just one pass once they enter the second area.
- Use any of the progressions or regressions from the original set-up.

Practice D: Counter-Press

The focus now shifts back to the players not in possession of the ball, beginning with the counter-press, with the level of difficulty increasing significantly compared with the previous practices for this topic. Additionally, the defenders now have to make a number of decisions as they attempt to win the ball. In the previous practices for the counter-press, the focus was on the player getting into the habit of reacting to losing the ball by attempting to win it back as quickly as possible. Quick reaction and attitude from the defender are still needed, but now they have to take a number of factors into consideration before making a final decision about what exactly they will do when they identify that they are not the team in possession of the ball.

The introduction of more players in terms of making it a two versus two, now increases the decision-making process for the defenders who need to react to their team losing possession of the ball. Where previously a player was reacting to losing the ball after having possession of it, the players are now reacting to losing possession when they are not directly involved in the turnover. Allowing the server to make the decision of who they pass the ball to means that the two teams are unaware of who will receive the pass, and therefore, when they do not receive it, they need to react quickly if they are to prevent the other pair from reaching the third area. This is made harder by the fact they will be set-up ready to receive the ball and will need to close down the spaces quickly. This set-up aims to replicate a team losing possession by a pass being intercepted and players needing to react to losing the ball when they are not right next to it.

Therefore, before making a decision where specifically they should go, they need to identify whether or not they are the player that immediately closes down the attacker who has just gained possession of the ball. Usually, it will be the closest player that applies the press, but where their partner is positioned also needs to be taken into consideration. For instance, are they in a better position to prevent the attacker on the ball from progressing forward? Another option is that both players close down the player on the ball, essentially 'doubling up' and try to make it extremely difficult for the attacker to keep possession. The risk with this, of course, is that if they do not close down the space quickly enough and the attacker is able to move the ball onto their partner or get away themselves with the ball, it makes it extremely difficult for the defenders to prevent their opponents from reaching the final area.

Practice D: Counter-Press

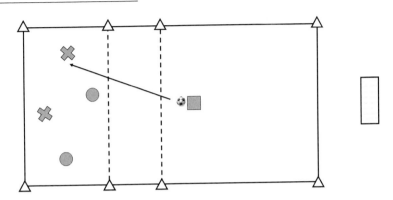

Alteration to Original Set-Up

- An additional area is added in between the two main areas.
- Two versus two in the first area.
- In the third area, a fifth player takes on the role of the server and defender.
- Server plays into one of the teams, which then tries to break into the third area to create a two versus one against the server, who now takes on the role of the defender.
- The pair who do not receive the pass must react quickly to prevent the other players from reaching the third area. If they do win the ball, they can break into the third area themselves.
- The team that receives the pass wins a point if they pass into the small goal/gates. If the other pair win the ball and pass into the small goal/gates they win more points.

Focus

- Immediate reaction to win back the ball: determination and aggression.
- Awareness of where in the area the opposition received the ball.
- Recognising where your partner is situated and what they are attempting to do.

Possible Progressions/Regressions

- Alter the size of the middle area.
- The team receiving the pass have to complete a very small number of passes first, before they can break into the third area.
- The defending pair are allowed to follow the attacking pair into the final area and support the defender in trying to win the ball.

Practice D: Cover and Support

This adaption provides another opportunity for the players to practise their understanding of where they should be positioned as the second defender. Once the practice becomes live, the second defender is allowed to enter the first area, and their first job is to identify where they need to position themselves to ensure that they effectively support their teammate. With no guidelines provided in this practice, there is a lot more emphasis on the player positioning themselves correctly, which is therefore more challenging for the players. This first instance of the defender having to identify where they need to go within the area to be in the correct position is, however, possibly the easiest part of the practice for the players. Because everything happens in front of them, it is much easier to see the picture and work out where they need to go. The real challenge for the defenders starts when there is a need for them to swap their roles.

When there is a transfer in the practice, the players usually find it really challenging to remember what they need to do in their new role. For instance, if the attacker decides to share the ball with their teammate, this usually means the defender who was previously providing cover and support now needs to engage the opponent who received the pass. This particular transfer in roles is usually one that the players pick up quite quickly; it is the other element of this change that the players find more challenging. Having been the player trying to win possession from the player on the ball, they now need to reposition themselves to provide cover and support. Quite often in this scenario, the defender will either be distracted by the ball or the movement of the player after they have played the pass, in other words, they will follow the pass and try to engage the new player on the ball or follow the run of the attacker on the ball. Either decision will result in the defending team being vulnerable because either the other defender will be exposed to a one versus one with no support, or the attacker will be completely alone, should the player on the ball be able to find them.

As the practice provides an environment where the defenders face constant changes to the picture, it is more than understandable that they will find it extremely challenging to always make the correct decision and will therefore make mistakes, which they, of course, will learn from, with support and guidance of the coach. This is a good example of where we need to remember the practice provides an 'extreme' environment that, in terms of the topic that it is focusing on, will be more challenging than the game itself.

Practice D: Cover and Support

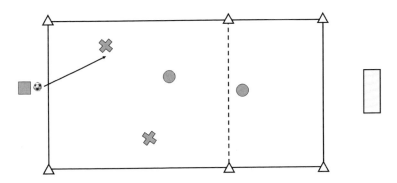

Alteration to Original Set-Up

- The first area is increased in size, which, in turn, decreases the size of the second area.
- Once the ball is played into the two attacking players, the second defender is unlocked from their area.
- All players are now free to go anywhere within the two areas.

Focus

- Identify where to position yourself in the first area as the ball is played in by the server.
- The second defender should be situated further back than the first defender so they are in a position to provide cover and support.
- If the player on the ball goes past the first defender, or if they pass the ball onto their teammate, the second defender needs to engage the player on the ball (i.e. they become the first defender). The other defender needs to recover and get back to being goalside and provide their partner with cover and support.
- Communication between the two defenders: where does the first defender want to show the attacker on the ball? Who is going to the ball, who is providing cover and support?

Possible Progressions/Regressions

- Both defenders begin the practice in the second area, and then both are released as soon as the server plays the ball into an attacker.
- Use any of the progressions or regressions from the original set-up.

CHAPTER 7
PRACTICE E

This particular practice is probably the best example of why, as coaches, we should consider using the same core practices in our sessions to help maximise player development and enjoyment. It is a fast-paced practice, in which the players develop lots of different aspects of the game, while also focusing on the main topic of the session. It is a practice that players also usually really enjoy, however, it does take a bit of time for them to fully grasp it and remember what to do. The transition from being an attacker to a defender is usually the main aspect of the practice that they forget. Entering the pitch as soon as the previous 'game' has ended is another part where they sometimes need a gentle reminder of what to do. Therefore, the first time, and possibly the second time that they take part in it, they will spend some of their time working out what to do and then also remembering to do it. So, it may take the players a few goes of the practice before they get the full benefits from it and start to enjoy playing it time and time again.

As well as the players really enjoying the practice, the other huge benefit is that it represents a lot of the characteristics that are found in the modern game of soccer. To have a greater chance of success, the attacking players need to break quickly away from their own goal and be in the position to have a shot as soon as possible. They also need to be direct in their play, and decisive and positive decisions need to be made to ensure that they make the most of the opposition players' disorganisation. With probably at least one of the defenders not being goalside and therefore attempting to recover, the attackers will often find just one or possibly even no defending players between them and the goal. With modern soccer matches usually played at a fast pace and the likelihood that this will continue in the future and probably increase, the players need support in all parts of their development: tactical, technical, physical, psychological and social to be able to play the game.

When looking at the practice design, there may be concerns around the players that are not involved, queueing off the pitch by the goal, waiting for their turn. And it would be right to have these concerns; a key ingredient of the most effective practices in the development of young players is a high level of ball rolling time or involvement. It is now possible for players to improve even if they are not involved in the practice. The best way they can learn is by doing, and they cannot do this if they spend more time standing around waiting for their turn than actually playing. Therefore, practices that are best described as 'drills', where players spend most of their time waiting for their turn, should usually be avoided or used sparingly. This type of practice usually removes the opportunity for the players to develop their decision making as well –any decisions have already been chosen for them by the coach, such as pass the ball to this teammate, then move to here, etc. First of all, this particular practice allows the players to make their own decisions, and the decision-making process is a key factor in whether or not they will be successful and, just as importantly, the waiting time for players is, in fact, very small. During their time on the pitch, players are fully involved in the practice and then, after they have completed their turn, by the time they return to the goal to wait to play again, they will usually be back on almost immediately, due to the speed of the games. This small amount of rest period is quite often needed due to the speed and physical demands of the practice, and the players can use the time between finishing their turn and going back to the starting position to recover. Therefore, though the practice may look as if it involves the players queueing and waiting for their turn, it does, in fact, provide them with lots of opportunity to play and develop numerous elements of the game. One thing we do need to be mindful of is the number of players within the practice. If there is a large number of players, there is a possibility they could spend too much time waiting. Therefore, if needed, two areas should be set up to ensure the players get enough playing time.

This particular set-up also provides the coach with an opportunity to provide individual support without affecting the rest of the group. While a player is returning to their starting position, the coach has the opportunity to speak to the player about what they just did in the practice. This could be to highlight something they did really well or provide feedback and support on an area they might need help with. While the player is working with the coach, all of their teammates can continue to play in the practice, which can lead to another element of player development: working with different teammates. In this practice, players usually prefer to work with the same teammate, not necessarily just because they are friends or that they want to play with them, but quite often they will keep the same partner as they presume that they have to, or it is what they always do. It is likely that unless they are told just to work with another teammate, they will wait for their partner to return before they enter the game again, even if it means missing a turn. Therefore, this is another aspect of the practice where they might need to participate in it two or three times before it becomes normal for them to go with any teammate who is ready to play. Producing this scenario of players pairing up with a variety of teammates means that not only do they get the benefit of playing with a range of partners with their unique characteristics who will make different decisions, but their opponents will also gain from it. Because the make-up of the pairs keeps changing, the opposition players will come against a mixture of combinations, making it more challenging for them to predict what they are likely to do, both in and out of possession.

Once the practice is up and running, a picture will often appear that indicates areas that the players need help and support in from the coach. As the attacking players enter the pitch, their movements are usually the same each time; their run will follow the same pathway, which is a straight line. This 'straight-line' running is usually seen in the movement of both attacking players – a railway track image helps the players understand what the player with the ball and their partner look like as they attack the opposition's goal. The movement of the player without the ball is particularly important; running forward in a straight line makes it much easier for the opposition players to defend. This straight run allows the defender or defenders to position themselves so they can easily deal with the player on the ball, and they can also either get across to the other attacker if the ball is transferred to them or intercept the pass. Therefore, it is the role of the attacker without the ball to make it uncomfortable for the defenders, and they can do this by coming off their straight-line pathway and making a movement across the pitch, meaning they will cross the pathway of the player on the ball. Doing this forces the defenders to make decisions, and it also provides their teammate on the ball with further options as new space is now available for them to drive into. At the same time, the pass into their teammate making the run can now be more dangerous, and the attacker with the ball making similar movements will cause the opposition players even more problems.

Practice E: Original Set-Up

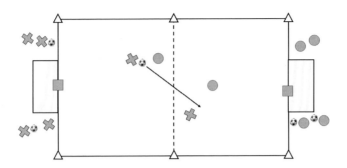

Set-Up

- The players are split into two teams, each team having a goalkeeper.
- Two players from one team enter the pitch and attempt to score a goal against the opposition's goalkeeper.
- As soon as they have had their shot, two players from the other team enter and attempt to score in the opposite goal. The two players who have just attacked become defenders and attempt to stop the other pair from scoring.
- The practice continues in this manner. New players enter the pitch when the attackers on the pitch have attempted to score, those players become defenders and the previous defenders leave the pitch and join the queue to play again.
- Once the players have attempted a shot, that particular game has finished, there are no rebounds, etc.
- If the defenders win the ball, they become the attackers and attempt to score. In doing so, they become defenders again, and a new pair of players from the other team enter.

Focus

- Positive in their play: always travel forward and do not turn back.
- Decisive decision making: when to retain the ball and when to pass it?
- If you decide to pass, where exactly does the player receiving the pass want the ball?
- The supporting player should consider where the run takes them: angled runs.

Possible Progressions/Regressions

- Alter the size and/or shape of the area.
- Move the goals away from the area.
- Attackers receive two points for a goal if they do not make a pass.

Practice E: Recovery Runs

Despite being a very attacking practice, it can also be used for a number of out of possession focuses, starting with this particular adaption that looks at recovery runs. Simply making one of the players run around a cone positioned close to where the new attacking players enter the pitch ensures that they will be in the wrong position and, therefore, they will need to make a recovery run before they can support their teammate. The scenario produced is very similar to the one found in chapter 6 for the same topic, and so the key messages are the same – they need to see what is occurring in front of them before making a decision about the best course of action.

To begin with, no decision is needed about which player should make the run around a cone before they can start defending. The main reason for this is to ensure that it is not too complicated for the players at the start, so the transition between the original set-up and this adaption is straightforward and easy for the players to understand. Giving the task to just one player means there are no decisions to be made; the player not on the ball knows they need to make the run around a cone, while the attacker who has the goal attempt understands that they can start defending straight away. The problem is that we are taking away an important moment in the practice that helps the players develop their decision-making skills. Obviously, when they are playing in a game, the players will not need to decide who makes a run away from the ball and around a cone, but they will need to decide which player goes to the ball or is in the best position to delay the opposition from progressing quickly. Therefore, once the players are ready, the progression of allowing either player to make the run around the cones can be introduced. By doing so, the two players that need to change from being attackers to defenders now need to make a quick decision about which player should make the recovery run. A number of factors need to be taken into consideration, such as which new player enters with the ball and the position of the players as they transfer into becoming the defenders.

An important element in all defending is communication between players to ensure that they remain compact and organised and that each player understands where they should be and what their role is at each specific moment in time. And the introduction of this progression emphasises the need for the two defending players communicating effectively with each other to ensure they both clearly know what each other is doing to make sure they have the best possible chance of delaying the attackers, before getting into a position to defend the goal more effectively and try to win the ball back.

Practice E: Recovery Runs

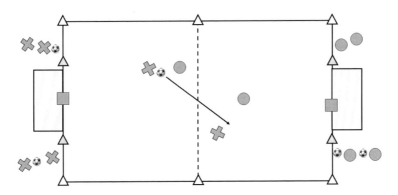

Alteration to Original Set-Up

- A cone is placed either side of both goals.
- As soon as the attackers have had their attempt on goal, the player who did not have the shot has to run around one of the cones situated next to the opposition's goal before they can help their teammate defend.
- If the ball goes out of play, either player can make the run around one of the cones. If the opposition players win the ball and start attacking, both attackers can start defending immediately.

Focus

- Identify what is happening ahead of you; where is the danger in the picture you see?
- If time allows, head towards the furthest post of your goal.
- Do not engage the attacker; try not to win the ball from the behind, unless there is no other option.
- If needed, angle the run so that it cuts off the passing line to the second attacker.
- Can the first defender delay the player on the ball to give their teammate making the recovery run enough time to get into position.

Possible Progressions/Regressions

- Alter the size and/or shape of the area.
- Change the positioning of the cones; they can be placed wider, further back from the pitch or slightly inside the area.
- Either player can make the run around one of the cones once they have had an attempt on goal.

Practice E: Cover and Support

By simply moving the positioning of the cones from next to the goals to the centre of the pitch, the focus of the practice can now be shifted from making recovery runs to cover and support. Making the defender run in the opposite direction after completing the task ensures they will usually be goalside of the ball and positioned behind their teammate, therefore, making them the second defender who needs to provide their partner with cover and support. As they complete their run around the cone, the defender needs to look at the picture that faces them in terms of the positioning of the two attacking players and their teammate. From this, they need to make an immediate decision of where they need to position themselves to provide the best possible support for their teammate. It could be that by the time they complete the task of running around a cone, the attackers have already managed to get past their teammate and rather than providing cover and support, they need to take on the role of first defender and engage the player on the ball. The focus of the coach in this situation shifts to the other defender who needs to recover after being beaten so that they can provide some support for their teammate.

Again, this practice has a number of similarities to the practice with the same focus from the previous chapter, as the player providing cover and support can see the picture in front of them and needs to act according to what they see, just as they would during a game. The significant difference in this practice however is that the picture they see is likely to be much more unstable compared with the one they would have seen in the other practice, which makes it considerably more challenging. In this practice, by the time the player has been able to move around the cone, the play would have been going on for a certain amount of time, therefore, the positioning of their teammate and the two attackers will be a lot less stable and structured; they are likely to be in full motion, meaning the picture they see will change quickly. This means it will be much harder to make the correct decision in terms of where and what they should do. It is possible that the first decision they make will need to change as they are travelling to the area on the pitch that they initially chose as the correct place to position themselves. There are numerous actions that could force the defender to change their initial decision, such as the player on the ball passing it onto their teammate or getting past the first defender, or the movement of the attacker who is not in possession of the ball. The new decision they make needs to be made quickly as any delay could result in the attackers being through on goal. This particular practice provides the players with an environment that will test and challenge their decision-making skills.

Practice E: Cover and Support

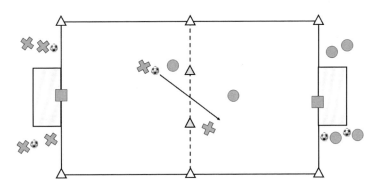

Alteration to Original Set-Up

- Two cones are placed on the halfway line.
- As soon as the attackers have had their attempt on goal, the player who did not have the shot has to run around one of the cones situated on the halfway line before they can help their teammate.
- If the ball goes out of play, either player can make the run around one of the cones. If the opposition players win the ball and start attacking, both attackers can start defending immediately.

Focus

- Once you have retreated to the cone, identify where to position yourself on the pitch.
- The second defender should be situated further back than the first defender so they are in a position to provide cover and support.
- If the player on the ball goes past the first defender or if they pass the ball onto their teammate, the second defender needs to engage the player on the ball, in other words, they become the first defender. The other defender needs to recover and get back to being goalside to provide their partner with cover and support.
- Communication between the two defenders: where does the first defender want to show the attacker on the ball? Who is going to the ball, who is providing cover and support?

Possible Progressions/Regressions

- Change the positioning of the cones; they can be placed wider apart or have two sets, with one set in each half of the pitch.
- Either player can make the run around a cone, once they have had an attempt on goal.

Practice E: Forward Passing

Just by altering the starting position of one of the attackers entering the pitch, the focus of the practice can be switched to the player starting the practice and the pass into their teammate. There is also an opportunity to use the exact same set-up and change the topic to receiving to play forward, with the focus now on the attacking player looking to receive the initial pass from their teammate. However, this adaption is more suited to the forward pass focus because it will not always be possible for the pass to be played into their teammate, therefore, there is a chance that they will not get enough opportunities to practise receiving the ball to play forward. Because there is a clear advantage in the attacking players getting the ball to the player already positioned high up the pitch, the defenders will try to prevent this from happening. Therefore, the main focus of the practice is the decision making of the player situated by the goal, in terms of whether they play the ball immediately and, if not, how both attacking players can affect the situation to allow the pass to be made.

Pictures within a game of soccer can change very quickly – space available can disappear in an instance. With the opponents already on the pitch and trying to react quickly to their change in roles from attackers to defenders, the space that the player on the ball sees in front of them is likely to alter as the defending players move to get back into position. Therefore, the player on the ball first needs to make a quick decision about whether or not to make the pass into their teammate. To take full advantage of the player's position high up the pitch, the ball needs to be played to them early before the defenders have time to recover and set up. The other decision that needs to be made is where they play the pass – is it into feet? Is it into space? The positioning of the defenders will definitely have an impact on this, as they might be cutting off one of the options so the decision has almost been made for them. The key is that they identify a possible pathway for the ball to travel quickly and then execute the pass effectively to ensure that it reaches its intended target.

If a pass cannot be made immediately, can the player waiting to receive the pass make a movement that puts them in a place on the pitch where they can receive the ball? They need to be in a position where the ball can travel safely to them and not be intercepted by an opposition player. The other option is for the player on the ball to create the pathway for the pass to be made. The player who travels with the ball for a short distance and manipulates it so that it travels on a different line will attract a defender who will try to close them down. All these actions will produce different spaces on the pitch, which could then allow the pass into their teammate to be made.

Practice E: Forward Passing

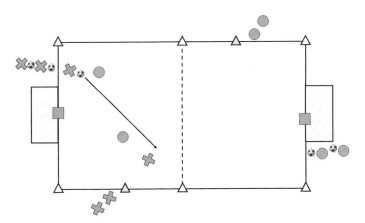

Alteration to Original Set-Up

- The starting positions of the players are now repositioned, as shown in the diagram.
- On starting the practice, the player with the ball can either pass the ball immediately to their partner or enter the pitch with the ball. Their partner without the ball can go onto the pitch at any time, once it is their turn to enter the practice.
- At the end of their turn (i.e. when they have finished defending), the players join the opposite queue to the one they were in before.

Focus

- Ensure that there is a clear pathway between the ball and the other player. If there is not, can you manipulate the ball so there is?
- Weight and accuracy of pass.
- If necessary, pass to where they will be, not where they are.

Possible Progressions or Regressions

- Alter the size and/or shape of the area.
- Change the start position of the player receiving the forward pass.
- Change the side in which the player receiving the forward pass is positioned.
- Give the defenders a task from the practices that have an out-of-possession topic.
- Use a smaller ball.
- Add two or three sets of gates on the halfway line that the attackers have to travel through before they can have an attempt on goal.

Practice E: Receiving Under Pressure

The starting positions of the players in is adaption is similar to the previous practice, however, instead of (hopefully) receiving a pass to go forward, they now have to drop into an end zone before they can receive the pass. By forcing them to travel to the end zone before they can receive the pass, and by making it the only way the ball can first enter the pitch, allows and encourages one of the defenders to follow and mark them tightly, putting them under pressure as they receive the ball. This will put the player in a similar position to the previous practices, which has the same focus. This will provide them with an opportunity to continue to develop this area of their performance. However, this practice also provides the coach with an opportunity to work with the teammate who is supporting the player on the ball.

Ideally, when a player receives a pass while under pressure, we would like them to find a solution that allows them to get away from their opponent while keeping the ball themselves. However, this is not always possible, and sometimes, the better option is to pass the ball onto a teammate. It is therefore important that the players have an understanding of how to provide effective support. Once the player has played the pass into their teammate, their initial thought is quite often to make a forward run beyond the ball, which is something that we would usually encourage them to do. But in some circumstances, it is not the right option as by doing so, they are no longer an option for their teammate with the ball who may use the support to either share possession or help keep it themselves.

Recognising the shape of their teammate on the ball and the way they are facing is key to where the supporting player should position themselves within the area. If they go past them while their teammate is facing away from the goal, they will be unlikely to be in a position to receive a pass. More often than not, a player will pass the ball the way they are facing, and the likelihood of this happening increases if they are under pressure from a defender who is preventing them from changing the direction they can play. Therefore, to begin with, the player who played the initial pass may need to position themselves so their teammate can see them and use them if needed. Movement to a particular side of the player on the ball may increase the effectiveness of this support. The movement may distract the defender or influence them to cover this side of the player in possession of the ball, allowing the other side to be exploited by the attacker, by turning into this space. The support the player provides their teammate on the ball can therefore be crucial in terms of whether or not they progress up the pitch.

Practice E: Receiving Under Pressure

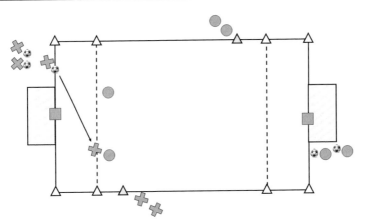

Alteration to Original Set-Up

- The pitch is split into three areas, with the two end areas much smaller than the central area.
- The starting positions of the players are now repositioned, as shown in the diagram.
- The player with the ball can only pass to their partner to start their turn, and they must wait until their partner has entered the end zone before they can do this.
- Only one defender can enter the end zone with the attacker.
- As soon as the first attacker has played the pass, they can enter the pitch.
- At the end of their turn (i.e. when they finish defending), the players join the opposite queue to the one they were in before.

Focus

- Awareness of the defending players' position.
- Body shape as they receive the ball.
- Which foot is chosen to receive the ball?
- Retain or share the ball?
- Positioning of the teammate to support the player on the ball.

Possible Progressions/Regressions

- Alter the size and/or shape of the area.
- Allow both defenders to enter the end zone with the attacker.
- Change the side the player receiving the pass is positioned.

Practice E: Pass or Dribble?

Similar to the adaptions that focused on out-of-possession topics, this practice is created by just adding a few cones to the set-up. In this instance, they are situated at the side, a small distance from the pitch. Forcing one of the opposition players to run around a cone before they can help their teammate defend provides a two versus one situation for the attackers until the other defender rejoins the pitch. If the attackers are quick enough in their actions, it should mean that, before the player has an opportunity to support their teammate defending the goal, the game will already be over. The key to achieving this is the decision making of the player on the ball and their teammate's actions when supporting them.

The first element needed to be successful is speed of play by the player entering the pitch with the ball. Any delay in their play could allow the first defender to get into the position they want to be in. This will likely provide the other opposition player enough time to get back onto the pitch, and the advantage that the attackers initially had will no longer exist. The attacker being direct in their play will give the defender no choice but to engage the player on the ball, which will then produce the opportunity to decide whether to pass or dribble. The decision the player on the ball has to make – before deciding whether to share it with their partner or not – is which direction they go when they enter the pitch. Not only do they need to identify where the first defender is situated but also whereabouts on the pitch the player making the run around the cone is likely to come back on. The decision the player makes is likely to have an impact on the next decision about whether to pass or retain the ball themselves, depending on what space will be available once they have moved into the area of the pitch they have selected. For example, if they travel towards the area where the defender is likely to re-enter the pitch, there is likely to be little space for them to continue into, so the pass could well be the better option. Therefore, they might actually do this on purpose, knowing they will occupy both defenders and leave their teammate in space, which they can then exploit provided they can successfully pass the ball to them.

With regard to the attacker without their ball, as discussed earlier in the book, their movement is key to ensuring they can be found with a pass or to act as a decoy for their teammate to go into a different area. What this practice offers – and more so than the others in the same topic – due to the size of the area, is the opportunity for the player on the ball to dribble and pass. If they can go past the first defender, they will attract the attention of the other opposition player returning to the pitch, so if they can travel and wait for this player to engage them, they can then release the ball to their teammate who, again, is likely to be free.

Practice E: Pass or Dribble?

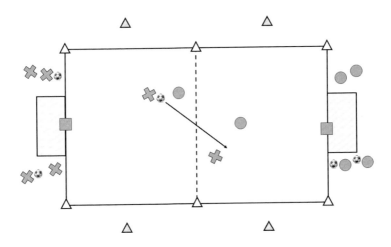

Alteration to Original Set-Up

- Four cones are placed as shown in the diagram.
- As soon as the attackers have had their attempt on goal, one player must run around one of the cones situated just outside the half of the pitch with the goal they are attacking before they can help their teammate.
- If the ball goes out of play, a player must still make the run around one of the cones. If the opposition players win the ball and start attacking, both attackers can start defending immediately.

Focus

- Decision making: when to retain the ball and when to pass it?
- Can you use the supporting player to help keep the ball individually?
- If you decide to pass, where exactly does the player receiving the pass want the ball?
- For the supporting player, what type of run could you make?

Possible Progressions/Regressions

- Alter the size and/or shape of the area?
- Change the positioning of the cones; they can be placed wider, further back from the pitch or closer.
- Use a smaller ball.
- Limit the attackers to just one pass.

Practice E: Finishing

Making a slight alteration to the shape of the pitch will encourage the players to have an attempt on goal more often. The original set-up and design of the practice already allows for lots of attempts on goal due to the size of the pitch and the players having to make the transition from being an attacker to a defender. The practice is designed to encourage fast attacking play, and it provides the players with an opportunity to achieve lots of success. However, when they are forced wide, which may happen quite regularly as the defenders will try to force them away from the goal, the attackers will then likely try to pass it on to their teammate, who they will perceive as being in a better position, to have a shot. Channelling the area towards the goal prevents the player on the ball venturing too far wide, as they will end up out of the area. Therefore, the shape of the area encourages the attackers to travel towards the goal and this, in turn, will persuade the player on the ball to have a shot on goal themselves, rather than share it with their teammate.

The progressions we introduce to the practice will have a real impact on the type of finishes that we can help the players develop. There are a number of additional adaptions within this one particular adaption that allows the practice to be used on numerous occasions in a number of different ways. Quite often, when we deliver a session with a focus on finishing, the types of finishes we provide for the players to practise are very similar in that the distances and angles are alike, similar to the way the player receives the ball before they have the shot. This obviously does not replicate the way in which a player will have a shot during a game of soccer; very rarely does a player attempt to score a goal in a match from a similar situation found within these more traditional practices.

If we look at one of these adaptions, we can see it provides a more realistic type of finish that is more closely related to that found within a match environment. Creating three channels that run the full length of the pitch and rewarding the players with extra points if they score from inside one of the outside channels encourages the attackers to shoot from these wide areas. This is a similar position to which they will try to score from during a game and, in this situation, we always encourage the player to shoot along the ground and across the goalkeeper into the far corner. By doing so, they put the ball into a difficult area for the goalkeeper to save, and even if they manage to prevent the goal, they are likely to push it into an area where another attacker might be able to get to the rebound first. But for the players to be able to practise this type of shot – which they are likely to try and execute in a game – we need to give them an environment where they can do it.

Practice E: Finishing

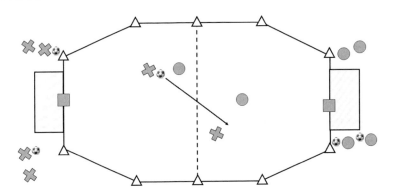

Alteration to Original Set-Up

- The shape of the pitch is changed as per the diagram.
- Everything else remains the same.

Focus

- Aim to have an attempt on goal at the earliest possible opportunity.
- Selection of shot: take into consideration where you are within the area and the positioning of the goalkeeper.
- Ensure that the shot is on target and struck with power.

Possible Progressions/Regressions

- Alter the size and/or shape of the area.
- Position the goals away from the pitch.
- Split the pitch into quarters so that each half is split into two. The players can then earn two points for scoring from the first area in the attacking half and one point from inside the second area (closer to the goal).
- Split the pitch into thirds by using channels the full length of the pitch. The players can then earn two points for scoring from inside a wide channel and one point if they score from within the central channel.
- Give the defenders a task from the practices that have an out-of-possession topic.
- Add targets inside the goal that the players get bonus points for hitting, such as a ball balanced on a cone.
- Change the angle/positioning of the goal.

Practice E: Turning

One of the simplest ways to introduce turning in a practice is to make it nondirectional. For this particular practice to become nondirectional, we need to allow the players to score in either of the goals. Therefore, we need to reposition where the attackers enter the pitch, and the obvious place to do this is halfway as it will create an equal distance to both goals. This then makes it unclear to the defenders which way the attacker will decide to go as they enter the pitch, which could then impact whether the players get the opportunity to practise the topic of the practice; turning. Since the defenders are unsure which direction the attacker is going to go when they enter the pitch, and because they have to transfer from being an attacker, it is likely that the player on the ball could identify a pathway to the unopposed goal, and there will be no need for them to complete a turn. The pass that the attackers need to complete before they can enter the pitch is therefore essential to the practice, as it provides the defenders with time to get organised. Allowing the defenders to get in a position where they can give some protection to both goals will ensure that the attackers do not get a free run to a goal. Instead, they will come up against an opponent and a turn is now a valid option to create a goal-scoring opportunity.

There is still a possibility that the practice may not generate enough turns as the players are finding success through other means, such as dribbling past a defender or sharing the ball with their partner who has made a forward run. If this happens, the progression of splitting the pitch into thirds is a good option to encourage the players to change direction and attempt to score in the opposite goal that they first attacked. Rewarding the attacking players with extra points if they do this is a really effective way to encourage them to complete a turn within the practice. The number of points we reward them with does not need to be restricted to just doubling it to two points; the number we decide upon should be influenced by how much encouragement the players need to produce a turn, and this can be increased.

Using scoring systems has been discussed in a number of different sections of the book already, but something that not been touched upon yet is the need to actually keep score. This may seem obvious at first, but quite often we do not keep an accurate score and the players will soon realise and not see the point of trying to gain the extra points. As coaches, we should not keep the score either as we should be concentrating on supporting the players. Therefore, a tactics board on the side of the pitch can be used by the players to keep a tally of points they have scored each time they complete their turn.

Practice E: Turning

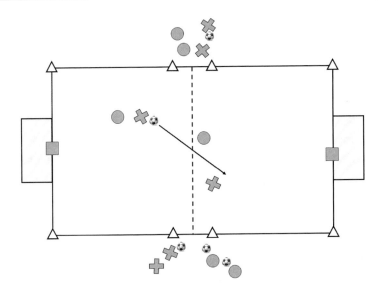

Alteration to Original Set-Up

- A gate is added to each side of the pitch on the halfway line.
- The two attackers now enter the pitch through the gates, one player through each gate.
- To start, the attacker with the ball, must pass across to their partner (the defenders are not allowed to block or intercept the pass). Both players can now enter the pitch.
- Once on the pitch, the attackers can score in either goal.

Focus

- Identify when you should turn.
- Which direction to turn? Away from danger and into space.
- Choice and execution of turn.
- Touches: use the smallest number of touches needed to execute the turn.
- Speed: sharpness of turn and acceleration away from the defender.

Possible Progressions/Regressions

- Alter the size and/or shape of the area.
- The pitch is split into thirds (the middle third is much smaller). The attackers get extra points if they score in the opposite end third to which they entered.

Practice E: Driving With the Ball

As in the previous chapter, this core practice can also be altered so it can be used for individual focuses, however, in this adaption and the next one, there is no element of sharing within them. However, they have similarities to those practices found in chapters 3 and 5. There is an option to introduce another attacker to make it a two versus one practice, however, the focus of the practice could be lost, so restrictions may be needed such as allowing the attackers only one pass. For this particular adaption, this pass also needs to be completed in the early stages of the practice so small areas could be added at each end, with the player on the ball only allowed to share it in this first area.

Unlike some of the previous practices that focus on driving with the ball, this particular adaption focuses on the actual technique rather than other aspects, such as getting your body between the ball and the defender. The set-up of the practice provides a clear lead to the attacker as they enter the pitch, and it is an advantage that they should retain, provided they are positive and drive forwards using the correct technique to ensure they travel at their maximum speed (with the ball). The challenge the players will probably face is to keep the ball under control while travelling at speed. Because they are aware that their opponent will start behind them, and because they can see a clear pathway to their target understandably, they will attempt to get there as quickly as possible. By doing so, they will often sacrifice the quality of the run over how quickly they can travel with the ball, and this can obviously affect whether they retain the ball or how long it takes them to reach the target. If they are not in full control of the ball, it will go off the pathway that provides them with the shortest and quickest route to their chosen gate. If the ball veers off to the left or right, the player will need to spend time adjusting their run to retrieve the ball. Not only will they have to move off their preferred pathway but they will likely need to slow down to readjust their movement pattern to allow them to collect the ball.

To have more of a focus on the attacker getting across the defender, there are a number of options available, and although they are listed as progressions, they can be used from the outset if this is the particular aspect of driving with the ball that you want to focus on. Either changing the gates that the attacker has to travel through to enter the pitch and score a point, or moving the central gate so it is set back from the area, stops the attacker from having a lead at the start of the practice. By removing this advantage, there will be more of an emphasis on the attacker protecting the ball while they are driving with it.

Practice E: Driving With the Ball

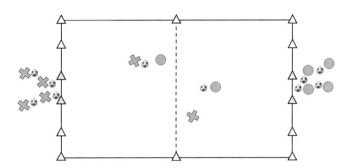

Alteration to Original Set-Up

- The goals are removed and replaced by three gates at each end of the area.
- When entering the pitch, the players must enter through the centre gate.
- To win a point, the player must travel with the ball through one of the two wide gates. They do not have to stop the ball; they can leave it as soon as they have passed through the gate.
- To increase ball rolling time for individual players, two pairs can go at the same time.

Focus

- First touch: strong touch out of your feet and forward.
- Identify whether or not you need to get your body between the ball and the defender.
- Strong controlled touches to allow long strides while running.

Possible Progressions/Regressions

- Alter the size and/or shape of the area.
- Give the attackers a task to do once they have travelled through a gate, for example they need to pass the ball into a small goal/gates.
- Move back the gates the attacker enters through, away from the pitch.
- The attacker enters through one of the wide gates and scores by driving through the middle gate.
- Use a smaller ball.
- Two small gates are added to the line that separates the two areas, with the attacker having to drive through one of them.
- Two sets of two small gates are added to the main area (four gates in total, two lines of two gates), and the attacker must drive through two of the gates.

Practice E: One Versus One Defending

The final practice in this chapter concentrates on defending in a one versus one situation and, as always, this adaption could be used to help the players develop the attacking aspects of this situation. To do this, it is recommended that only one goal is used at each end of the pitch instead of two. Having two goals will probably make it too easy for the attacking players to find success, as it is difficult for the opponent to defend two separate targets situated so far apart. The difficulty created by having two goals is that it is not the right environment for the players to develop specific aspects of defending.

Because the players must defend two goals quite far apart, there is not really a specific direction in which the player can be shown. The defender can, of course, try to force the attacker out of the area, but this can be extremely challenging as there will clearly be space on the other side of the area, where the player on the ball will be happy to move into because they will likely have an opportunity to score a point. The practice also increases the challenge for the defender because the attacker has the opportunity to score a point from near enough anywhere in the area; the attacker may not even need to get past the defender to score a point, they could attempt to pass the ball into one of the small goals as soon as they enter the pitch. Although there is a clear advantage to getting past the defender as it will allow the attacking player to get much closer to the goals and make the final pass much easier, there is still the danger that the attacker could attempt to win a point at any time. Therefore, the most effective tactic that the defender can employ is to try and win the ball as soon as possible.

When providing this type of environment for the defender, it may be a challenge for the coach to support the player in being aggressive to win the ball while making sure that they are not too enthusiastic, which may result in the attacker manipulating the ball and going past their opponent quite easily, because they have overly committed themselves. However, at the same time, it is important that the defender closes the attacker down quickly to ensure the pathways to both goals are closed off. Once they are in this position, the defender then needs to be aggressive in their play and take charge of the situation. They do not want the attacker to be in control and dictating the practice – it is the defender who needs to be on the front foot, forcing the player on the ball backwards or into making a mistake. Doing this should ensure the attacker is not able to create any type of space that will allow them to progress forward or attempt the pass into the small goals.

Practice E: One Versus One Defending

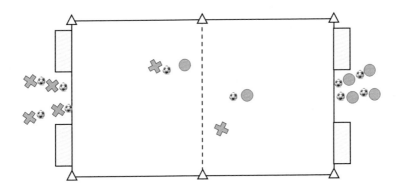

Alteration to Original Set-Up

- The goals are removed and replaced by two small goals/gates at each end of the pitch.
- The attacking player enters the pitch between the two small goals/gates.
- To win a point, the player must pass the ball into one of the small goals/gates.
- To increase ball rolling time for individual players, two pairs can go at the same time.

Focus

- Angle and line of approach.
- Slow down as you get closer to the attacker.
- Body position to be side-on and knees bent.
- Aggressive in trying to win the ball back, take control of the situation.
- How early can you win back the ball?

Possible Progressions/Regressions

- Alter the size and/or shape of the area.
- Add a gate in between the small goals/gates the player enters through, which can also be used as a third goal.
- The pitch is split into thirds, and the attacker is not allowed to pass the ball into the small goals/gates from the first third or from the first third and the middle third.
- Two small gates are added to the line that separates the two areas, with the attacker having to travel through one of them.
- Use a smaller ball.

CHAPTER 8
INTERVENTION STRATEGIES

Creating the right environment for players to come and play soccer while training and learning is, without doubt, the most important thing we can do as coaches to help them in their development. And the main focus of this book is to help create such an environment by providing game-like practices that the players recognise and understand, so that they spend most of their time having fun with their friends and playing a game that they find challenging and motivating. When placed in such an environment, the learning and developmental process will, to an extent, look after itself, as the players will find themselves in similar situations to those within an actual match, where they can practice all the different aspects of their performance through what is essentially trial and error. However, for this particular chapter, the important element is that the learning and development process is taken care of to 'an extent', therefore, if the players are to achieve their full potential, or at least get close to it, they will, at times, need some support from the coach. If we look at the school environment and, in particular, the early stages of their schooling where children spend a lot of their time learning through experimenting and problem solving, it is clear that teachers plan activities their pupils will find fun and challenging with the opportunity to discover the solutions themselves. But when the pupils are struggling to find the answer, the teacher is on hand to provide them with the guidance and support they need to progress in their understanding and learning. As coaches, we need to do exactly the same: to provide the environment where the players have an opportunity to find the answers themselves but, when required, we need to be available to provide them with the support that they not only need but quite often want.

There are, however, also times where we can be too eager to provide the players with some form of help. Coaches are often seen by the player, the parents and sometimes even themselves as the person who has the knowledge and all the answers. When this occurs, it is understandable that the coach wants to step in and help whenever they can, as they believe this is the right thing to do because providing the support that the players need will aid them in their development. The problems that this usually creates, however, are that the players lose out on ball rolling time and the opportunity to find the answers themselves. If we stop the practice too often to give information or to provide support, it is likely we will prevent the players from having enough time on the ball. It is also likely that the practice will lose its momentum and tempo, which can also have an impact on their development during that particular session. And stopping the practice too quickly to provide support could prevent the players from having the chance to work it out themselves, which can be significant as we are taking away an opportunity for them to learn.

Striking the right balance of allowing the players to play and work out the solutions themselves while also supporting them is an extremely difficult skill to get right, and it is highly unlikely that we ever will. Plus, we will never know whether we did get it right, as it is impossible to say whether a player or players would have gone on to find the solution themselves if the practice had not been stopped by the coach for guidance or support. But what we can do is allow the players to try and work out the problem themselves and then look for signs that they need some help and would benefit from the support of the coach. These signs could be one of a number of things, such as the players getting frustrated because they are unable to do the task they have been set, or they continually make the same mistakes and struggle to progress in terms success. The amount of time we give the players to solve the problems themselves will, of course, vary, and this forms a part of why it is important that we get to know and understand the players we work with as individuals.

Once it has been decided to provide some form of support, the first decision that needs to be made is how many players are we going to try and help? Will it be an individual intervention or are we going to work with a group of players? Sometimes, we may be influenced by the type of practice that we are delivering. For instance, if it is a larger, squad-type practice, where all the players are playing in the same area (examples of which are in the next three chapters), we will often use a group intervention. Or it could be that we prefer supporting the group as a whole, because we feel that individual interventions are too personal and players may feel uncomfortable in that situation. And this, in some instances, may be the case, but it is the role of the coach to change that mindset, by making it normal for players to receive one-on-one coaching and help them see the benefits of receiving this personal support.

Once we have decided whether we are going to support an individual player or a group of players, the next decision is how we are going to support them? Is it verbally through using a question-and-answer technique, by giving the players information, or it could be more of a visual strategy, such as a demonstration or by 'painting pictures'? Again, we can be influenced by a number of factors, including individual preferences of the coach. If we are not overly confident in our ability to complete a demonstration effectively, then we may not use them as a tool to support the players' development. Instead, we might try to use more of a verbal strategy, giving the players information rather than showing them. However, we need to be mindful that everyone has their preferred method of learning and receiving information; as a rule, we either prefer to see things (visual learners), hear things (audio learners) or do it ourselves (kinaesthetic learners). Therefore, when we do try to support a player or players, we need to ensure that we cater for every need. We should be constantly addressing the kinaesthetic learners anyway, by giving the players the opportunity to work out the solutions themselves before we provide any help. Therefore, we just have to meet the needs of both the visual and audio learners by providing support in a way that the players can both see and hear the information.

When it comes to providing support, we need to be comfortable and confident using all the different methods and strategies are available to coaches. This is really important as the coach needs to be able to select and use the intervention strategies that are the most suitable for that specific moment during the session. Numerous factors will be considered in the decision-making process, such as which strategies should be used, for instance, the particular player or group of players we are working with and whether we have already given some support previously for the same aspect of the performance. As ever, there is not a definitive rule that states when each particular type of intervention should be used. However, there is definitely some guidance that we can follow, which highlights the benefits of each type that will then help us in the selection process when deciding which strategy should be used.

Individual or Group Intervention?

The first questions we need to ask ourselves when deciding whether to use a group or individual intervention are: who specifically needs the support and who would benefit from it? If we look at the first aspect of this – who needs the support? We ask ourselves if the support we are about to provide is needed by just one player or are there a number of players struggling with the same aspect of the performance. If it is just the one player, there is no reason to stop the whole practice, which will impact the amount of ball rolling time the players will achieve during the session. Players will benefit from having more time on the ball, rather than standing watching and/or listening to the coach provide support for something they do not need any help with. As discussed earlier in the chapter, we should only provide support when the players really need it. If, however, a number of players are finding a particular part of the topic really challenging, then it would make sense to deliver the support in one go, through a group intervention.

However, there will also be times when not all the players need the support that the coach wants to provide, but they will definitely benefit from it. This will often happen within group practices but can also occur within smaller practices, such as those seen in the two previous chapters. For example, in a larger squad practice, a player might be struggling with their decision making, for instance, they might select the wrong option or not attempt the pass that we want them to. By stepping in with a group intervention, we can show this player which option they should be selecting, but we can also discuss it with the rest of the group why it is the better option, in other words, what does it allow the team to do? What does it do to the opposition? It provides us with an opportunity to check the players' understanding because they are doing something that we want them to do, but do they know why they are doing it? So, different players will benefit in different ways from the same intervention. We just need to decide whether enough players will benefit from the full session being stopped.

Individual Interventions

Providing a player with an individual intervention can have the biggest effect on their development as they benefit from the full attention of the coach and receive support specific to their needs. It also allows the rest of the group to continue playing, which will increase their ball rolling time and provide them with an opportunity to develop other areas of the performance that are more beneficial for them.

For each of the practices, a number of coaching points are provided that can be used to support the players in their development. A small number of these (two or three) should be used for each session to help the players progress around the main focus. So, for instance, if the session focus is one versus one (attacking), the coaching points that could be used are: shift the ball quickly in a different direction, explosive acceleration to exploit the space they have created and move away from the defender. Therefore, all the support that we provide the players should be around these two coaching points, and they should be introduced gradually and revisited during each practice.

At the start of each practice, the players should be given the opportunity to have a go at the practice and to start to work out the different ways that they can be successful and, while doing this, we can observe them to see how they are getting on and decide which coaching point we should introduce first. Quite often, there is a logical order that we should use the coaching points, but it is possible we do not need to use them all. If the players are already doing something really well, we do not need to provide them with any support in this area of the performance. Instead, we can move to the next coaching point and allow them to have time to concentrate on the aspects that they do need to develop. Once we have introduced a coaching point – for example, when you are trying to go past the defender, can you shift the ball quickly in a different direction? – our sole focus should now be on this coaching point, and any support we provide to an individual player should be around this specific part of their performance. We can easily get distracted trying to support them with other parts of their performance, but if we try to fix too much, we can end up actually not helping them with anything.

Once we have identified a player who needs support with a specific coaching point, the decision then needs to be made about how we support them visually and verbally. Usually, it is recommended that verbal support will come in the form of questions and answers, and this should definitely be used at the start of the intervention. The key factor in this process is to make sure we know exactly what we are going to ask the players when we first approach them. The question needs to be short, to the point and linked directly to the coaching point. It can be directed in a number of ways, depending on the player we are working with and their level of understanding of the topic. For instance, we could use an open-ended question, or to make it less challenging for the player, we might ask them a question where the answer is yes or no, or where we offer choices, for instance, do you want to play quickly or slowly? Once we have gone through this process, we might use direct instruction. This is normally only used when the player is unable to provide the correct information and we need to give them the answer. If we continue to ask questions until they give the correct information, we put the player in a really uncomfortable position; we are preventing them from returning to the practice and it is likely that the only reason they finally provide the right answer is because they have stumbled across it or it is the final option. Within this process, it is really important to provide the players the opportunity to give us the information rather than the other way around (open-ended questions). If they are unable to do this, we can give them some guidance to help them (yes or no questions or multiple-choice questions) and then, finally, if needed, we may have to give them the answer. Throughout this process, it is important that the 'why' is discussed – it is essential the players do not just know the answer but the reason for it as well.

To supplement this verbal support, we also need to provide players with visual aids, which can come in a range of different formats. First of all, we could provide the players with a demonstration so that they can see exactly what we want them to do. If we decide to use this particular form of visual aid, it is really important that we complete it exactly the way that we want the players to do it. If we want them to explode past the defender, then our demonstration needs to be explosive'. Should we be in a position where we feel that we are unable to provide an effective demonstration, we can use another player from the session that we have seen complete the action how we want it to be performed. We could either ask the player we are supporting to watch the other player when they perform the specific action, or we could ask this particular player to come over and complete the demonstration. Another option available to a coach is to use a tactics board. This particular option might be more suitable when the focus is more around positioning or decision making. For example, if the practice topic is cover and support, we may use a tactics board to get the player to show us where they should be positioned as a second defender. So, in this instance, the coach would be using verbal and visual support alongside each other: can you show me where you should be positioned? Similarly, we could ask the player to position themselves within the practice where they believe they should be. Again, this can then be further supported with questions for the player to answer: why have you positioned yourself there? What does this allow you to do?

When delivering these individual interventions, it is also really important that we do not impact the players' self-esteem in a negative way. Understandably, players can see an individual intervention as criticism or as being singled out for doing something wrong. Therefore, we should always look to begin the intervention with lots of positive comments before we go into the details of supporting them. So, if we refer back to the one versus one attacking focus and the coaching point, how to shift the ball quickly in a different direction when trying to go past the defender, we could start the intervention by praising the player for being positive and direct in their play and demonstrating really effective skills to go past the defender, or any other part of the performance they are doing well. Highlighting specific aspects of performance that they are doing well will help increase their confidence and encourage them to approach the intervention with more of a positive outlook. This is essential in any learning environment; learners need to be engaged and involved in the process to fully benefit from the support they receive. Therefore, if they enter the intervention with a negative mindset, they are unlikely to take anything away from the process.

Group Interventions

There are a number of similarities between group and individual interventions. For instance, any intervention with the full group needs to be linked directly to the session's coaching points, and the players will need both visual and audio support and to be involved in the learning process. Probably the most significant difference is when and where we deliver the intervention. We will often deliver an individual intervention just after the player has attempted to complete the action and possibly while the rest of the players continue to play. We can see this in the practices in chapter 7. Here, once a player has completed their turn, it is possible to speak to them and deliver an individual intervention. With the practices in chapter 5, we could just remove the role of the server for a short period of time while we work with one specific player. Whereas in a group intervention, it is likely that we will provide the support while the players are still active within the practice, or the whole practice is stopped and a discussion takes place with all of the players.

Where possible, it is more beneficial to stop the practice so that we can 'paint a picture' for the players. So, for instance, we could stop the practice and show them a picture where they could have made a different decision that would have brought about a more favourable outcome. This, however, can be quite challenging for the coach as the picture is constantly changing due to the movement of the players and the ball and identifying a coaching moment can, therefore, be difficult. One of the reasons that we often find it challenging to identify the right moment to stop the practice is that we are not entirely sure what we are looking for or that we are looking for too many things. This is when we should revert back to the coaching points we have selected as the key focuses for the session. If we pick just one of these, it allows us to have a much narrower focus when we observe what is happening in front of us. We can then wait for the right opportunity to pause the practice because there is a teachable moment for this specific coaching point. Once we have done this, we can then move on to the next coaching point or stay with the existing one, depending on the needs of the players at that specific moment in time.

If we are going to use this form of intervention, it is essential that once we have stopped the practice, we try to ensure that the players return to the positions they were in when we first identified an opportunity to highlight something to the group. Of course, this can be extremely challenging, and we can never hope to get it all completely right, but the important part is to get the main 'pieces' in place, otherwise whatever it is we are discussing will be incorrect. For instance, if we are discussing passing lines and we position a defender in a different place, the picture that the player on the ball saw when we stopped the practice will differ from the one that they see now. Therefore, any information discussed with them will likely be wrong, and instead of helping the player, it could, in fact, confuse them, which could then have a negative impact on their learning and understanding of the topic. The only way we can improve in this area of coaching is to spend time practising so that we start to get more experience and knowledge of when we should stop the practice and make sure that we recreate an accurate picture of what happened.

Another issue that can arise with this form of intervention, is that we stop the practice too often and for too long. Quite often, the reason for both of these problems, is that we are overly keen to help and support the players and believe that the information that we can share with them, is essential to their development. However, it is likely to have the opposite effect on the players, in that it is shifting the focus away from them and onto the coach. If we first look at the number of times that the practice is stopped, this impacts the player's development in a number of different ways. Stopping the practice too much reduces the ball rolling time and limits the opportunities the players have to solve problems themselves and practise the session topic. In addition, if we keep stopping and starting, we are also likely to affect the flow of the practice and the players will struggle to find any kind of rhythm. To prevent this from happening, we can restrict the number of times we allow ourselves to stop the practice, for instance, this could be two or three times. Not only will this ensure that we do not stop the practice too often, it will also help us to be more patient and use the stoppages more effectively, in that we will look to save them for when they are really needed. This can be difficult to implement because after we have reached our limit of the number of times we are allowed to stop the practice, we will always be tempted to stop it *just one more time*. To help with this, we can enlist the help of the coach that we work with and ask them to enforce the rule and stop us from making any additional stoppages once we have reached our limit.

We can also use the help of the coach we work with to ensure that when we make a stoppage it is short and to the point. If we spend too much time talking in the stoppage, it is likely that the players will lose concentration and will no longer be engaged in the learning process. In addition, if the players stand still for long periods of time, it will impact their ball rolling time and the opportunity to practise the session topic. Therefore, we need to get the message across to the players quickly, and whatever methods we decide to use need to be delivered in the quickest timeframe possible, while ensuring that the information is clearly received by the players. To help achieve this, a time limit can be set for how long each intervention lasts, and as soon as this timeframe has been reached, the players must resume playing immediately. And this is where the other coach can be used again; they can keep track of the time and, as soon as the allotted time has been reached, they can instruct the players to start playing again, whether the coach has finished the intervention or not. This can be quite challenging at the beginning for everyone involved; for the coach it can be frustrating to get interrupted and not be allowed to finish the message that they want to get across, while for their colleague, it can be uncomfortable and the players can find it awkward and confusing. However, once these initial teething problems have been overcome, this strategy of restricting the amount of time the coach has to complete the intervention can be highly effective. Once in place, the coach will soon start to adapt their approach and the interventions will be delivered in a clear and precise manner.

Another strategy that we can use in a group intervention, and specifically when we are using question and answers, is 'snowballing'. After an initial question is asked and a response received, a further question can be asked to a different player. This second question can either be used to reconfirm the first question or progress the question. So, for example, the first question could be, 'show me a good position to receive the ball', and a teammate could be asked, 'would you agree with this?' Alternatively, the question could progress to 'why is that a good position?' This enables the level of the players' understanding and knowledge to develop and grow. This strategy can also be used in an individual intervention, however, we have to be very careful that we do not make the player feel uncomfortable or pressured by continuing to ask them questions. Doing this within a group intervention removes all the focus and possible pressure from one player and allows it to be shared across a number of players.

Group interventions can be extremely effective in getting key information across to the players in one go and allow the players to learn collaboratively. It also provides opportunities for the coach to show the players pictures that are more closely related to what they will see during a game (mainly due to the number of players involved). It can also be said that they save time; sometimes, with individual intervention, the coach may find themselves providing the same help to a number of different players, which means they will have less time looking at other areas of the session topic. We just need to remember that group interventions should only be used when it is relevant for the full group of players, or at least the majority of them and that we only use them in moderation and they are delivered quickly but precisely.

Check Learning

One of the biggest mistakes that we often make as coaches when supporting players is checking their understanding after we have just delivered an intervention. This might be because we have just delivered an individual intervention and are eager to watch players in another area, or after a group intervention we want to move on to another important coaching point. However, it is important to remember that we need to ensure that a player or players are ready before moving on to the next stage of their development. Just because we have provided them with some help does not mean they will automatically become competent or an expert in this specific area of the game.

Once we have completed the intervention, it is essential that we continue to observe to identify whether or not there has been a change in their actions. Ideally, the player or players have been able to make changes to their performance as a result of the interaction. If we are able to identify an alteration in their performance, then it is important we let the players know that we have seen these changes and that what they are doing is right. This should be the same if they are still not able to do what we want them to do but they are attempting to do it. Whichever it may be, we should make the player aware that there has been some form of improvement by providing them with specific and accurate praise. For example, 'Sammy, much better, you accelerated away from the defender really well' or 'Connor, well done, I could see that you tried to shift the defender's body weight that time, keep trying to do that'. Once we are happy they have understood what we want them to do, we can turn our attention to another player or another area of the performance.

As coaches, we face a more difficult challenge if there are no signs of improvement. As with the original intervention, we have to decide when exactly to provide the support, as we need to give them the opportunity to work out the solution themselves before we step in and help. However, at the same time, if they are unable to show any signs of improvement after the first intervention, we should not be reluctant to provide additional support. It is understandable that we may not want to go back and work with a player if we have only just provided them with support, as this may affect their self-esteem and, for this reason, we should definitely not keep returning to the same child. But it is important that if after the first intervention they are unable to demonstrate an adjustment in their performance or that they are attempting to change what they do, then we need to provide further support. It is possible that they did not fully understand what they needed to do or that they just need a bit more help. What is important is that if there is an improvement, we let the player know this, as outlined before. If not, we provide them with praise and encouragement: 'Hugo, great effort, keep working on the weight of your pass'.

It is important to check learning when first introducing a coaching point to the players. So, for example, if we stop a practice and ask the players to 'check their shoulders' before they receive the ball, it is really important that we observe their performance to ensure they are doing what we have asked them to do. Quite often, we will ask the players to do something, allow them to continue within the practice and then introduce a further aspect of the performance before we have actually provided any support around the first part. If we are going to ask the players to do something, it is essential we check to ensure they are doing it and, if not, we need to provide some form of support. We have asked them to try and do something because it is an important aspect of the performance. For instance, if we refer back to 'checking their shoulder', the reason they need to do this is so they are aware of what and who is around them, which is essential as it will influence what they do next in terms of their movement and first touch. Therefore, once we have shared this key information, we need to make sure that they understand it and are trying to implement it within their play; we need to check their learning.

Let Them Play

The final vital aspect of delivering interventions during a session may well contradict the key messages at the very start of this chapter that has been reinforced throughout the book – at times, players need support from the coach to support their learning and development. However, we just need to be careful that we do not take this too far and prevent them from having playing time to implement their learning and, more importantly, affect their enjoyment of the session; we need, at times, to just allow them to play. The importance of ball rolling time, not stopping the practice too often and ensuring the interventions are short and precise have already been discussed, and these will definitely provide the players with lots of opportunities and time to practise the topic of the session. We can support this further by allowing the players to have some free play at the end of the session, where they get the opportunity to just play the game of soccer and put into practise what they have learned.

The game at the end of the session is often played because we want to give the players what they want. The most common question asked by a player during a session, is 'when are we playing a game?' And this is more than understandable because, at the end of the day, they started to play soccer and continue to play it because they enjoy playing the actual game. They will enjoy going to training and having the opportunity to play with their friends, but the most enjoyment that they get is from playing the actual game. But it is also an opportunity for them to implement what they practised in the session into their play. While they are playing the game, it can be tempting to provide the players with some form of support, whether this is an individual intervention or a group intervention. However, we need to be mindful that the players have already been provided with support during training, and they have now reached the stage of the session that they have been looking forward to, so they are unlikely to be open to receiving any further help, resulting in missing out on some of their playing time.

Allowing the players to just play in a game at the end of the session provides the coach with different benefits and opportunities. It gives the coach a chance to observe the players in a realistic and relevant environment, which will provide them with the ultimate challenge that will test their ability to perform the topic of the session. Although the practices give the players an opportunity to learn and develop the session focus, the most effective environment we can place them in is the game itself. Allowing the players to just play the game provides the coach with an opportunity to observe them and then analyse whether the session has been successful in achieving its aims. What we cannot expect is for there to be a significant difference in their performance – they have, after all, only been practising the topic for a short period of time. But what we can look for are any indications that the next time we deliver the topic, they are ready to progress to the next stage or whether they need to revisit the same coaching points before they are ready to move on?

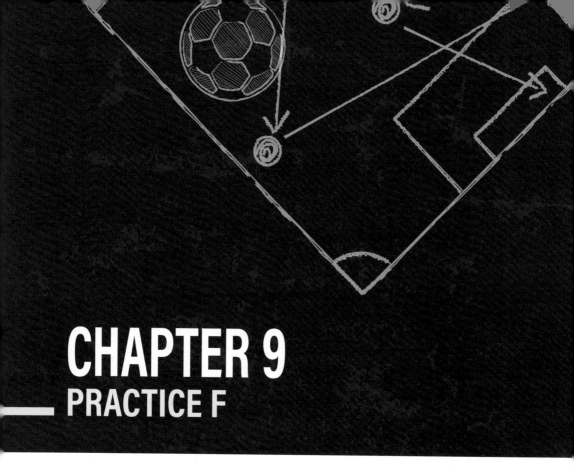

CHAPTER 9
PRACTICE F

This chapter and the next two focus on practices where all the players are involved in the same practice and are playing the same game. These types of practices are often referred to as squad practices. Because all the players are involved, there are greater numbers involved in the practice and therefore there are different types of challenges. For instance, there are now more teammates and therefore increased options for the player on the ball. They have progressed from having to decide whether to keep it themselves or to pass it onto their partner, to now deciding whether to retain possession or give it to a teammate, and if so, which one? There is also the increased difficulty of more defenders, which is caused not only by the fact that there are more opponents to avoid but also because it is now much harder to be aware of the positioning of these opposition players. Therefore, we need to be sure that the players are ready for these types of practices and decide if reduced numbers should be used to help their transition from the smaller number practices to these squad practices. This can be achieved by having two different practices running alongside each other, with the players transferring between the two. So, for instance, alongside a practice from this chapter, a practice with the same topic from chapter 5 or chapter 6, could also be used so that fewer numbers are active within the squad practice. This reduces the increase of difficulty for the players, while still allowing them to experience this type of practice.

This particular practice starts to move away from the players trying to retain the ball individually or, by sharing it with a partner, keeping the ball as a group or a team. When introducing this part of the game to the players, it is important to remember the purpose of why a team needs to retain possession of the ball, which is to progress up the pitch and create goal-scoring opportunities. Quite often, we plan and deliver a possession-based practice that has no real purpose other than keeping the ball for as long as possible. Where possible, we should have an additional target for the players to achieve, as well as keeping the ball for a set amount of time. The focus of retaining possession as a team needs to remain, but there needs to be a purpose to it, so for example, the teams might be set the initial task of keeping the ball for a set amount of time or minimum number of passes, and then, once they have achieved this, there needs to be an additional task. This second task can be anything relevant to what the players would do in a game after they have retained the ball for a period of time, such as an attempt on goal, a forward pass or a player driving with the ball. The players need to be shown that there is a reason to keep possession of the ball and the opportunities that come from doing it.

This particular core practice, however, does not have this additional task and focuses primarily on retaining possession of the ball. The reason for this is to make the practice simplistic for the players to understand, and also to get the players active quickly, which, of course, are essential ingredients for all the core practices. Therefore, this initial set-up should only be used for a short period of time, before the adaption is introduced. As with all the adaptions, they are a progression of the original practice and we can use the core practice to get the players active, before introducing the change that allows it to focus on the topic of the session. This tactic is, of course, used with all the core practices, but it is particularly important with this specific core practice: that we do not leave it too long before introducing the adaption. The players need to have the mindset that they are retaining the possession of the ball for a specific reason.

Another common theme of possession-based practices is restricting players to a maximum number of touches two, for instance, or sometimes even one. The reason for this is that we may want the players to play quicker or to work on their first touch. And though these are definitely valid reasons for introducing these types of restrictions, the outcome it often produces can be unrealistic to the game and detrimental to the development of the players. For example, how often have we seen a player use up all their touches and be forced to try and protect the ball without touching it until a teammate is able to come and collect it from them. Or a player's initial first touch does not allow them to make the pass they wanted to play, so they end up playing a different pass or just clearing the ball. Often all that was needed was for them to take an additional touch, which would have allowed them to make the pass that they wanted to play – and should have played, but they could not do this as we have restricted them to just two touches. Instead of restricting the players to these very small numbers of touches, we should look to first support them and help them understand that they do not always need to take the additional touches and help them understand that the consequences of doing this can be that the opportunity they first saw has now disappeared. If we want to introduce restrictions as we feel the players are holding onto the ball for too long, then a limit of three or four touches should be introduced. This allows them to play normally, should some of their previous actions or the actions of the defenders force them into needing an additional touch or two.

The set-up of this practice shows the players being split into three teams of four players, which allows a four versus four in the area, and then a further set of players supporting the team on the outside with one player on each side of the area. Therefore, a total of 12 players is used within the practice. However, as we are fully aware, this 'perfect' number of players for a practice very rarely materialises during training, so we need to adapt to the number of players that we have. If there are more than 12 players, there are a number of options available. As mentioned earlier in the chapter, an additional practice that accommodates the extra number of players can be set up next to this practice, with players being rotated around the two. Or the area size can be set out to accommodate the extra numbers, so for instance, it could be a six versus six with four support players and, when the roles are switched, two players from the team (who are now the support players) can remain within the area and join the team of four. There is also an option to have an additional support player within the actual area. We should not be too concerned if the two teams in the area do not have the same number of players, for example it is four versus five or four versus three. Although the game of soccer is usually played between two teams with the same number of players, it is very often the case that in a moment of the game, one team has more players than the other. For instance, if a team is playing out from the back, more often than not they will have more passing options (teammates) than the opposition trying to prevent them. And this particular practice actually provides an overload for the players in possession of the ball, due to the support players, therefore, teams having the exact same numbers is not that essential. And should there be less than 12 players, then the game within the area can be reduced to a three versus three (no less) and/or fewer support players can be used on the outside.

Practice F: Original Set-Up

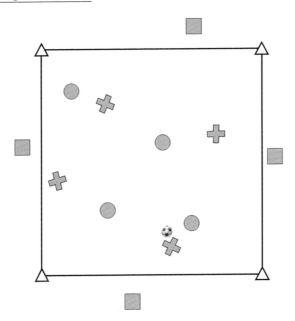

Set-Up

- Square area relevant for the group of players.
- Players are split into three teams, with two teams inside the area and the third team on the outside supporting the team in possession of the ball.
- Teams have to complete a set number of passes to win a point.
- Role of the support team is changed regularly or after each point.

Focus

- Positioning of teammates to support the player on the ball: distance and angle.
- Supporting players: can the player on the ball see your feet?
- Decision making: when to pass the ball and to whom?
- Weight and area of pass: what does the player receiving the ball want to do with it?

Possible Progressions/Regressions

- Alter the size and/or shape of the area.
- Change the number of passes that have to be completed to win a point.
- Use a smaller ball.

Practice F: Team Possession

The only change to this first adaption is a slight change to the rules and an additional task for the players to complete once they have achieved the set number of passes. Because the key principle of the practice is a team retaining possession of the ball, there does not need to be many changes, just some small alterations to emphasise the topic further and a task at the end to provide a purpose to retaining the ball. The final task that the team has to complete after they have completed the set number of passes has not been stipulated as it can be anything you want. Some of the tasks from the other adaptions could be used, and you may choose one that the players enjoy doing or something that you think they need extra time practising. The important thing is that they do something at the end of completing the set number of passes, so they are working towards something and trying to move the opposition players out of possession for a specific reason. What the players might try and do is complete the task as soon as they have achieved the set number of passes. Here, they may need a reminder that the set number of passes is the minimum amount they need to achieve and not the exact number and that they should aim to complete the final task when it is the right time to do so, not as soon as the number of passes has been achieved.

The main element of the practice is the players completing the set number of passes, plus when and how they use the support players. In this adaption, the support players are in place for the 'free' or 'easy' pass and represent certain situations found within a match, for example, a midfielder passing back to a centre-back. This type of pass helps the team retain possession of the ball but does not help them be progressive or creative; it is played with the sole purpose of retaining the ball. Although this type of pass is definitely needed in some moments of a game, a more progressive and riskier pass is most definitely preferred. Therefore, the main of aim of this practice is for the players to develop their ability to keep possession of the ball in tight areas, trying to escape the pressure through passes that split the defenders and find a teammate in a better position. They also need to recognise that, at times, there is a need to make the safe pass to ensure that they do not lose possession of the ball.

Another key element of the practice is the need for the player passing the ball to recognise where their teammate wants to receive the pass. It is not enough for the players just to pass to a teammate; they need to pass it into the right area. So, if the player receiving the pass has a defender closing them down to their right, they need the ball to be played to their left foot to allow them to protect it. It is integral that players pass the ball in a way that allows their teammate to complete the next pass effectively and efficiently.

Practice F: Team Possession

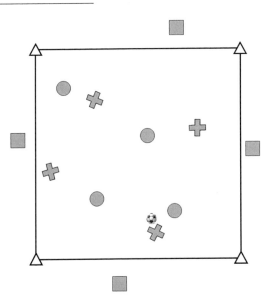

Alteration to Original Set-Up

- The support players can still be used, but the number count returns to zero.
- On completing the set number of passes, the team has to complete an additional task, chosen by the coach, to win the point. It could be one that is used in one of the other adaptions in this chapter.

Focus

- Identify where your teammate wants the ball to be played to them.
- Recognise when to release the ball.
- Safe or risky pass?
- Understand when to progress, for example, identify the opportunity to complete the final task.

Possible Progressions/Regressions

- Alter the size and/or shape of the area.
- Change the number of passes to be completed before the team can attempt to win a point.
- Use a smaller ball.

Practice F: Individual Possession

Although squad practices have increased number of players in them, they can still be used for individual focuses. We just need to be mindful that the players will not get as many opportunities to practise the session topic and that some may dominate the game and have more attempts on completing the focus. So, in this particular adaption, the number of times a player has an attempt at retaining the ball themselves (i.e. dribble through the two gates), will be considerably less than when they participate in the practice with the same focus, in chapter 6. Plus, the players who are more confident in this element of the game will most likely attempt to win points more frequently than those who are not as self-assured; these players will be more willing to pass the ball onto a teammate. However, there are other returns that we get from this type of practice but do not necessarily always see. First of all, as the number of players on both teams is equal, it is likely that when they are in possession of the ball, players will come under pressure from a defender, meaning they will be practising to keep the ball as an individual, before passing it onto a teammate. Another positive factor with this practice is that it allows the players to retain individual possession of the ball in an environment closer to the game of soccer; rather than just protecting the ball from a partner, they may now have to protect it from multiple defenders.

The need for players to travel through two gates to win a point is key to the players being able to practise retaining the ball as individuals. It is likely that the player with the ball will attempt to win a point when they have some space around them. Therefore, when they travel through the first gate, they will likely do so under no pressure, however, as they move towards and through the second gate, the defenders has time to react and close down the player on the ball. Additionally, if they are successful in getting through a second gate, they still have to find a teammate to pass to, which gives the opposition additional time to try and win the ball. If they only have to travel through one gate, players will likely achieve the point without coming under any pressure at all.

This task also provides an environment where the players on the ball will be closed down from defenders who will approach them from different sides and angles. Because of this, they need to keep changing how and where they protect the ball while still trying to achieve the task to win a point. This will therefore likely include manipulating the ball and changing the original pathway that they had selected when first deciding to try and win the point. They need to be able to travel with the ball while having the awareness and ability to protect it, using both their left and right foot and different parts of their feet.

Practice F: Individual Possession

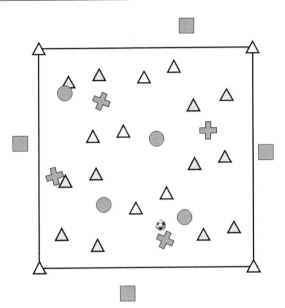

Alteration to Original Set-Up

- A number of gates are added to the area.
- Teams no longer need to complete a set number of passes.
- Teams win a point if one player is able to dribble through two sets of gates in one go and then pass the ball to a teammate.
- On winning a point, the team retains possession.

Focus

- Protect the ball, keep your body between the defender and the ball.
- Use the foot furthest away from the defender.
- Use feints/disguise to move away from the defender.
- Identify/predict the most effective pathway.

Possible Progressions/Regressions

- Alter the size and/or shape of the area.
- Change the number of gates within the area.
- Players receive an additional two bonus points if they travel through a third gate, but lose their initial point if are unsuccessful.

Practice F: Receiving to Play Forward

As with all practices that focus on receiving to play forward, this adaption requires the players to consider several things: their angle of approach, their body shape, receiving the pass on their furthest foot, etc. However, unlike the previous practices, which allowed the players to receive the ball unopposed so they can concentrate on the actual act of receiving the pass to play forward, in this adaption, they do not have the safety of receiving unopposed. Therefore, there is great emphasis on the players scanning and being aware of what is around them to identify when there is space to enable them to receive the ball and move forward. A key requirement of this is the players scanning the area and timing their movement so that they can drop into the space, receive the ball and exit before the opposition have the opportunity to close it off. If they enter the area where they want to receive the ball too early, they will likely attract the attention of a defender, who will then look to get tight and prevent them from receiving the ball and playing forward. The players will begin to learn to use strategies, such as moving away from where they want to receive the ball, before quickly changing direction to allow them to receive the pass in space so that they can receive and play forward.

Once the action of receiving the pass and moving forward with the ball into the central area has been completed, the topic of the practice has been achieved and it is important that it returns back to the focus as soon as possible so that the players have the opportunity to keep developing this area of the game. Therefore, once the player has reached the central area, the game needs to be re-set by the player passing the ball to a teammate or one of the support players. An additional task can be introduced to the practice to further challenge and motivate the players, but we need to make sure it does not take away from the primary focus of the session, and it must be over quickly. It also needs to lead in to what the players would do in a game after receiving the ball and travelling forward with it. Therefore, in the game of soccer, after completing this action, we would ideally like them to continue playing forward, to keep the momentum going and help the team progress up the pitch. A further task can be added where the player has to complete a forward pass once they have entered the central area. As discussed earlier in the book, this should be done by rewarding the players with additional points, rather than adding this onto the task, as they have completed what we want them to focus on. Therefore, an additional bonus point can be awarded to a player if, after they have reached the central area, they are able to play a pass into the support player directly opposite the support player that played the initial pass. On doing so, they would have received a pass from someone behind them, driven forward and then played a forward pass, which is exactly what we want them to do in a game.

Practice F: Receiving to Play Forward

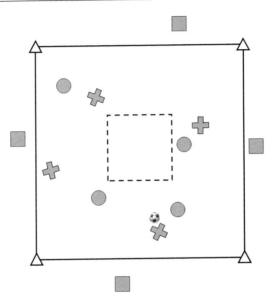

Alteration to Original Set-Up

- A small square area is added to the centre of the main area.
- Teams no longer need to complete a set number of passes.
- To win a point, a player must receive the ball from a support player and drive into the central area, entering the side facing the support player.
- Once they have entered the area, the practice continues.

Focus

- Identifying when there is an opportunity to receive the ball from the server and drive forward.
- Angle of approach and body shape to receive from the server.
- Pass from the server onto the furthest foot of the receiving player.
- First touch from the receiving player, positive and forward, towards the central area.

Possible Progressions/Regressions

- Alter the size and/or shape of the main area and/or the central area.
- A set number of passes need to be completed before a player can attempt to receive the ball and drive into the central area.

Practice F: Forward Passing

This practice follows the same type of principles as the previous adaption in that the tasks that the players must complete force them in a forward direction and, subsequently, to play forward. The central area is used again, but this time, it is much easier for the players to enter it – either driving in with the ball or standing inside it or receiving a pass from a teammate. The rule that an opposition player is not allowed in the area further reduces the difficulty of the task. This is to ensure that it is quite simple for the players to get inside the central area with the ball, and if needed, they can also take a bit of time to decide which side they exit, taking into consideration the positioning of the defenders. Both of these characteristics of the practice are in place so the players then complete the final part of the task – passing into the small goals/gates – which is the element linked to the focus of the practice. If we wanted, we could alter how they are allowed to enter the central area by only allowing them to receive a pass inside it, in other words, they can no longer drive into it with the ball. This then gives the practice even more of a focus on passing.

As the players exit the central area, they are faced with the choice of two small goals/gates to pass the ball into to win a point. The small goals/gates are positioned in the corners and just outside of the area, and this will help ensure that the pass the players play will be forward and diagonal. There is a small possibility that the players may travel with the ball towards a small goal/gate, and the pass will then become straighter. But this is unlikely to happen often, as the longer they take to make the pass, the increased chance that they will get closed down and possibly lose the ball. Therefore, the players should be encouraged to make the pass as soon as they exit the area. If the passing line between the player and the small goal/gate is clear, the pass should be made straight away, not after they have taken unnecessary touches. The players should only take additional touches if the passing line is blocked and the ball needs to be manipulated so that the pathway to the small goal/gates is clear. The pass that the player makes is set up to be forward and diagonal to replicate the type of pass often needed in the final third of the pitch, where a forward pass is needed to penetrate the defensive line. Making it diagonal makes it more difficult for the defenders to read and intercept. This type of pass also makes it easier for the teammate to collect the ball and execute whatever it is they want to do next, such as dribble, pass, shoot, etc. A straight-line pass will always be running away from the player waiting to receive it, and there is a possibility that when this type of pass is made in the final third of the pitch, it can run out of room, in other words, it goes out of play or can run through to the goalkeeper. The forward diagonal pass is therefore an essential area of the game that the players need to be given time to practise.

Practice F: Forward Passing

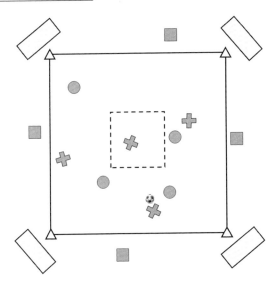

Alteration to Original Set-Up

- A small square area is added to the centre of the main area.
- Four small goals/gates are situated just outside the area in the corners.
- Teams no longer need to complete a set number of passes.
- To win a point, a player must dribble into, or receive the ball inside, the central area and then exit the area. They must then pass the ball into one of the two small goals/gates facing them.
- Players from the team defending are not allowed inside the central area.

Focus

- Ensure that there is a clear pathway between the ball and the small goal/gate. If not, can you manipulate the ball so there is?
- Weight and accuracy of pass.

Possible Progressions/Regressions

- Alter the size and/or shape of the main area and/or the central area.
- A set number of passes needs to be completed before a player can attempt to receive the ball and drive into the central area.
- Change the position of the small goals/gates.

Practice F: Receiving Under Pressure

In previous practices, where the focus was also on receiving under pressure, once the player received the ball, they were either required to keep it themselves or, in some practices, they were given the option to share it with a teammate. In this practice, the players are now asked to receive the ball under pressure and then pass it onto a teammate. The players will, therefore, try to hold onto the ball for a very short period of time, as they will be aware of the need to move it onto a teammate to get closer to achieving a point. How the players decide to receive the ball could be different to how they received it in previous practices with the same focus. Previously, they may have tried to secure the ball more, knowing that they were likely to retain possession themselves for some time, whereas now, they may look to take a first touch that allows them to pass the ball almost immediately. Although we want the players to be brave and have the confidence to get out of these situations individually, there will be times in a match when it is not the right decision to do so, especially when they start playing the full version of the game. Therefore, we need to provide them with opportunities to practise this particular element of the game.

Not allowing the players to play back to whoever passed them the ball forces them to remain positive and confident when in possession. Once they have received the pass, they need to manipulate the ball and change the direction they are likely to be facing. However, due to the set-up of the practice, they have numerous options of where and whom they pass the ball to. For instance, if the ball is played into them by a support player, they still have the option to pass to the other support player that can help in that particular zone, plus the two teammates whose zones connect with their own. This makes it more challenging for the defenders as there are a number of different ways that their opponent will try to manipulate the ball. Therefore, if the practice is not challenging enough, we can restrict who the player on the ball can pass to even more. So, for instance, if they receive from a server, they can only pass the ball onto a teammate within the area, or vice versa, thereby changing the number of options available to the player from three to two.

Support can also be given to the players about where they position themselves when looking to receive a pass. Getting too close to the area where the ball is coming from reduces the amount of space they have to work in once they are in possession. Not waiting in one place to receive the pass but instead starting elsewhere and making a movement to receive the ball, gives them a chance of receiving the ball in a position where they have more options in terms of where they can go with the ball.

Practice F: Receiving Under Pressure

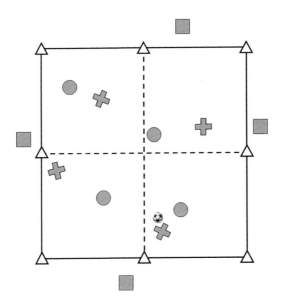

Alteration to Original Set-Up

- The area is split into zones, with a player from each team locked into each zone.
- The ball can only be passed between zones (i.e. players cannot dribble into it).
- Players can pass to the two teammates whose zones are attached to theirs.
- The support players can help the two zones on their side of the area.
- Players cannot pass to whoever (teammate or support player) passed them the ball.

Focus

- Awareness of their partner's position.
- Body shape as they receive the ball.
- Which foot is used to receive the ball?
- Positioning of the teammate to support the player on the ball.

Possible Progressions/Regressions

- Alter the size and/or shape of the area.
- Change the number of passes that have to be completed to win a point.
- Support players can be used, but if they are, the pass count returns to zero.
- Limit further who the players can pass to.

Practice F: Finishing

By simply adding four goals and giving the team on the outside of the area dual roles (support players and goalkeepers), the practice now becomes a fast-paced finishing game, where the players get lots of opportunities to have a shot on goal. Once the small number of passes is completed, the player on the ball should be able to have a shot on goal almost immediately. If not, they should be able to either create an opportunity so that they can – this could be by simply completing a turn – or pass the ball onto a teammate in a position to have the shot. The key point is that they get lots of opportunities to practise the focus of the session.

The set-up of the area and the position of the goals naturally provides an environment where the players will try all different types of finishes, all of which are realistic and relevant to the game of soccer. This includes where they take the shot from, the different distances and the range of angles, what is between them and the goal, are there defenders in the way, making it more difficult, or is there just the goalkeeper to beat? In addition, each time they have a shot, they will likely perform a completely different action just before, so this could be nothing, in other words, they shoot first time, or if the pass comes from a wide area they may even attempt to score with a header. Alternatively, they might complete a turn or dribble to go past a defender, or they might take a touch or two before executing the actual shot. If we compare this with more traditional finishing practices where the players continuously shoot from the same position, one they are most likely not going to be in during a game, then this adaption provides an environment that is much closer to the actual game of soccer. Therefore, this more chaotic and random environment can only be a better learning experience for the players and more beneficial for their long-term development.

We are often deterred from using practices such as this as we do not have all of the necessary equipment needed. In this particular scenario, we may not have four goals available for a training session, however, this should not prevent us from delivering the practice. We need to remember that it is not what the practice looks like but what is actually happening in it. When children play soccer with their friends outside the training environment, they can be extremely resourceful in creating a game without any proper equipment. This does not affect their enjoyment or how the game is played. This tells us that they are not overly concerned whether they have all the correct equipment. Yes, they would prefer to have actual goals, but if they are not available, they would sooner play in the practice using something else rather than not play in it at all.

Practice F: Finishing

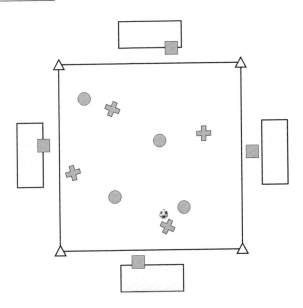

Alteration to Original Set-Up

- Four goals are added to the practice, one on each side of the area (set back).
- After completing the set number of passes, the team tries to win a point by scoring in any of the four goals.
- After completing the set number of passes, the support players become goalkeepers.

Focus

- Try to have an attempt on goal at the earliest possible opportunity.
- Selection of shot: take into consideration where you are in the area and the positioning of the goalkeeper.
- Ensure that the shot is on target and struck with power or placement.

Possible Progressions/Regressions

- Alter the size and/or shape of the area.
- Move the goal closer or further away from the area.
- After a goal has been scored, teams can no longer score in that particular goal until another goal has been scored.

Practice F: Driving With the Ball

As with other practices within this chapter, this adaption provides a different concept to its topic. In previous practices that focused on driving with the ball, the players either start with space already in front of them or they look for the opportunity to drive with the ball when the space opens up. Either way, the player driving with the ball usually only has to concern themselves with an opponent approaching them from behind and decide whether to change their pathway to get their body between the ball and the recovering defender. In this practice, however, they are likely to make the initial decision to drive with the ball when they have identified that there is space in front of them. There is a strong possibility that, as well as opposition players recovering from behind them, they will also have defenders approaching from ahead of the ball. Due to the number of players in the practice, and as it is nondirectional, there will more than likely always be at least one defender ahead of the ball. The players, therefore, now have the opportunity to develop this aspect of driving with the ball.

If a player initially decides to leave the half of the area they are situated in with the ball in an attempt to drive through one of the far gates, it is likely that they have made this decision because there is space in front of them. Therefore, when a defender closes down the player on the ball, they will not be directly in front of them as they will have an angled approach. So, when driving with the ball, the attacker needs to decide whether to travel away from the approaching defender or, alternatively, cut back and attack the space where the opposing player has come from. A number of factors will influence this decision, such as how far away they are from the gates, how quickly the defender is approaching and where they are positioned within the area. It is important they do not slow the play down as it can then turn into a one versus one, and the advantage they have over the defender is reduced. By driving with the ball at pace, any changes in direction made by the attacker are difficult for the defender to react to, especially when they are travelling at speed but in a different direction.

There is also the possibility that the attacker may decide to drive with the ball, even though there is a defender situated directly in front of them. In this situation, their touch to manipulate the ball to produce space is vital, but just as important is the need to explode into the space and drive away from the defender. Physically, the players need to be able to produce high levels of acceleration so they are able to manufacture as much of an advantage as possible, which they initially created with their sudden change of direction.

Practice F: Driving With the Ball

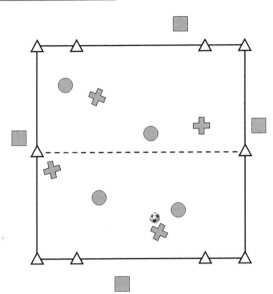

Alteration to Original Set-Up

- The area is split in half.
- Two gates are added to two ends of the area (opposite each other).
- Players now win a point if they can travel out of one half and through one of the sets of gates located at the end of the other half.

Focus

- Identify when there is an opportunity to drive with the ball.
- First touch: strong touch out of your feet and forward.
- Identify whether or not you need to get your body between the ball and the defender.
- Strong controlled touches to allow long strides while running.
- Shift the ball off the initial line when needed.

Possible Progressions/Regressions

- Alter the size and/or shape of the area.
- Increase the number of gates to three at each end.
- Give the attackers a task to do once they have travelled through a gate, for example, pass the ball into a small goal/gates.

Practice F: Shielding

Placing two players in the central area puts them in a tight area that gives them little space to receive and protect the ball. Therefore, there is a real emphasis on the player receiving the ball being able to shield it from the defender that is locked in the area with them. How long they will need to shield the ball for depends on how long it takes for one of their teammates to get into a position where they can receive a pass. However, just having a teammate in a position to receive the pass is not enough, as the player shielding the ball also needs to identify that they now have someone to release the ball to. Therefore, not only do they need to shield the ball they also need to be aware of the positioning of the defender who is trying to win possession from them and all of the other players in the main area. When shielding, players naturally look down at the ball to see where it is positioned to work out whether they need to move it to provide further protection. Therefore, they will find it quite challenging to shield the ball while scanning the area.

Another key aspect of the practice is the direction the ball arrives at the player in the small area. Because the game is played all around them, they need to keep repositioning themselves to be in a position to receive the pass. The ball is also unlikely to come to them from a player positioned directly in front of them, which it does in the practice outlined in chapter 5, which makes it more challenging to control and protect. The other challenge they face is the change in possession between the teams in the main area, meaning the roles of the two players in the central area also change. They change from being the player waiting to receive the pass to the defender and vice versa. This is particularly important when their role moves from defender to attacker, as they now need to try and get themselves in front of their opponent to be in a position to receive the ball. When this happens, they may need to use double movements to get themselves ahead of the defender or delay their movement until their teammate is ready to make the pass, giving their opponent little time to react. Then once they are in this position, they need to ensure that the defender is unable to get ahead of them and intercept the pass. An understanding of where exactly the defender is positioned behind them is critical for ensuring the attacker stays in front, and as they need to keep their eyes on the ball so they know when the pass is being played to them, the use of their hand and forearm is important. These can be used to stop the defender getting too close and also gives the attacking player a reference to their positioning; any movements by the defender can be felt and counteracted. The final ingredients are strength and determination, The attacking player needs to be strong enough and determined enough to keep the defender behind them.

Practice F: Shielding

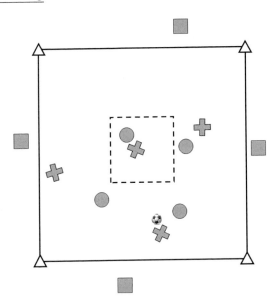

Alteration to Original Set-Up

- A small square area is added to the centre of the main area.
- One player from each team is locked inside this area.
- Teams win a point if they play a pass into the player in the central area and they pass the ball back out.
- When playing the ball out of the area, they cannot pass it back to the teammate who played it in. They must pass it to a server or a different teammate.
- Once the ball has been played in and out the central area, the players in it are changed.

Focus

- Body shape to receive the ball: wide stance and side-on.
- Knees bent and arm up against the defender.
- Control with the outside of the foot, using the foot closest to the player passing.
- Use your body to protect and shield the ball.

Possible Progressions/Regressions

- Alter the size and/or shape of the main area and/or the central area.
- The ball cannot be played out on the same side that it entered.

Practice F: Counter-Press

When working on counter-pressing, it is important to remember that you are supporting the players with what they do when they lose the ball and, therefore, they must be in possession of the ball initially. So, we need to ensure that they do not spend too long in possession, meaning they will not have much time to practise the actual focus of the session – counter-pressing. Normally, a two-touch restriction would not be recommended (as discussed at the start of the chapter) but, in this instance, it is needed not to help the players develop their touch or passing but to manipulate the environment so the team with the ball find it challenging to retain possession. We do not want a team to retain possession for long periods of time, therefore, reducing the number of times they get to react to losing the ball. By restricting teams to just two touches, they will likely lose possession quite regularly, which will significantly increase the number of times the focus of the session can be practised.

A key element of counter-pressing involves not allowing the opposite team to escape from the area where they won the ball, or, at least, delaying them sufficiently so that they cannot take advantage of the team being unorganised. The gates in the practice set-up represent spaces in a congested area where the team are aiming to escape after winning the ball. Providing them with a number of choices of how they can escape (i.e. pass to a server through any of the gates or drive through one with the ball) gives them the same options they would have in a match. Plus, encouraging them to complete the task of passing or dribbling the ball out of the area in a set number of passes characterises the team trying to exploit the opposition before they have time to organise themselves. The environment, therefore, is ideal for the players to work on their ability to counter-press.

As discussed earlier in the book, the ideal outcome of the counter-press is that the team that has just lost possession wins the ball back almost immediately, and if they do not achieve this, they should look to delay the opposition. The scoring system for this adaption is also really important to help the players understand the need to win the ball back quickly. Rewarding the teams with additional points for winning the ball back after a set number of passes encourages the players to try and win back possession straight away, which they should do since the other team has a number of ways and options to escape the area and win the points if they do not do it quickly.

Practice F: Counter-Press

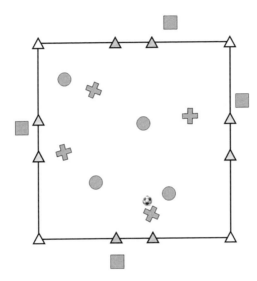

Alteration to Original Set-Up

- A set of gates is added to each side of the area.
- The team with the ball plays two touches and has to complete a set number of passes.
- If the other team wins the ball, they need to escape the area by a player dribbling or passing the ball to a server through one of the gates. They earn two points if they do it in a set number of passes (two or three) or one point if they do it in more.
- The other team wins three points if it wins back the ball in the set number of passes – two if it is in the set number of passes or one point if it goes out of play.

Focus

- Immediate reaction to win back the ball: determination and aggression.
- Awareness of where in the area the team has lost the ball.
- Recognising where your teammates are situated and what they are attempting to do.

Possible Progressions/Regressions

- Alter the size and/or shape of the area.
- Decrease the number of gates the players can escape through.
- Change the set number of passes.

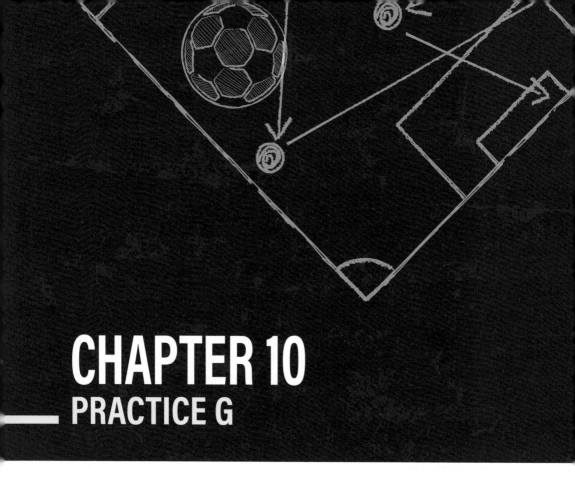

CHAPTER 10
PRACTICE G

The core practice in this chapter provides an environment for the players where they will play a game with a lot of similarities to soccer and a number of the principles of soccer as well. The basic characteristics of soccer, as with all invasion games, are that it is a team game with an equal number of players where the overall aim is to attack the opponent's territory to score some form of goal or point. As well as these main characteristics, there are other key factors that make a sport an invasion game. These include the game being played on some form of field or court, which has clear boundaries; some form of object is used to score the goal or point, these can be in a range of forms including a ball, puck and disc; the practice resembles the area in which the game of soccer is played (i.e. it is a rectangle), which each team attempts to protect and attack from opposite sides of the pitch; and within the practice, each team has an equal number of players.

As well as resembling many characteristics of soccer, the practice also includes the key principles of the game and many of the different components that make up these principles. The three main principles common to all invasion games are in possession, out of possession and transition (this can be from possession to out of possession, or from out of possession to in possession). Each of these principles is made up of different components, for example, components of in possession include width, depth, progression, penetration, support, creativity and retention. All the practices in this book include a number of these, which is one of the many reasons they have been selected. However, this particular practice is the closest to achieving them all, until we reach the game practices, which, as the name suggests, are practices that are very close to the actual game. The shape and size of the practice area encourage the team in possession to provide *width* and *depth* and, to win a point, teams must receive the ball from one server and *progress* up the pitch, *penetrating* defensive lines to get the ball to the other server. To achieve this, they need to *support* the player on the ball to help the team *retain* possession and, at times, will have to be *creative* in their play. Although it may look simplistic in its set-up, it provides a very effective environment for the players to practise and develop their understanding of the key principles of the game.

Having two servers at each end of the area is quite important to the set-up of the practice, however, if the number of players does not allow for it, one server can be used. It is preferable to have two servers at each end of the area rather than one because it allows for a number of crucial elements to occur within the practice. Having just one server, first of all, can make it quite challenging for the team in possession to make the final pass and win a point because they only have one target that they can aim for. The servers are allowed to move along their line, but if there is only one, defending players will, quite often, position themselves in front of them to stop the attacking team playing the pass into them. It could be argued that this might happen in a game, especially when we reach the full version, with a central midfielder standing in front of a striker, preventing the pass from being played into them. The difference here, however, is that if this did happen, the player on the ball would most likely have another option positioned ahead of them that they can play the ball to. This could be another striker if the team is playing with two forwards or a player moving from outside to in, in a formation that uses wide attacking players. Therefore, it is likely that teams will be able to reduce the options of the player on the ball, but it is less likely that they will eliminate all of them.

The other key element of the practice that benefits from having two servers at each end of the area is when they are in possession of the ball. It is important that we allow the players in the area to close down the servers when they have the ball. This makes the practice more realistic and relevant to the game, in that defenders within a match would have the option to either set up a block or apply pressure to the player on the ball. Whichever choice they make creates different problems and opportunities for the player on the ball. The problem this creates, however, is that if there is only one server the only direction they can play is forward. Although we want them to try and play forward as much as possible, they also need to recognise when they can and cannot do this, and when they are unable to play a forward pass, they should look for a teammate who can. This can be seen a number of times in a game when a central defender is in possession of the ball. They will try to play forward into one of their midfielders or, if there are no suitable options or they are being closed down, they will try to transfer the ball across to one of their teammates, usually their centre-back partner. Therefore, we need to try to replicate this within the practice, and the most effective way in to do this is to have two servers, so if one is unable to play forward, they can switch the ball across to their partner.

A particular part of the play to look at within this practice is the distances between players when their team is in possession, particularly when the servers have the ball. Quite often, players will come very short looking to receive the pass and, therefore, get very close to the servers. By doing so, they create unrealistic distances between themselves and the player playing the pass; they are trying to receive the ball from a teammate in a position that they would not try to do within a game. By being so close to their teammate, they do not force the defender into making a decision. The defender can close down the space for the player on the ball while also being in a position to cover their teammate looking to receive the pass. By increasing the distance between themselves and their teammate, players can force a defender in to making a decision: follow the ball or follow the player? And if they choose to do neither, the defender can get caught in an area where they are not affecting either player, therefore, making it much easier for their opponents to retain possession of the ball.

By coming close to the server to receive the ball off them, players also reduce the space in which are play. Dropping into an area that is only a short distance from the edge of the area limits how much room they have to operate in once they receive the ball. This space will be reduced even further if the defenders follow them, which you would expect them to. When the players are out of possession, we ask them to make the pitch small so they are compact as a team and reduce the space in which the opposition can play, making it more difficult for them to retain the ball and to penetrate and progress. However, in this instance, the defending team does not need to make the pitch small as the attacking players are doing this for them in terms of where they want to receive the ball from. The players therefore may need some support with their distances and understanding that they may need to start away from where they want to receive the ball before dropping into the space when they see the server is ready to play the pass.

Practice G: Original Set-Up

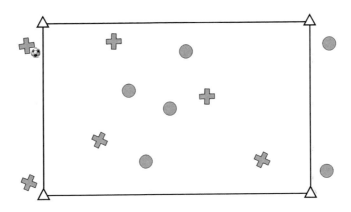

Set-Up

- Teams are split into two teams. Each team has two servers at each of the area who support whichever team is in possession of the ball.
- Teams win a point if they successfully get the ball from one set of servers to the other set without the opposition touching the ball.
- On winning a point, the team retains possession and attempts to transfer the ball back to the other set of servers.
- If the other team wins the ball, it tries to get it to any set of servers before attempting to transfer it across to the other set.

Focus

- Ensure that there is a clear pathway between you and the player on the ball. If there is not, can you move into an area so there is?
- Can you be on a different line to the rest of your teammates?
- When you receive the ball, can you play forward? If not, can you pass it onto a teammate who can play forward?

Possible Progressions/Regressions

- Alter the size and/or shape of the area.
- Introduce support player within the area.
- Server can step in with the ball when their team has possession and they must be replaced by a teammate.
- Use a smaller ball.

Practice G: Team Possession

Splitting the area in two is key to this adaption as it allows different tasks to be completed in each half. Whichever area the players receive the ball from the servers is labelled the 'first area', and then the area that players then look to make the final pass to the other set of servers is the 'second area'. This will constantly change during the practice due to it being multi-directional. The first half replicates the 'build-up' phase in a game, where teams are often more cautious and patient in their play, retaining possession of the ball until it is the right opportunity to play forward. This phase often includes 'ball circulation', where a number of passing options are needed for the player on the ball so it can be moved around the pitch, constantly shifting the opposition to create and exploit spaces. Once the ball has progressed up the pitch and out of the build-up phase, it moves into the 'creative' phase where players often need to attempt more risky passes, which are needed to produce goal-scoring opportunities.

With the first area representing the build-up phase, the teams can be challenged to complete a set number of passes before being allowed to transfer the ball into the second half. This allows the players to develop their ability to retain possession of the ball as a team while waiting for the right opportunity to play the ball forward. Once the ball has been transferred into the next area, we want the players to be positive and quick in their play. Rather than being patient, they now need to take more risks, replicating the creative phase. Therefore, we do not want to force the players into making a set number of passes before they can play into the server, instead we want them to play it in at the earliest opportunity; we want them to be brave with their pass. If needed, we can restrict the number of passes they have in the second area to encourage them to play the pass earlier when they would not normally do so. Instead of playing a safer pass, they may now risk the pass into the server.

The other element of the practice that helps develop the player's decision making is allowing the team in possession to have freedom in the area. By allowing this, the players have the choice to go and support the players to retain the ball in the first area and achieve the set number of passes. However, if they decide to provide support in the first area, they need to recognise when to move into the second area. If the team does not have any players in the second area, they will not be able to progress there, but if they go too early, an opponent can easily mark them, so timing of their movement is key.

Practice G: Team Possession

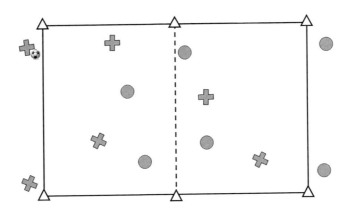

Alteration to Original Set-Up

- The area is split into two halves.
- Players in the team that is out of possession are locked into their designated halves.
- Players in the team in possession are free to go anywhere in the whole area.
- On receiving the ball from a set of servers, the team must complete a set number of passes before they can transfer the ball into the next half.
- Once in the second half, teams can play into the servers whenever they want.

Focus

- Identify where your teammate wants the ball to be played to them.
- Angle and distance of support.
- Recognise when to retain and when to pass the ball on.
- Understand when to progress into the next area.

Possible Progressions/Regressions

- Alter the size and/or shape of the area.
- Change the number of passes that must be completed before the team can progress into the second half.
- All players are unlocked.
- Ball cannot be played back to the support players.
- Gates are added to the line that separates the area in half, and the ball must be passed through one of these when transferring the ball between halves.

Practice G: Individual Possession

Having a small number of players and locking the same number of players from each team in a half will almost ensure that the team out of possession will use a man-to-man marking strategy. Therefore, when they have the ball, players are likely to come under pressure from a defender and they will need to try to retain possession of the ball while awaiting support from the server. They do have the option of passing it onto their teammate locked in the area with them. However, because they will likely be closely marked by the other defender, it is probably riskier to pass the ball than it is to keep hold of it.

The decision-making process that this practice creates, which the other adaptions with the same focus do not provide as much, is should the player try to retain the ball until support arrives or should they risk trying to progress forward without the help of the server? Because the defender will try to win the ball before the server enters the area, as this creates an overload for the team in possession, the attacker may well be able to take advantage of this by identifying opportunities to progress forward. The defender needs to take some risks when trying to win the ball, before the level of difficulty increases with the introduction of another attacker. Therefore, the player on the ball needs to try to identify if they can create space where they can travel in the other half of the area or if they can play the ball to a teammate already located there. To win possession, the defender needs to attack the ball and will probably commit to attacking one side of the player with the ball. The attacker needs to decide whether to exploit the space on the other side (if there is any) or try to hold onto the ball until support arrives. If they decide to wait for support, they can still attempt to go it alone by using the movement of the server entering the pitch. The defender may well expect the pass to go to the server entering the area and, therefore, there is a chance that this can be taken advantage of by the player on the ball as they keep hold of the ball and drive forward themselves.

There has, so far, been very little mention of the other attacker locked in the area with the player on the ball. As mentioned earlier, playing a pass into them can be extremely risky, but that does not mean they do not have a role to play in the practice or their team playing forward. But their movement can help create uncertainty in the defenders as decisions need to be made about whether they change their positions and strategy. Forcing the defenders into making a decision can create mistakes or delays in their actions, which, in turn, provides the attacking players with opportunities.

Practice G: Individual Possession

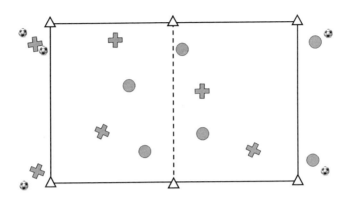

Alteration to Original Set-Up

- The area is split into two halves.
- All players are locked in their designated halves.
- On receiving the ball from a set of servers, the team tries to transfer the ball into the next area.
- Once they have played into the area, the servers have to complete a set number of passes between themselves. Once completed, the server whose team has possession of the ball can move into the area and join the play.
- To transfer the ball into the next area, players can either pass it or drive with it.

Focus

- Protect the ball, keep your body between the defender and the ball.
- Use the foot furthest away from the defender.
- Use feints/disguise to create space and time.
- Pass or retain?
- Await support or progress forward individually.

Possible Progressions/Regressions

- Alter the size and/or shape of the area.
- Increase or decrease the number of passes the servers have to complete.
- The server is not allowed to enter the area.
- Use a smaller ball.

Practice G: Receiving to Play Forward

Within this adaption, the players can continue to work on their movement to receive the ball and play forward before completing the actual technique. As this practice has direction in its set-up, it allows the players to practise realistic movement patterns they can transfer into a game. Allowing players from either area to enter the centre channel also provides an opportunity for them to rehearse receiving to play forward by dropping-in or making a movement to get ahead of the ball.

To begin with, the players have the opportunity to collect the pass unopposed, unless they are already in a position where they need the challenge of having to lose the defender, so they can receive to play forward. When the practice begins where the player receives the pass unopposed, it is important they are not allowed to wait in the central area. They need to understand the importance of making the movement at the right time so they arrive at the place they want to receive the pass either just before or at the same time as the ball. Therefore, within the practice, the players cannot be allowed to wait within the area; once they have entered it, they must leave it almost immediately with or without the ball. However, we must not get too focused on ensuring the players comply with this rule. For instance, if we place a rule that they cannot spend more than, say, three seconds in this area, and then we start counting each time a player enters it, we can easily become distracted and will end up spending most of our time enforcing the rule, rather than observing and supporting the players.

By allowing a player from either of the two areas to move into the central area to receive the pass, we are now also introducing them to the decision-making process of where, specifically, they need to support the player on the ball. This is particularly important for the players in the first area who need to understand and recognise when they need to provide support further up the pitch so their team can progress forward. They can only do this when they can be sure that their teammate on the ball and the team as a whole have good or safe possession of the ball and are in a position to play forward. What they do not want to do is leave the main area when their teammate still needs them to help retain possession of the ball. At the same time, they need to recognise or even predict when the player on the ball can play forward so that they can make a movement into the central area to be in a position to receive the pass, as soon as their teammate is ready to play it. If not, the opportunity for the player on the ball to make the pass could well disappear.

Practice G: Receiving to Play Forward

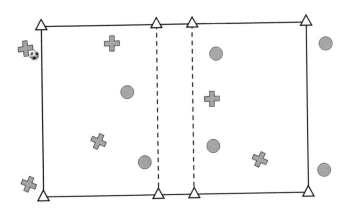

Alteration to Original Set-Up

- A central channel is added to the area.
- All players are locked into their designated areas. Each area has the same number of players from both teams.
- To transfer the ball from one area to the other, a player can move into the central channel to receive a pass. If they came from the area that the ball needs to be played into, they can pass or dribble out of the channel. They are only allowed to pass the ball out of the channel if they come from the area the ball is being played from,.

Focus

- Identifying an opportunity to receive the ball within the channel: is the teammate on the ball able to play the forward pass?
- Angle of approach and body shape to receive the pass.
- Pass from the player on the ball needs to be early and onto the furthest foot of the receiving teammate.
- First touch from the receiving player should be positive and forward.

Possible Progressions/Regressions

- Alter the size and/or shape of the area.
- Allow one defender to enter the channel.
- Server can step in with the ball when their team has possession.

Practice G: Driving With the Ball

This adaption continues to provide the players with the opportunity to practise driving with the ball, and it also allows them to really experience how it can affect the opposition and what they then need to do in these situations. An important aspect of the practice needed to provide this environment is to allow a defender from each area to engage the player driving with the ball. A defender leaving the same area as the player on the ball and chasing after them ensures that the attacker has to drive at full pace, otherwise they will be caught by their opponent. This is essential because if this is not allowed to happen, the topic of the session may not be achieved. If there is no pressure coming from behind when the defender approaches the attacker from the area they are travelling to, it is possible the attacker will slow down, and it turns into a one versus one. Therefore, the pressure that comes from the defender that is chasing is essential to produce the situation we want to focus on: the decision the attacker makes when a defender closes them down.

Giving the defenders a choice of whether or not they exit their area replicates what happens in a game of soccer; defenders either decide to leave their position and engage the player on the ball or stay where they are in an attempt to remain compact. The player driving with the ball, therefore, needs to experience both of these situations and develop their decision making around each one. If none of the defenders approach the player driving with the ball, they need to make the decision to pass the ball early or enter the final area before releasing it. Or if a defender does approach them, do they look to release the ball before they reach them or do they change the line they are travelling with a view to getting closer or into the area? Either way, the player driving with the ball needs to be able to scan and assess the situation while travelling at speed.

Ideally, the attackers will look for a pass that is directly to one of the servers, winning the point immediately. The players defending may not recognise, at first, the need to defend in a way that prevents the pass going into the servers, but this will soon change if the attacking players continue to pass into them straight away. Therefore, when driving with the ball, the player will likely have to identify which of their teammates is available to play the pass to. The challenge they then face is executing the pass while travelling at speed. If they attempt to use the inside of the foot, they are likely to advertise the pass and they will need to adjust their body shape and stride pattern. Therefore, using the front or outside of their foot allows them to pass it more effectively with disguise.

Practice G: Driving With the Ball

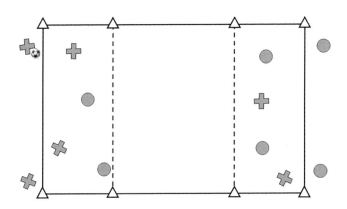

Alteration to Original Set-Up

- The area is split into thirds, with the central area bigger than the two end areas.
- Players are split and locked into one of the end areas.
- To transfer the ball from one end area to the other, a player must leave their area with the ball and drive to the opposite area.
- When driving with the ball, players must pass the ball before they reach the other end area, or they can enter it but then must release the ball with their first touch. The pass that they play can be straight to one of the servers.
- When driving with the ball, one defender from both areas can try to win the ball back within the central area.

Focus

- Identify when there is an opportunity to drive with the ball.
- First touch: strong touch out of your feet and forward.
- Identify whether or not you need to get your body between the ball and the defender.
- Strong controlled touches to allow long strides while running.
- Shift the ball off the initial line when needed.
- Technique to play the pass while driving with the ball.

Possible Progressions/Regressions

- Alter the size and/or shape of the area.
- A server can enter the area when they receive the ball, but they must attempt to drive with it to the other end area.

Practice G: Finishing

This adaption focuses on the movement and body shape of the server/forward player, which will allow them to create a goal-scoring opportunity for either themselves or a teammate. The team out of possession will likely attempt to block the pass into the server, which will be easier to do now that there is only one option for the attacking players to play into instead of two. As a result, it is also likely that the defending players will position themselves just in front of the end zones, therefore, they will be in a position to close down the server quickly once they have received the ball. This creates a situation where the server needs to be decisive in their decision-making process, and they will also need to execute whichever action they have chosen quickly before they are closed down by the recovering opponent. They also need to ensure their movement allows them to get in an area where they can receive the ball with the correct body position for whichever decision they make next.

As you would expect, this adaption is also really effective for the goalkeepers within the squad as it is a finishing practice, but it does allow for more than just 'shot stopping' to be developed. If there are specialist goalkeepers in the squad, instead of having one player from each team in the end zones, we can place a goalkeeper in there, and a player who acts as the attacker for both teams. Therefore, when the ball is played into the end zone, the goalkeeper can always be the player who retreats to the goal. But in addition to this, when they are acting as one of the servers playing into the main area, they can also practise similar types of receiving and passing that they will use within a game. We can do this throughout all the practices in the book that focus on finishing. Where there is a role of a goalkeeper, or where players are asked to complete dual roles, like in this adaption, we can leave the goalkeepers in the squad in these roles throughout the practice.

The other thing to consider when delivering a practice that focuses on finishing, especially when there is more than one goal, is that everything does not need to be identical. So, for instance, in this practice, we do not have to use two goals that are the same size, and they do not have to be positioned equal distances away from the area. Having different sizes and/or distances provides the players, including the goalkeepers, with a range of challenges, which we can then link to a scoring system. Or we may just choose to have a different set-up to meet the different needs of the players, for instance, one goalkeeper may need to be challenged more than the other and so they are allocated in a larger goal, or their goal is situated closer to the area.

Practice G: Finishing

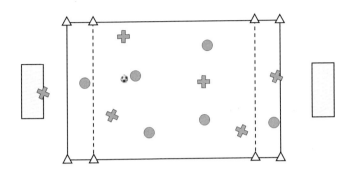

Alteration to Original Set-Up

- The servers are situated within end zones rather than outside the area.
- Two goals are added, one at each end, away from the area.
- Servers continue as normal when playing the ball into the area. But then when the ball is being played towards them, the server whose team is out of possession retreats to the goal and becomes the goalkeeper.
- Teams look to receive off one set of servers and then play the ball to the server on their team at the other end of the pitch.
- On receiving the ball, the server can either attempt to score themselves or lay it off for a teammate to have a shot.
- The attacking players have a maximum of three touches to have the shot, and one defender can recover into the end zone to apply pressure.
- If the ball goes out of play, the game restarts with a set of servers.

Focus

- Take the shot yourself or lay it off for a teammate.
- Selection of shot: consider where you are in the area and the positioning of the goalkeeper.
- Ensure that the shot is on target and struck with power or placement.

Possible Progressions/Regressions

- Alter the size and/or shape of the area.
- Move the goals closer or further away from the area.
- Change the number of touches the attacking team can have to get their shot off once it has been played into the server.

Practice G: Shielding

This particular practice focuses on the final part of the shielding process, specifically, the lay off to a supporting player. The set-up of the practice means the server receiving the pass has to shield until they have identified a teammate, who they can lay the ball off to. Therefore, the players still get the opportunity to develop the actual technique of shielding the ball before they move on to the next step of playing the pass. The key element of the practice that provides the opportunity for players to work on this part of the performance is the rule that states that the player making the pass through one of the gates must do so with a first-time pass. Making it a first-time pass means players must support the server who is shielding the ball in exactly the right place, and the pass from the server must also be played with the correct weight and into the right space. If any of these components are not done correctly, it will make it really difficult for the team to achieve the point.

Quite often, when a player tries to support a teammate shielding the ball, they will look to do so in the wrong place and either get too close to or make a supporting run beyond the ball. By getting too close, they are restricting the space in which they can play once they have received the pass; they are, in fact, making it easier for the opposition to defend as they are helping them to stay compact. By positioning themselves further away from the ball, they are likely to have more space in which to operate, as the opposition players will be attracted to the ball. Another decision players sometimes make is to run beyond the ball, even though their teammate is not in a position to play a forward pass, because of a defender being positioned behind them and preventing them from turning. Initially staying away from the player shielding the ball before making a movement into an area where they can receive the ball and play the pass into a gate provides a better opportunity for success.

Once teammates get into better areas to provide support, the player shielding the ball needs to understand the role that they play in terms of where they should place the pass. To allow a player to make a one-touch pass through a gate, they ideally need the ball to be played in front of them so they can just move or step onto it. Providing this situation encourages the players to pass the ball into this area, which is a skill they will transfer into a game. Doing this in a game allows the player receiving the ball to be positive in their play, whether this is with their first touch, a pass, a shot or any other action – it encourages them to play forward. This element of the practice also encourages the players to consider where they are playing a pass in all aspects of the game.

Practice G: Shielding

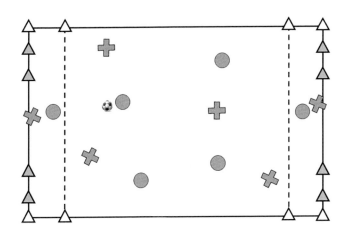

Alteration to Original Set-Up

- The servers are situated in end zones rather than outside the area.
- Two sets of gates are added at each end of the area.
- Servers continue as normal when playing the ball into the area. When the ball is being played to them, the server whose team is out of possession becomes a defender.
- Teams try to receive off one set of servers and then play the ball to the server on their team at the other end of the area.
- On receiving the ball, the server tries to lay it off for a teammate to pass the ball through one of the two sets of gates with a one-touch pass.
- If the ball goes out of play, the game restarts with a set of servers.

Focus

- Body shape to receive the ball: wide stance and side-on.
- Knees bent and arm up against the defender.
- Control with the outside of the foot using the foot closest to the player passing.
- Use your body to protect and shield the ball.
- Identify the supporting player and select the correct area to pass the ball.
- Teammates: where to support the player on the ball.

Possible Progressions/Regressions

- Change positioning of the gates or add more gates.

Practice G: One Versus One Attacking

Before going into a one versus one situation, this adaption allows the players to work on creating an opportunity to isolate a defender into this situation. This can be achieved through individual players creating the opportunity for themselves or teammates to work together to create an opening for one player. This will help to get players into the mindset of trying to do this within a game. As highlighted throughout this book, if a player can go past a defender, it often results in that opposition player being taken out of the game, and it will also force one of their teammates to leave their position, creating spaces that can be exploited by the attacking team. Therefore, it is really important that we encourage the players to try and get themselves in this situation so they can isolate a defender into a one versus one situation and then have the confidence and ability to get past them.

The set-up of the practice allows the attacking players on the ball to be creative in terms of how they approach the defenders and the strategies they use to attempt to get past them to win a point. Because the defenders are locked into their own specific areas, which are joined together, the attacking players have an opportunity to be creative in their play, as they can move with the ball towards one defender with the intention of entering that specific area before changing direction and entering the adjacent area. When doing this, there is the possibility they will catch the defender unaware, giving themselves an increased chance of winning a point. Although this is not necessarily related to something in particular that happens within the game, what it does provide is an environment where the players develop some of the key elements needed to be successful in a one versus one situation. For the player on the ball to keep the defenders guessing about which area they will enter and try to catch them by surprise, they will need to use effective feints and demonstrate high levels of agility, balance and speed.

This particular practice also provides lots of opportunities to make changes that will have a significant impact on the level of difficulty for the attacker when they get themselves in the one versus one situation. The area sizes in which the servers are situated can be easily altered, for instance, a third area can be added in between, which is a 'no go' space that will dramatically reduce the space the player on the ball has to win their point. Or the area the servers are located can remain the same, and we can allow them to enter each other's area to help prevent the attacker from scoring a point and provide a two versus one situation. These easy changes can also be used to introduce differentiation, as whatever change is introduced does not have to be for both teams.

Practice G: One Versus One Attacking

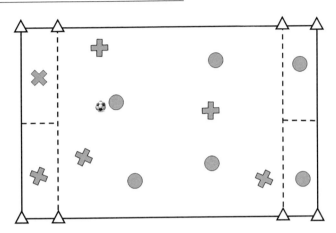

Alteration to Original Set-Up

- The servers are situated within end zones rather than outside the area. Each end zone is split in two with a server allocated in each half.
- The game is now directional, with a team starting the practice with their servers and attacking the other set of servers.
- To win a point, a player must enter one of the end zone areas occupied by an opposing server, dribble past them and exit through the back line.
- If the ball goes out of play at any time, the game restarts with the servers for whichever team is in possession.

Focus

- Before entering the end zone, try to shift the ball to the left or the right to make the defender move and shift their body weight.
- Feint and disguise to shift the defender's body weight in a selected direction.
- Shift the ball quickly in a different direction.
- Explosive acceleration to exploit the space and move away from the defender.

Possible Progressions/Regressions

- Alter the size and/or shape of the area and/or the end zones.
- Allow a defender to recover into the end zone as well.
- Add an additional task after getting past the defender.

Practice G: Pass or Dribble?

The focus is mostly on the players not in possession of the ball in this particular adaption and how they can support their teammate, who is deciding whether to pass or dribble. Quite often, the actions of teammates can almost make the decision for the player on the ball. A clever run can, sometimes, force the player into making the pass, or if their movement takes a defender or defenders with them, it may well persuade them to retain the ball and dribble with it instead. Therefore, when a player is in possession of the ball, the positioning and movement of their teammates is key to whether or not the ball can be transferred through one of the two gates, and which strategy is used to achieve it.

The two attacking players waiting in the half of the area where the ball will be played to them through the gates are likely to position themselves close to the gates. They will do this as they believe this is the best way to support their teammates in the other half, as they are in a position to receive a pass. However, by doing so, it is likely they will be closely marked by their opponents, so if they do receive it, they will come under pressure immediately, and it will be difficult for them to play forward as they will have little space to operate in as they will be positioned too close to the other half of the area. The other problem it will cause is that they will limit the opportunity that their teammate, who has possession of the ball, will have to enter the half by dribbling. By positioning themselves close to the gate, they will have dragged the defenders into an area where they can defend against the pass being played through the gates or engage the attacker in possession of the ball if they decide to dribble. Therefore, it is important that these attacking players initially position themselves away from the gates and observe what is happening within the other half of the area so they can identify when is the right time to move into an area where they can receive the pass through one of the gates. They need to ensure that the player on the ball is looking to make the pass and also able to play it. As soon as this happens, their movement into the correct area needs to be decisive, and the ball needs to be played immediately so that it reaches the player while they are still able to receive it.

Similarly, they also need to recognise when their teammate is likely to dribble through the gates; their movement needs to take them into a different area. When their teammate travels through a gate, one of the defenders will likely close them down and, therefore, this player needs to make the decision whether to go past the opponent or pass the ball on. Therefore, the supporting players need to be in a place where, if their teammate on the ball wants to release it, they are in a position where they are a valid option to receive a pass.

Practice G: Pass or Dribble?

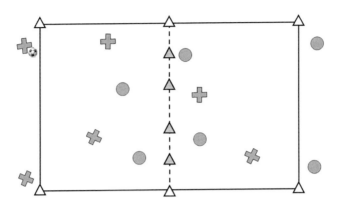

Alteration to Original Set-Up

- The area is split into two halves.
- The players in the team that is out of possession are locked into their designated halves.
- The players in the team in possession are free to go anywhere within the whole area, but as soon as they lose the ball, they must return to their designated half.
- To transfer the ball from one half to the other, it must travel through one of the sets of gates, this can be with a pass or by a player dribbling with it.

Focus

- Decision making: when to retain the ball and when to pass it?
- Can you use the supporting players to help keep the ball individually?
- Do you need to go past the defender? Draw them in, before releasing the ball.
- For the supporting players, what type of run could you make?

Possible Progressions/Regressions

- Alter the size and/or shape of the area.
- Change the number of gates.
- All players are unlocked and can go anywhere in the area.
- Use a smaller ball.
- Server can step in with the ball when their team has possession and they must be replaced by a teammate?

Practice G: Counter-Press

When a team initially loses possession, the closest player to the ball needs to press immediately to prevent the opposition from playing forward quickly, as this will probably result in them achieving a point. When possession is initially lost, if the player nearest to the ball can either force their opponents to play backwards or delay them from playing forward immediately, there is a possibility they will help prevent the opposition from scoring a point. As this initial reaction is taking place, the decision-making process of the player's teammates, in terms of what they do while this is taking place, is key to whether or not the team goes on to win back possession or the opposing team eventually wins the point.

Ideally, as one player goes to close down the opposition player who has just gained possession of the ball – whether this is from winning the ball themselves through a tackle or interception or because they have received a pass from the teammate who won the ball – their teammates should join them in the counter-press. Several players quickly closing down the space where the ball is situated makes it extremely hard for their opponents to progress with the ball or even retain possession. However, players need to be mindful that this is not always possible, and if they do not get enough players there quickly enough, it is likely that the other team will be able to play through the counter-press as the spaces have not been closed off quickly enough. If this happens in a game, the opposition will be able to progress forward and bypass a number of players. Therefore, within this particular adaption, once the team loses possession, the players need to decide whether to help their teammate try to win the ball back immediately or retreat instead so that they create a 'block' and have a more patient approach to winning back possession.

Allowing one of the servers to enter the area as soon as their team has lost possession of the ball can help promote good habits. Because of their positioning, they will always be ahead of the ball in relation to the direction the opposing team needs to go to win a point. Therefore, they will be making some form of recovery run and need to make a similar decision to that of the rest of their teammates: do they press or help form some type of block? When it is the right decision to help the team in the counter-press, the direction they come from to help press the ball can be very effective in winning the ball back. Joining a teammate who is already pressing and doubling up on the player in possession of the ball significantly reduces the amount of space available to them and reduces their options. However, the defender needs to ensure they can reach the play in time to affect it before the ball is moved on; otherwise, they have made the wrong decision.

Practice G: Counter-Press

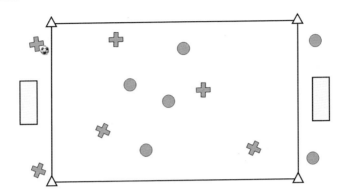

Alteration to Original Set-Up

- A small goal or a set of gates are added to each end of the area. They are situated centrally, just outside the area.
- The team starting with the ball try to win a point as normal. The team out of possession win a point if, when they win the ball, they can pass it into the small goal/gate positioned by the servers that last played the ball into the area.
- If the team starting out of possession are successful in winning the ball and playing it into the correct small goal/gate, they retain possession.

Focus

- Immediate reaction to win back the ball: determination and aggression.
- Awareness of where in the area their team has lost the ball.
- Recognising where your teammates are situated and what they are attempting to do.
- Counter-press or move into a block?

Possible Progressions/Regressions

- Alter the size and/or shape of the area.
- Add an additional small goal/gate to each end of the area.
- The team winning possession of the ball must complete a small number of passes before they can attempt to play into the small goal/gate.
- One of the servers from the team that just lost the ball can enter the area.
- One of the servers from the team that just won the ball can enter the area.

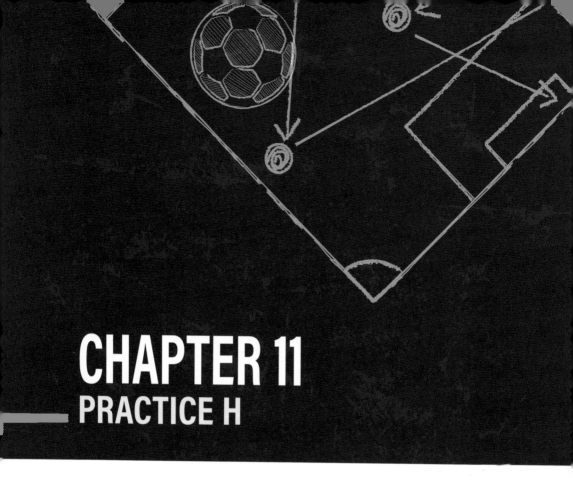

CHAPTER 11
PRACTICE H

The final squad practice before we end with some game practices provides the coach with even more opportunity for flexibility and creativity, both in terms of the final task that the players have to complete and whether we want it to be a directional or nondirectional practice. Having two separate ends to the practice area provides the coach with the opportunity to set the players a range of challenges to complete once they have achieved the initial task. We do have to be careful, however, as it has always been maintained, and rightly so, that a session should just have one focus so that the players can concentrate on this one aspect of the game, which will help maximise learning. Therefore, in most cases, the separate tasks the players have to complete once they have broken out of the main area will either be linked or the same. But it does still provide flexibility when we want it. So, for instance, if we have one goalkeeper in the group of players we are working with, we could put a goal at one end of the practice, and the task that the players complete if they break out this side of the area would include a shot on goal. The set-up used for the core practice shows two completely different tasks: at one end of the pitch the players have to complete a pass to win a point and, at the other end, they need to drive with the ball. This is to demonstrate the flexibility of the practice, and the adaptions going forward will have tasks that are either identical and linked to the session focus or are different but still relevant to the topic.

In terms of whether the practice is directional or nondirectional, a number of factors need to be taken into consideration. The main aspect that influences whether the practice is directional or not is if the session topic has a focus around players being in possession or out of possession. If the session topic looks at the players not having the ball, it is likely that the practice will need direction. A key principle of defending is to protect; the players need to have something to defend, and in the game of soccer, this is obviously their goal. In this particular practice, it is the line that separates the areas, therefore, when it is nondirectional the players have to defend two separate targets, which are situated in opposite directions. In this situation, it is extremely difficult to get key messages across to the players and for them to develop around the focus of the topic as they are placed in an environment that will be nothing like the situation they find themselves in the game of soccer. They could defend correctly, protecting one of the lines, but the opposition then finds success by simply changing direction and attacking the other end. In soccer, this would be seen as a great success for the team out of possession, as it would mean they forced the opposition to play back towards their own goal, but this would not be the case in this practice if it were nondirectional. When the practice is nondirectional, it is very difficult for the team out of possession to defend correctly and, as a result, any of the key coaching points we attempt to get across to the players cannot be properly applied.

With sessions that focus on the team being in possession, there is an opportunity to be more flexible in terms of whether the practices are directional or nondirectional. Although there is an argument that if an in-possession practice is nondirectional it loses key principles, just as out-of-possession practices do. For instance, key in-possession principles of any invasion game are progression and penetration, and it is likely you will lose these in a nondirectional practice. However, you will still retain other key principles, such as support and retention, and there is also the possibility that a further principle – creativity – will become more evident, as the opportunity to find success in multiple directions helps enhance the players' awareness and encourages them to be more resourceful in their play, for instance, they may be likely to attempt to make more turns and skills, as well as complete a wider range of passes. Because there will be more opportunities in terms of space in the practice, they will have the option to attack the opposition in multiple directions. Once they have identified this space, it will usually just take one action to exploit it before they can obtain a point. When considering whether to make the practice directional or nondirectional, we need to assess what we will gain and lose from both options and then select the one most suitable for what we want to achieve from the session.

Another consideration for this practice is the distribution of the players within the area. The selected set-up for the core practice has the players split into two teams. The danger with this is that it will be difficult for the players to retain possession of the ball. If we ask them to complete a set number of passes before they are able to break out of the main area, they could spend too long trying to complete this element of the practice and will not have enough time to develop around the focus of the session; this will depend largely on the ability of the players as a group to be able to retain possession and complete the number of passes set. If they need support in achieving the passes, there are a number of options available that will allow them to complete the target number with more ease. Support players can be used inside or outside the area, or both, and this will then give the team in possession an overload, making it easier to keep the ball. Another option available is to increase the area size, which will provide the team that have possession more space to operate in, which, in turn, makes it harder for the opposing players to close down the ball. The final option is, of course, to reduce the number of passes they have to complete before they are allowed to break out of the area. This rule could be removed completely, allowing players to break out whenever they want. As with all these options, the focus of the practice will influence what we introduce specifically. And we can, of course, introduce more than one of these changes; we just need to select the option or options that will be the most effective in meeting the needs of the players.

Another part of the practice that we can adapt and, again, it will depend on a number of factors, such as the needs of the players, the topic of the session, etc., is how the players are allowed to exit the area. The option that has been selected for the core practice is that a player can exit the central area by breaking out with the ball so they will either dribble out or drive out. We can, of course, change this to the players being allowed to exit by receiving a pass from a teammate, or they can do it through either of the two options. If we give the players the option to break out through receiving a pass, we need to decide how they are allowed to collect the ball – are they allowed to exit the area before the ball is played or are they only able to exit once the pass has been made? Only allowing them to exit after the pass has been played provides the opportunity to work on the offside rule as the line that separates the central areas and the other areas can also act as the offside line. We should only do this if the players are playing a version of the game that includes the offside rule – we should not introduce this too early, even if is to prepare them for it. Allow the players to play the version of the game they are currently playing; they will have plenty of time to play the other versions when it is the time to do so. We can encourage them not to just wait outside of the area but, instead, delay their movement, which will make it harder to defend against.

Practice H: Original Set-Up

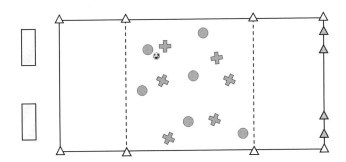

Set-Up

- An area that is relevant for the group of players.
- The area is split into thirds (the middle third can be a different size to the end thirds).
- The players are split into two teams and are all situated in the middle third.
- Teams have to complete a small number of passes before one player can break out into either of the other areas. One player from the other team can follow and defend.
- In one area, the player must pass into one of the small goals/gates, and in the other, they must travel through the gates with the ball.

Focus

- Positioning of teammates to support the player on the ball: distance and angle.
- Supporting players, can the player on the ball see your feet?
- Weight and area of pass: what does the player receiving the ball want to do with it?
- Identify the correct time to exit the middle third and the correct direction to travel.
- Technique to complete required task.

Possible Progressions/Regressions

- Alter the size and/or shape of the area.
- Change the number of passes that have to be completed to win a point.
- Use a smaller ball.
- Alter the final task that the players must complete.
- Make the practice directional.
- Increase the number of defenders that are allowed to leave the middle area.

Practice H: Cover and Support

In this adaption, allowing the players to break out of the central area by passing or travelling with the ball themselves provides the defenders with a wider range of challenges and more realistic situations that will occur within a game. If we only allow the players to break from the central area by travelling with the ball themselves, it makes it easier for the defenders to identify where exactly and when the opposition will enter their area. This makes it easier for the defenders to understand which role they will undertake to begin with, in other words, will they be the first defender, the player that closes down the attacker on the ball, or will they be the second defender, who provide the cover and support. Allowing the teams to break out of the central area in several ways means it will become more random and therefore more realistic for the defenders, it will also be much harder to predict/identify when an attacker will break out. Because of this, the defenders will have less time to react in terms of which one closes down the player on the ball and who provides the cover and support. Communication is a key factor in whether or not they react quickly enough to get themselves organised, which is essential if they are going to be able to defend effectively. As soon as one of the defenders has identified who should press the ball, this needs to be communicated to their teammate (i.e. 'I will press' or 'you press, I will cover').

The number of small goals or gates that the defenders have to protect is an important aspect of the practice. If there is only one, it is likely that at least one of the defenders will be tempted to wait in front of it while their teammate tries to win the ball back. This is understandable and also quite clever because it is an effective way of stopping the opposition from winning a point. The problem this creates, however, is that if they do not defend correctly, they will get into bad habits and will not provide support to their teammate attempting to win back the ball. Therefore, a minimum of two goals are needed to ensure that the players defend correctly and in a manner similar to the way they need to defend in a game. They may try to implement the same strategy as there are two targets and two defenders, so each one of them may attempt to block the small goal/gate. However, this does not usually happen as this would mean that the attackers would have the ball with no pressure applied to them. Therefore, even if the targets are blocked, it will still be quite easy to score a point as they will be able to move and manipulate the ball quite easily and, therefore, will be able to find a gap to play the ball through to achieve the point. So, we just need to ensure that the defenders are not tempted to just sit and block; we need to make sure that they defend 'correctly'.

Practice H: Cover and Support

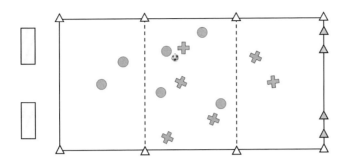

Alteration to Original Set-Up

- The practice is now directional, with each team defending a specific end of the area.
- Two players from each team are situated within the end area and act as defenders.
- Two players are now allowed to exit the middle area and attack the end protected by the two opposition defenders, creating a two versus two.
- If the defenders win the ball, they look to pass into one of their teammates within the central area and the practice continues.

Focus

- Who presses and who provides the cover and support?
- The second defender should be situated further back than the first defender to be in a position to provide cover and support.
- If the player on the ball goes past the first defender or passes the ball onto their teammate, the second defender needs to engage the player on the ball (i.e. they become the first defender). The other defender needs to recover, get back to being goalside and provide their partner with cover and support.
- Communication between the two defenders: where does the first defender want to show the attacker on the ball? Who is going to the ball, who is providing cover and support?

Possible Progressions/Regressions

- Alter the size and/or shape of the area.
- Allow three attacking players to exit the central area, creating a three versus two.
- Increase the number of small goals/gates that the attacking team can score in.

Practice H: Recovery Runs

The foundations of this practice mean that recovery runs take place by players from the team that is out of possession. When an attacking player exits the central area with the ball, one opponent is also allowed to leave and defend, therefore, they are making a recovery run. However, it is often likely they will be able to get in a position that allows them to get in front of the attacker quite quickly and easily, meaning the actual recovery run is either not needed or is quite easy to achieve. To help players develop and improve, we need to put them into challenging situations where they are not comfortable so that they have to do something different if they are going to be successful. Therefore, placing an attacking player inside these safe zones where a teammate can pass to them from almost anywhere within the central area ensures that the attacker will break out with a considerable advantage over the recovering defender. The additional area that is added where the attacker must reach before they are allowed to pass the ball into a small goal or gates, ensures that the defender does actually have a chance to recover. If this area was not added, the attacker could just attempt to make the pass immediately, therefore, there would be no opportunity for the defender to make a recovery run.

Because the attacking players get such an advantage, a key aspect of this practice, which the defenders need to develop, is their ability to identify or anticipate danger. Players mainly react to danger; they will only change their behaviour when they actually see a problem happening. For instance, they may watch a teammate try to defend against an attacker in possession of the ball and will only react to this situation if the defender is unsuccessful and, by then, it is quite often too late. Players rarely think about what could happen and reposition themselves so that if it does happen, they are in a better place to provide support or deal with it themselves. In this practice, if the team that is out of possession waits for the ball to be played into the attacker in the safe zone before they react to it, it is likely that they will not be able to prevent this player from scoring a point. Instead, they need to identify when they believe the pass into the attacker will happen and react to this, rather than waiting until it actually happens. The difficulty around this for the players is that they get drawn to the ball and do not consider other dangers. Although the immediate danger is most definitely the player on the ball, if this danger is being dealt with by some of their teammates, players need to recognise the next possible danger, which, in this case, is the pass into the attacker in the safe zone. So, not only do they need to predict when the pass will be made into the safe zone, but they also need to recognise when they are the best player to make the recovery run and prevent the attacker from scoring a point.

Practice H: Recovery Runs

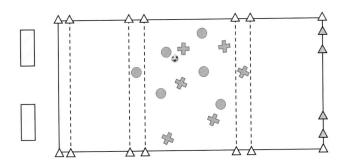

Alteration to Original Set-Up

- At each end of the central area, an additional line is added to create further areas or safe zones.
- One player from each team is situated within a safe zone. These players are attackers that their teammates try to play into.
- On receiving the ball, the attacker breaks out of their safe zone and tries to score into one of the small goals/gates.
- As soon as an attacker receives the ball, a player from the opposition team can exit the central area and try to prevent the attacker from scoring.
- If the attacker is passing the ball into small goals/gates, a further area is needed, which they must enter before they can attempt the pass.

Focus

- Do not wait for the danger, try to predict it.
- Identify what is happening ahead of you – where is the danger in the picture you are seeing?
- If time allows, head towards the furthest post of your goal.
- Do not engage the attacker. Try not to win the ball from the behind, unless there is no other option.

Possible Progressions/Regressions

- Alter the size and/or shape of the area.
- Allow one attacker and two defenders to exit, creating a three versus two.
- Position the safe zone further away from the central area.

Practice H: Counter-Press

This adaption provides the players with an environment where they have to react quickly and defend with intensity after they have lost the ball, and because the focus is on this small period of time just after the ball has been lost, it is one of few out of possession practices that can be nondirectional. By actually making it nondirectional, if the team does not win the ball back almost immediately after losing it, it will be too late, and their opponents will go on and steal all of the points.

It is therefore, essential that not only do individual players react quickly but all of their teammates respond and work together to close down the opponent on the ball and the space around them. It will, of course, not be possible for all the players to get to the player on the ball quickly enough, as they would have been set up as if they were in possession, that is, they would have been positioned to make the area as big as possible, making it difficult for the opposition to win the ball. Therefore, because of these big distances between themselves and their teammates, when the team does lose possession of the ball, some players will not be able to cover the distance quickly enough. These players will need to identify or predict where the ball is likely to go next. Once they have done this, they need to reposition themselves so they can close down the opposition after the ball has been moved into this part of the area. This is particularly important because it is likely that once the ball has been moved on from where it was initially lost, this will be the last opportunity to win it back before the opposition breaks out of the area and wins the points.

The additional central area is key to the practice as it encourages the team starting with the ball to play it as often as possible through the middle of the area. They are also likely to attempt more risky passes in this part of the area as they will be rewarded with a point if it is successful, similar to how teams attempt riskier passes when they are close to the goal in a game, as it could lead to a goal-scoring opportunity. Encouraging the team to make risky passes in the centre of the area increases the likelihood that this is where possession of the ball will be lost, which is vital if there is any chance of them being able to win it back. If the ball is lost close to the edge of the area, there is very little opportunity for them to regain possession, whereas if it is lost close to the middle, the players can practise the focus of the session. We may just need to monitor how hard or easy it is for the defending team to win the ball; if needed, the number of supporting players may need to be altered or the team in possession could be restricted to two or three touches. We need to ensure that it is not too easy or too hard for the defending team to win the ball.

Practice H: Counter-Press

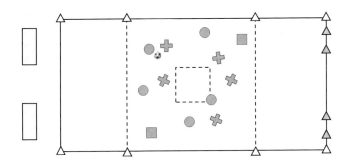

Alteration to Original Set-Up

- An additional small area is placed within the central area.
- The team starting with the ball begins with one point and earns an additional point every time a player receives a pass in the additional small area.
- Two support players help the team that starts with possession of the ball.
- When the opposition team wins the ball, it looks to break out and either drive through the gates or passes the ball into one of small goals. If successful, the team wins all the points that the other team won; if unsuccessful, the other team keeps the points.

Focus

- Immediate reaction to win back the ball: determination and aggression.
- Awareness of where in the area their team has lost the ball.
- Recognising where your teammates are situated and what they are attempting to do.
- Counter-press or move into a block?

Possible Progressions/Regressions

- Alter the size and/or shape of the area.
- Change the number of supporting players.
- Team in possession are restricted to a number of touches.
- The team attempting to win the ball back, have to get it back to the additional area to win all of the points after they have gained back possession. If they fail, they only win one point.

Practice H: One Versus One Defending

In this adaption, both of the end thirds are split into two and the ball is now released from the middle third by a pass played into a teammate locked into one of these areas. Splitting the end thirds in half and allocating one player from each team in both halves will ensure that the attacking player can receive the ball unopposed and, therefore, it allows for the one versus one situation. This, in turn, ensures the players can concentrate on the focus of the session, rather than finding themselves in situations that relate more closely to other topics. As with any other practice where the players are split between different roles, in this particular instance there are two types of roles — either playing in the central area or in one of the end thirds; it is important to remember to regularly rotate them. If we do not do this, then some players will get a very limited amount of time, or possibly even no time at all, developing the aspect of the game that the session is focused on. We need to try and ensure that all the players get the same number of opportunities.

The first aspect of the practice that the players need to work out is their positioning, which needs to change as possession transfers between the two teams, in addition to the ball changing position within the central area. When their team has possession of the ball, the players in the end thirds need to keep readjusting where they are situated so they can, hopefully, find a position where they are able to receive a pass from a teammate playing within the middle third. The other player within the end third needs to react to this movement, as their team will be out of possession and, therefore, they need to be ready to defend, should the ball be played into the opponent they share the end third with. They need to ensure that as their opponent changes their position in the area, they reposition themselves as well, so they are in the correct place to defend if, or when, the attacking player receives a pass. Because they are locked into their own particular half of the end zone, they will not be able to get as close to the attacker as they would like — so a one versus one situation occurs. However, they can ensure that they get goalside and position themselves as close to the line that splits the end third in two so that when the ball is played into the attacker, they can close them down as quickly as possible. This then leads on to the other key aspect of the practice that the defenders will need to develop: how they approach the attacker once they have received the ball. They need to make sure that the line along which they approach the attacker allows them to protect the goal or gates that they are defending, as well as forcing their opponent away from them. They also need to ensure that as they get closer to the attacker, they identify when they need to slow down and start to get themselves in the correct body shape to make it difficult for their opponent to get past them.

Practice H: One Versus One Defending

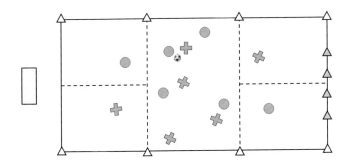

Alteration to Original Set-Up

- The end where there were previously two small goals, there is now just one, placed centrally. At the other end, the two gates are placed closer together.
- The two end thirds are split in half, with a player from one team in one half and a player from the other team in the other half.
- Game stays nondirectional and teams look to pass the ball to one of their players in the end thirds, once this happens both players in that end zone are unlocked and it becomes a one versus one.
- If the defender wins the ball, they try to play it back into the middle third.

Focus

- Angle and line of approach.
- Slow down as you get closer to the attacker.
- Body position to be side-on and knees bent.
- Aggressive in trying to win the ball back, take control of the situation.
- How early can you win back the ball?

Possible Progressions/Regressions

- Alter the size and/or shape of the area.
- Make the game directional and release the players from their allocated halves of the end third.
- Add additional small goals/gates for the players to score points in.
- Allow one of the attacking players' teammates to support them after a set period of time to create a two versus one.

Practice H: Forward Passing

By ensuring that the final task is a pass into a small goal or through a set of gates, the practice now has two elements, which requires a forward pass, giving it a clear focus around this element of the game; a forward pass is needed to release a player and then also to score a point. However, there are also likely to be two different types of forward passes. It is likely that the final pass to win the point will be played while the player is on the move as a defender will be chasing them, trying to prevent them from scoring a point. While the pass that allows the team to break from the central area could come in all types of different scenarios – such as the ball being passed back from a player to allow their teammate to play forward, a first-time pass or a player receiving on the back foot to play forward – it could also come from a player playing it when they are on the move. Therefore, the practice provides the players with an environment where they can constantly practice playing the ball forward. If needed, the challenge of playing the ball forward in this practice can easily be increased by making it directional. By doing so, the number of options available to play the pass out of the central area will be reduced by half, due to the number of gates now available.

One of the decisions you will need to make with this practice relates to the rule of how a player can receive the pass to allow them to break from the central area, in terms of whether they are allowed to exit the area before the pass is made. Although this can be linked to the offside rule, it does not necessarily just need to be linked to this, and restricting players from exiting the area until the pass is made can also be used with young players as well. If we are going to use it with younger players, the word *offside* should not be mentioned and, instead, the rule is used to help them understand where they need to pass the ball sometimes, especially when they are playing a forward pass. Quite often, young players will try to play the ball to where their teammates are situated when they first identify them as a possible option for a pass. What they do not take into consideration is whether the player is stationary or on the move, or whether there is space for the player to move into. Restricting the player to only being allowed to break out of the central area once the pass has been made not only provides the players off the ball a chance to practise their movement to run onto a pass, it also gives the player on the ball an opportunity to develop their understanding of when they should play to feet and when they need to pass into space. Passing the ball through the gates and into a space where there will not be any teammates waiting for the pass allows the players to develop the mindset of playing a pass into an area where the player will or could be, rather than where they are.

Practice H: Forward Passing

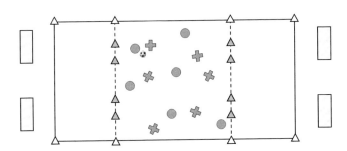

Alteration to Original Set-Up

- Two gates are added to each line that separates the central area and the two end areas.
- For both end areas, the players must pass the ball into one of the small goals/gates.
- To break out of the area, the ball needs to be played through one of the gates situated on the line between the central area and the two end areas.
- The line that separates the central area and the two end areas can be used as an offside line if required.

Focus

- Ensure that there is a clear pathway between the ball and the small goal/gate. If there is not, can you manipulate the ball so there is?
- Weight and accuracy of pass.
- When needed, pass to where they will be not where they are.

Possible Progressions/Regressions

- Alter the size and/or shape of the area.
- Make the practice directional.
- Move the small goals/gates, closer or further away from the area.
- Change the size of the gates that the ball has to be passed through to break out of the central area.
- Add a further gate to the lines that separate the central area and the two end areas.
- Allow an additional player from each team to leave the central area to make it a two versus two (if a player chooses to pass to their teammate, it must be a forward pass).

Practice H: Team Possession

The original set-up of this practice lends itself to team possession and therefore very little changes need to be made to it to give it a focus around this particular topic, in fact, it could be done without making any changes. However, the introduction of the support players makes it slightly easier to retain possession of the ball, which is important as the number of passes that need to be completed before a team can break out of the central area has been increased. The support players also provide an 'overload' for the team in possession, which allows it to replicate game-like situations. In soccer, when a team tries to keep hold of the ball, it will often have more players in the area of the pitch where the ball is situated compared with the opposition. The number of passes also needs to be increased, otherwise the teams are not really retaining possession; they are just completing a small number of passes. The practice needs to provide an environment where the teams are required to keep possession of the ball for prolonged periods of time before identifying the appropriate time to release a player. And because everything else they need to do in the practice involves passing the ball – releasing a player from the central area and scoring the point – it provides further opportunities for the players to develop an important aspect of team possession.

One of the progressions that can be used within this adaption is adding the rule that a support player must receive and pass the ball before a team is allowed to break out. This completely changes the role of the support player in the practice; previously, they were there to help the team with possession of the ball, now they are integral to whether or not the team is successful. This particular progression can be a really effective way of bringing differentiation into the practice. Because the defending team is aware that the ball has to be played into a support player, quite often, the team will be happy for the other players to have the ball and, therefore, it will focus its attention on the support players. This will often result in the support players being man-marked by players from the defending team. The support players now have to work really hard to get on the ball and pass it on successfully to someone in the team that they are supporting. So, instead of every player having an attempt at this role, it can be just the players who have been identified as needing to be challenged within the group. The other players will still practise the focus of the session, but at the level that is appropriate for them. Alternatively, all the players could have a turn in the role of the support players, but the rule of the ball having to played to them can just be used for those players that need to be challenged.

Practice H: Team Possession

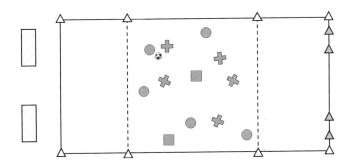

Alteration to Original Set-Up

- One or two support players are added to the central area.
- The number of passes the teams are required to complete before they can break out of the central area is increased.
- Teams can only break out of the central area with a pass, players are not allowed to drive out.

Focus

- Identify where your teammate wants the ball to be played to them.
- Angle and distance of support.
- Recognise when to retain and when to pass the ball on.
- Understand when it is the correct time to play the pass that releases a teammate out of the central area and when the ball needs to be retained.

Possible Progressions/Regressions

- Alter the size and/or shape of the area.
- Change the number of support players.
- A pass has to be played into a support player before the team is allowed to break out of the central area.
- Add gates to each line that separates the central area and the two end areas. The pass that allows the team to break out of the central area needs to be made through one of these gates.
- Make the practice directional.

Practice H: Individual Possession

The difficulty of this practice can be easily altered by allowing a defender to enter the channel when an attacking player receives the ball within it. With the initial rule of the defenders not able to engage the player on the ball until they exit the channel, this alteration allows this player to do a number of things. First of all, it provides them with all the time and space they want to make the decision about when they leave the channel and in which direction to go because they will not come under any pressure from an opponent; they can scan the two different areas and carefully select which one they enter. If they want to, they can also travel inside the channel, which allows them to enter an area in a different place to where they received the ball, so they can look for and choose an easier route. Once they exit the channel, they obviously still have the same challenge of having to break out without the support of any of their teammates. Having that time to evaluate the situation and carefully select where they want to go gives them a better chance of breaking out successfully. Once we allow a defender or defenders to enter the channel after the attacker has received the pass, we take away all the time and space the player on the ball had to make these decisions. Therefore, they now have to make these decisions while the ball is travelling to them, and their first touch will now be a lot more important as it will dictate how much pressure they come under immediately after receiving the pass and how quickly they can travel into the area they want to go.

With this practice, there is a real emphasis on the players not just retaining possession as an individual but also keeping the ball and creating opportunities with it. To successfully break out of an area, the attacker will, undoubtedly, have to go past some opposing defenders and then go on to complete the final task: the pass into the goal, the drive through a gate or whatever has been set up within the practice. This ability to keep hold of the ball and go past players before completing another action is priceless and definitely something we should encourage all players to do from the moment they start playing the game. However, what we also need to remember is that it is also extremely difficult and possibly the most difficult part of the game, therefore, it is very likely that the players will find it very hard to be successful within this practice. The width of the channel is important; the wider the channel, the easier it will be for the players as it will reduce the size of the areas they have to travel through before they can break out. And, of course, what we can do is position the channel so it does not split the central area exactly in half; it can be laid out so that it creates two different area sizes on either side of it. By doing so, we can award different points depending on which side the players break out of, and it also provides the players with a choice of travelling through an easier or harder area.

Practice H: Individual Possession

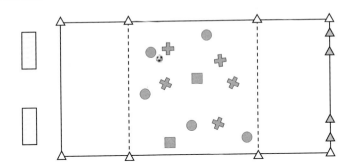

Alteration to Original Set-Up

- The central area is split into two with a channel running down the middle.
- Players are still free to go anywhere within the central area, and the ball can be passed through the channel.
- Teams can try to exit the central area at anytime (i.e. a set number of passes no longer needs to be completed).
- To break out of the central area, a player must receive a pass inside the channel; on doing so, they must break out without any help from their teammates (i.e. they cannot pass the ball).
- Defenders are not allowed to enter the channel, they can only travel through it. Therefore, they cannot attempt to tackle the attacker until they exit the channel.

Focus

- Protect the ball, keep your body between the defender and the ball.
- Use the foot farthest away from the defender.
- Use feints/disguise to create space.
- Identify/predict the most effective pathway.

Possible Progressions/Regressions

- Alter the size and/or shape of the area.
- The channel is made narrower or wider.
- Defenders can enter the channel when an attacker is in there with the ball.
- Add gates to the end areas, The attacker must travel through one of the gates before they can attempt to score a point.

Practice H: Receiving Under Pressure

The basis of this practice forces teams to complete a number of passes before they can release a player, which ensures that in this particular adaption, several players will need to receive the ball while under pressure. And due to the level of difficulty that this involves, it is likely that the players will get lots of opportunities to practise it due to the number of turnovers in possession likely to occur. The sizes of the areas that they are locked into with an opponent will also make it difficult for the players whose team has possession of the ball. When receiving a pass, there will be little space for them to operate in and keep the ball before offloading it to a teammate. Because of this, their first touch, which they will need to complete while under pressure from the defender, needs to be executed well so that it enables them not only to retain possession of the ball but also to have an opportunity to move it on to a teammate.

Allowing players to pass to any teammate and not just those situated within a connecting area means they need to be ready and available to receive the ball at all times. It also means they will receive all types of passes, such as a lofted pass played in the air, driven passes along the floor and short quick passes. Therefore, they need to be able to receive and control the ball in a number of different ways while under pressure from the defender. This brings with it several challenges that they will have to deal with and work out the solutions to. For instance, a pass played to them in the air will be extremely difficult to bring down and control, even when there is not a defender putting them under pressure. Not only will they need to develop their technical ability to control the ball, but they will also need to display physical ability to hold off the defender and provide a stable base that will make it easier to bring the ball under control.

Rotating players around the different areas (consider moving one team clockwise and the other team anti-clockwise) provides them with different experiences. They will play against different opponents who defend differently from the previous defender, and they will also have different options available in terms of where they they can play the ball. When they occupy a middle area, they have options either side of them as well as in front or behind, while an end area will reduce these options as they will only have one player available to them to the side. Therefore, not only will it make it more difficult to move the ball on but it will also make it easier for the defender to try to win the ball as the attacker receives the pass, as they can be more aggressive in their play knowing that if they do not win it, they still have an opportunity to recover and still prevent the attacker playing the pass out.

Practice H: Receiving Under Pressure

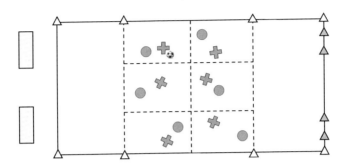

Alteration to Original Set-Up

- The central area is split into areas equal to that of the number of players in each team.
- One player from each team is locked into one of the areas.
- Teams complete the set number of passes before one of the players is allowed to break out into the end area next to the area they are locked in.
- When a player breaks out, the opposition player that was locked in the same area is also released and allowed to defend against them.

Focus

- Awareness of their partner's position.
- Body shape as they receive the ball.
- Which foot is used to receive the ball?
- Positioning of the teammate to support the player on the ball.

Possible Progressions/Regressions

- Alter the size and/or shape of the area/areas.
- Change the number of passes that must be completed before a player can break out of the central area.
- Have a support player who can travel anywhere within the central area.
- Defenders cannot attempt to win the ball until their partner has had their first touch.
- Make the practice directional.
- Use a smaller ball.

Practice H: Turning

The real focus for this adaption is on the players' ability to identify where they need to go and where the defender is approaching from to ensure that the turn is executed effectively and that they are able to escape from the central area quickly before their opponent can get close enough to try to win the ball. Once the set number of passes have been completed, all the players from the opposing team, apart from one, need to block all the gates, except for the one that has been called out by the coach. Therefore, initially, the player on the ball will be unaware of which opponent will be the one that tries to close them down until they actually start to do it. While they are trying to identify which player is closing them down and where they are approaching them from, they also need to look for which gate they can escape from. It is important that while they are doing this, they continue to travel with the ball so that it is more difficult for the defender to close them down and win the ball off them. Once everything has been identified and worked out, the player on the ball will then need to change the direction they are travelling, so that they can head towards the relevant gate.

It is a possibilty that the players may get slightly confused with the practice to begin with and, therefore, may need some help. When the coach selects which gate is to remain open, it is possible that the players from the defending team may get confused in terms of who should go to which gate and who should close down the attacker in possession of the ball. This could lead to more than one gate being left open and a number of defenders closing down the player on the ball. To help prevent this from happening, each player on both teams can be allocated a specific coloured gate, therefore, when the coach calls out which coloured gate is to stay open, the players know which of them closes down the attacker and which gate they should block. This will definitely help the players understand their roles once the number of passes has been completed, and it will also allow the focus of the practice to be achieved. However, if we leave it as it is, then it is likely that chaos will occur within the practice, which can, in fact, help produce a more relevant environment for the players to develop their turning. Because of the confusion, more than one defender might end up engaging the player on the ball and, therefore, this could result in them having to complete numerous turns. It also means there is more than one place where they can escape the central area, and this means they will have choices, which increases the number of decisions they have to make. Just because the players are not doing exactly what they should be doing in a practice in terms of the rules, it does not mean that learning is not taking place or that it should be stopped and the rules explained again; chaos often provides the most effective environment for development.

Practice H: Turning

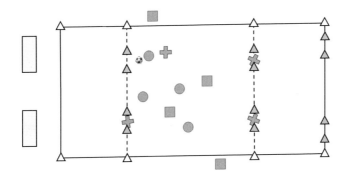

Alteration to Original Set-Up

- Players are split into three teams. Two teams play the game, the other team acts as support players, some within the central area and some on the outside.
- Two gates are added to each line that separates the central area and the two end areas. Each gate is a different colour.
- Once a team has completed the set number of passes, they cannot make anymore passes (i.e. the player on the ball cannot pass it and must be the player that breaks out).
- Once a team has completed the set number of passes, the other team must block all the gates apart from one, leaving one player to defend against the attacker on the ball. The coach will call out the colour of the gate that is to be left open.
- The player on the ball looks to break out of the only gate that is free.

Focus

- Identify when you should turn.
- Which direction to turn? Away from danger and into space.
- Choice and execution of turn.
- Touches: use the smallest number of touches needed to execute the turn.
- Speed: sharpness of turn and acceleration away from the defender.

Possible Progressions/Regressions

- Alter the size and/or shape of the area.
- Increase the number of gates to provide the attacking player with more options.

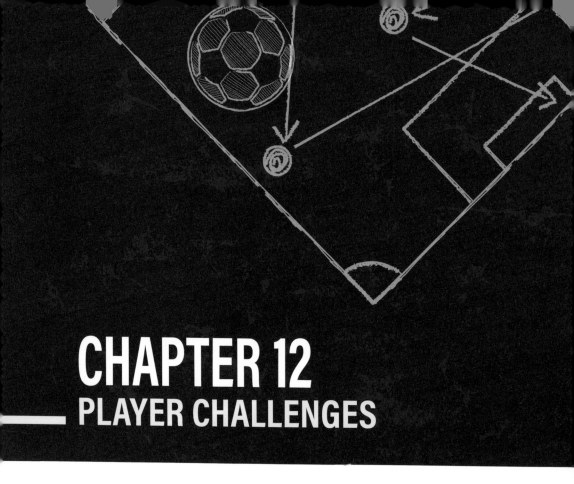

CHAPTER 12
PLAYER CHALLENGES

In chapter 8, the importance of interventions was discussed, along with a number of strategies of how they can be delivered. One strategy not discussed that has become a popular way to support players, both as a group and as an individual, are player challenges. Although this can be an effective tool for developing players, it is something we often use without fully considering how it will affect the player, and also the practice as whole, as well as the way it links into the topic of the session. If we are truly going to use challenges as part of the way we support players, then they should become part of our planning process. By doing this, we can prepare a bank of challenges that directly link to the session focus and can be used as and when needed.

A challenge often used with players is 'number of touches', where they are required to use a small number of touches, and we do this to encourage them to move the ball quickly, in other words, pass it early. Because it is a strategy we like to use and one we see as important, coaches will regularly use it. Therefore, it is likely that a lot of the times we give it to a player or a team of players, it may be the wrong time to do so as it may not be relevant to the session topic. So, for instance, we may challenge the players to have only two or the touches when the session topic is on finishing or turning or even dribbling. Although the intention is correct as we have recognised that the player or players need to be challenged, we need to ensure that the challenge is directly connected to the session topic. We decided to use the challenge either because we identified that they are doing well within the practice or that they need some support, and therefore it is the 'topic' of the session, which they are excelling in or need help with. If we use a challenge not directly related to the session topic, we are not going to help them to improve this particular part of their performance, in fact, we might even hamper their development. Where previously, they were doing well in a practice with a focus on finishing, the challenge that they have been given — only having two or three touches — could now actually prevent them from even having an attempt on goal. Therefore, we need to ensure that we are challenging them around the area of their performance that the session is helping them to develop,

Another key consideration is the terminology we use when we are issuing a challenge. If we say to a player that they can only have two touches, or if we say to a team they must pass the ball at least five times before they can attempt to score a goal, we are not giving them a challenge, we are actually restricting them or adding an additional rule to the practice for them. When we use a challenge in a session, it needs to be something we want them to *try* and do but not something that they *have* to do. Therefore, the words we use when we give a challenge are very important for instance, instead of saying, 'you can only', we should say, 'when you can'. Instead of telling a player that 'you can only use your left foot', we now challenge them, 'when you can, use your left foot'. This is essential when we use challenges as an intervention strategy as it not only helps the players with their decision making but also prevents the players from doing something you would not want them to do in a game; it prevents them from falling into bad habits. If we return to the example of a player using their left foot, restricting them to using this foot only they will not be able to develop the decision-making process for when they should use it. Plus, they have to use the left foot when they should use their right foot, for example, the player is in space and has the opportunity to receive the ball on their back foot and play forward, but because they are restricted to only using their left foot, they are unable to do this as their furthest foot is their right foot. We want them to understand when they should use it and then attempt to use it. If we use the same scenario, but with the furthest foot as their left foot, the aim is for them to recognise that they should use this foot as it allows them to play forward and then try to use it when they receive the pass. If they still use their right foot, we can use questions and answers to help remind them of their challenge: what is your challenge? Was it a good time to try to do it then?

To help ensure we provide the players with the correct challenge, we should aim to include individual and team challenges as part of our planning. Identifying and producing a number of challenges when planning the session will help ensure they are directly linked and relevant to the topic. It also allows you to have a bank or library of challenges with you when you are at the training session. Therefore, when you have a player or group of players needing a challenge, you can select one from the library suitable for their specific needs. We can take this a step further by producing actual cards that have the challenges written on them, so that when we want to give a player or players a challenge, we can hand them the card to read before returning to their practice. This provides a number of advantages for both the players and the coach. For the coach, it allows them to continue to watch and observe the practice while the player reads the card. If they did not have a card, they would need to explain the challenge to the player verbally, which would involve moving their focus away from the practice. For the player, instead of receiving the information verbally, during which, it is unlikely they will be fully focused on what the coach is saying as they will, understandably, be distracted by the practice going on, they just need to read the information on the card. Reading information, rather than listening to it takes more concentration and focus; therefore, it is likely that they will understand what they are being asked to do more effectively through reading the card. This opportunity for learning also provides the players with a slightly different experience. Rather than going through the same process of talking with the coach, they have more control of how they obtain and understand the information. For instance, once they have read the card, they can either return it to the coach or retain it to refer back to, should they need to remind themselves what they are being asked to do. Or it could be that after they have read it, they are not quite sure what it means, and they can be proactive in their learning and ask the coach for further information.

Now that we have a better understanding of what a challenge is and how it can be used, the main decision we need to make is whether we are going to issue it to an individual player or a group of players. As with individual and group interventions, there are advantages and disadvantages to both, and it is just a matter of analysing the situation at the time and making a decision in terms of what is the best strategy at that specific moment in time. Will an individual challenge support the one specific player it is aimed at and provide them with the help they need around the theme of the session or is it something that a number of players will benefit from as they are all performing in a similar way within the practice? On the other hand, it could be that the challenge is given to certain players to support another player or players within the session.

Individual Challenges

These are usually given to a player if they need to be encouraged to do something or if they are excelling within the practice and need to be taken out of their comfort zone and moved into an 'ugly' zone. This ugly zone is where a player is put into an environment or situation, which is just beyond their current level of ability and where they will try and mostly fail, but with support and encouragement and by learning from their previous experiences, they will start to find success. Individual challenges are an effective tool to support players and help them move from one level of performance to the next one. It also allows them to do it at a pace that suits them as they get to choose when and where they attempt to do it because it is a challenge and not a rule or restriction.

For players needing encouragement, this usually involves encouraging them to either try and complete some of the tasks in the practice, which is often the case when it is an individual practice (i.e. a one versus one) or trying to get them to take on more responsibility, usually within a multi-player practice. Within all the adaptions of Practice B, there will undoubtedly be players that do well and others that find it much more challenging. The players who find it difficult can quickly lose confidence and motivation and will, therefore, need some support so they can experience some form of success. Therefore, we need to give them something they can work towards, which will help them start to find some elements of achievement. For instance, in the adaption with a focus on one versus one attacking where the player on the ball has to enter the central area and exit through a different side, we could challenge the player to try and beat the defender before they even enter the central area. The reason that the player will not have much success is because they lose possession of the ball once they have entered the central area, where the practice becomes opposed. Therefore, we need to encourage them not to enter the central area until they are in a favourable position where they can enter the central area almost unopposed, meaning they will have a good chance of successfully exiting the area, as well. To do this, they need to manipulate the ball so their partner has to keep changing their position in the central area, and they need to keep doing this until they identify an opportunity to win a point. By doing this, they are doing the majority of the work needed to go past the defender unopposed, rather than attempting to do it once they have entered the central area, where there is a much greater risk and likelihood that they will lose possession of the ball. This will then enable them to achieve more success and, in turn, increase their levels of confidence.

Another example of providing an individual challenge to support a player finding a practice difficult and needing some help from the coach can be found within Practice C, and in particular, the adaption that has a focus on driving with the ball. In this practice, players low on confidence or who believe they will not get to the end area usually try to slow down and allow the defender to go past them so that it turns into a one versus one situation. As the topic of the session is driving with the ball, we do not want the players to do this, we want them to keep going forward and try to keep the defender behind them. Therefore, the challenge that we can give them could be, can you keep running whatever happens? Or can you get to the end area without slowing down at all? Similarly, in the same practice where the adaption now has a focus on receiving to play forward, once they have taken their touch and progressed forward, they might then try to turn back as the defender approaches to try and protect the ball. The purpose, however, to receive to play forward so the player/team can progress up the pitch. Therefore, the last thing we want them to do is turn back and face their own goal. So, the challenge in this instance would be, once you have received the ball can you stay facing forward? The purpose of these challenges is mainly to change the mindset of the player and get them to do at least an element of what is needed to perform the session topic. Doing so will provide them with a starting point from which they can build upon.

When the player needs encouragement and the practice involves multiple players, the challenge they are given is often just the task they must complete in the practice. So, for instance, in Practice D where the topic is finishing, it is likely that the player who needs some help or encouragement does not attempt to score and, instead, passes onto their partner for them to try to score the point. Therefore, the challenge can simply be, can you have more shots at goal than your partner? For Practice F, where there is a focus on individual possession and the players must dribble through two gates to win a point, the player can be given a challenge of, can you try to win a point for your team the next time you receive the ball? In these instances, the player who needs encouragement is passing on the responsibility to complete the task or win the point to their teammates and, therefore, they are not practising the actual focus of the session. It is important that we push them a little so that they at least attempt to perform the area of the game that the session is focused on, as this is the only way that they will be able to develop this specific element of soccer.

For those players finding the practice relatively easy, we need to give them a challenge that will make it more difficult for them and harder to experience success. So, if we revisit the same practices we used as examples for when a player needed some form of encouragement, we can see how the challenges we provide differ, depending on the needs of the individual player. For Practice B, where the focus was on one versus one attacking, the player could be given a challenge of only having two or three touches outside the central area. This will mean that, at times, the player will enter the central area when they would prefer not to, in other words, if the defender is in a good position to win the ball. It also means they will not get many opportunities to rest and will find the task increasingly difficult as their levels of energy reduce. For the driving with the ball adaption for Practice C, the players could be challenged to start closer to the defender so that the defender has a better chance to catch them. And for the same practice where the topic is now receiving to play forward, the player who is excelling could be given the challenge of, 'can your first touch go into the second area?' Because we want them to go forward, we want the players to have a positive touch that drives them forward. The difficulty with this challenge is that the player needs to be accurate with the touch – if it is too heavy, it might run through to the defender. Therefore, the player receiving the ball needs to be very careful when trying to complete the challenge.

When it comes to the multi-player practices, the players still have to be challenged in a similar way in that they need a challenge that makes the task harder for them. By using the same practices that we used when providing examples for the players that needed to be encouraged, we can now provide further examples of how we can support those in the session that need to be taken out of their comfort zone. For Practice D, where finishing is the topic, players could be given a challenge of trying to score with their first touch inside the second area. In Practice F, where the topic is individual possession, they can be challenged to try and dribble through three gates or not to use the support players, so they have fewer options when they are on the ball, meaning that they will need to keep hold of the ball for longer.

When using individual challenges to support players in a practice, we need to remember that the challenges must be relevant to both the needs of the player and the topic of the session. This will then help ensure that the challenge will be beneficial in terms of the players' development and that it keeps them focused on the session theme. The challenge can encourage them to try something new or move them out of their comfort zone and into the ugly zone where the most effective levels of learning and development can take place.

Group Challenges

Often in sessions and, in particular, during squad practices and game practices (which will be covered in the next two chapters), a group of players need to be challenged rather than just an individual player. This is usually required because the groups in the practice are performing differently. If the players were performing at a similar level, we would not need to give them a challenge, instead, we would just either progress or regress the practice. Therefore, the purpose of a group challenge is usually to make it more difficult for the group dominating the practice, or as with the individual challenges, we can challenge the group finding it harder than their opponents. The difficulty with these types of challenges, is that we have to ensure they are relevant for all members within the group. It is possible that if a particular set of players are doing well in a practice, that it is because of two or three members of the group are excelling and possibly dominating not only the game itself but also their team. Therefore, in these instances, giving the whole group of players a challenge that makes it more difficult would not be the correct decision as some players are not ready for this increase in difficulty. By doing this, the stronger players could then dominate the practice even more, restricting the development of the rest of the group. However, when all the members of the group are contributing to its high level of success, then a group challenge can be an effective strategy to help not only the development of the players in this particular team but all the other players in the practice as well.

An example of how this can be achieved can be seen in Practice G and the adaption that focuses on team possession. If in this particular practice, one team is dominating and retaining the ball quite easily, a team challenge can be given so that possession between the two teams is shared more evenly. Not only does this make the practice more difficult for the team that is excelling it also provides more opportunities for their opponents to practise the session topic. Providing a team challenge of always having the same number of players in each half of the area or asking them to try and play with just two or three touches makes it harder for the team to keep hold of the ball. To achieve the same levels of success that they were experiencing before they received the challenge, the players now have to show higher levels of ability around key aspects of retaining the ball as a team. For instance, if they are asked to try and play with just two or three touches, they need to ensure they have a really good first touch to begin with so they can play a pass with either their next touch or the one after. Or if they are asked to try and retain an equal balance of players between the two halves of the area, the number of options available to the player on the ball is likely to be reduced and, therefore, they will need to ensure that they make the correct decision of when to make the pass and who they should share the ball with. At the same time, their teammates need to work harder and smarter to find positions in the area to support the player on the ball.

These particular challenges also demonstrate really well why we sometimes need to use challenges rather than restrictions. If we restrict the players to a maximum number of touches, we can create unrealistic situations, which would never happen in a game, and that can really disrupt the flow of the practice. Sometimes, a player needs extra touches of the ball due to the pressure they are put under by their opponents, the first touch they had or the quality of the pass received from a teammate. Therefore, if we restrict the number of touches they are allowed, we can produce a situation where the player runs out of touches and end up trying to protect the ball until a teammate can collect it from them. Whereas, if we issue it as a challenge, it allows the player to have an extra touch if or when it is needed. Similarly, if we only challenge them to have an equal number of players in each half of the area, it allows a player to move from one side to the other if they have recognised that their teammates are struggling to retain possession or progress the ball forward.

The final two practices that make up the ten core practices – and are covered in the next two chapters – are game practices, which essentially are games of soccer with some form of rule or restriction added to them. Within these practices, we can use a different type of group challenge where we can give a team or group of players a scenario. When using a scenario, we give the players a situation that might occur within a game of soccer and ask them to adapt or alter how they are playing to meet the demands of the given situation. As with any challenge, we need to ensure that the scenario we provide will change how the team plays in a way that is linked to the topic of the session. It is also important that we do not use the scenario for too long and that we keep giving them different scenarios. The scenarios need to be used as an intervention with a short and sharp impact on the players to give them a real focus for a few short minutes before they can return to just playing the game. The best way to achieve this is by giving it to the team at the start of the game and letting them know it is just for the first five minutes (or whatever timeframe you decide to use) or towards the end of the game. Also, when we tell the players what the scenario is, we also need to help guide them by helping them think about what they might need to do and ensuring it is linked to the session topic.

For instance, if the session topic is on finishing, we might provide a scenario that the team is losing with just five minutes to go in the game. Giving a team this scenario will probably not be enough to encourage the players to do what we want them to do; we will need to use questions and answers to guide them to what we would like them to try to achieve. So, once we have given them the scenario, we could follow it up with a question, which could be, 'what will you need to do now?' There are, of course, numerous responses that the players can give, which will all be correct, but we need them to provide the one that is directly related to the topic of the session. Therefore, if they come back with answers, such as get the ball forward quickly or take more risks in possession, we should definitely praise them for giving some really good information, but we need to help them get to the answer we want them to provide. So, a further question needs to be asked. Brilliant answers, but to score an actual goal, what do we need to do? This should then lead to the players providing the answer we wanted, which we can then praise and reinforce. Fantastic answer, so we need a goal, so we need to make sure we actually try and score, therefore, whenever you have a chance, can you look to try and score a goal?

Other possible scenarios we can give to the players include being a goal up with five minutes to play, which we can link to out-of-possession topics and also some in-possession topics, such as team possession. For the team-possession scenario, we need to get the players to think about keeping the ball so the other team do not get the opportunity to score an equaliser. Alternatively, we could link it to counter-pressing, encouraging the team to win the ball back as quickly as possible after losing possession. A scenario does not always have to be related to the scoreline; we can link it to the context of the game or the way that a team plays, either the team that is receiving the scenario or their opponents. For example, we could provide a scenario where it is a two-legged tie and therefore the main priority for the team is not to concede, but if they can snatch a goal as well, it will be a bonus. This can be used for a topic that is linked to counter-attacking, such as driving with the ball or forward passing. Another way they can be used is to tell a group of players that they are a team that like to play from the back, when the session has a topic of receiving to play forward.

There are a number of different ways we can use a scenario as a group challenge, and the players will usually enjoy them regardless of which type we decide to use. This is because they are scenarios that they will do themselves when playing with their friends outside the training environment. Quite often, children will place themselves in the context of a specific game and/or player that they want to emulate. When they do this, they are creating their own scenario and attempting to play like the player or team they are pretending to be. So, in using scenarios, we are just taking advantage of the creative way that children like to play and placing them into an environment they often place themselves in when playing with friends.

So, to summarise, both group and individual challenges can be an effective way to support players in their development of the session topic. It allows players to be moved away from the environment in which they are comfortable and placed in one they will find more challenging, which will help to provide them with an opportunity to progress and improve around the focus of the practice. In addition, they also help other players in the session as it is likely that challenging one set of players will provide some of their teammates with more opportunities to practise the session topic, therefore, boosting their own development. And although they can be used on their own, they can also be used alongside other types of interventions and, in particular, restrictions, which will increase the impact that it has on the players. An example of how this can be achieved can be seen in Practice G, where the focus is on team possession. One of the possible progressions put forward for this particular practice was to prevent the players from being able to pass to the support players, in other words, they are restricted to being able to pass to only one of their teammates in the area. Along with this restriction, we can also challenge a player or players to try and play with only two or three touches. Therefore, we are not only reducing the number of options available when they are in possession, but we are also challenging them to pass the ball on more quickly, which highlights again how effective a challenge can be when supporting the players in their development.

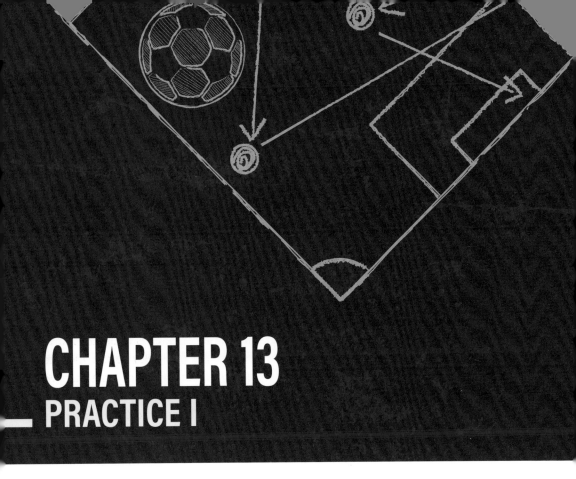

CHAPTER 13
PRACTICE I

The two remaining core practices, are game practices, which are usually used towards the end of the session before the players are given the opportunity to have some free play. During this time, they get to play the game of soccer without any additional rules or restrictions or stoppages by the coach. We usually finish a session with this free play as it is what the players want to do and we want to reward them. However, this free play is a key element of the players' development and the learning process taking place within the session. Giving the players this time to just play the game without any stoppages or interventions gives them an opportunity to try to apply what they have learnt during the previous elements of the session. But before we do this, we need to place them in a game that is conditioned to promote the topic of the session. By doing so, it provides them with the final link of the learning process: a connection between the practices and the game of soccer. These game practices provide the players with this connection by putting them in an environment where they are encouraged or forced to perform the session topic that is very close to the actual game. In this type of practice, the players can develop their understanding of how they need to perform the particular aspect of the game that the session is concentrating on, as well as improving their decision-making skills regarding when to apply it. Additionally, they will also be able to start to build an understanding of why they do it.

This particular game practice uses four small goals rather than the usual two goals, which introduces a number of elements that you would either not find in a normal game of soccer or that you might find, but in smaller amounts. However, with this, you will, obviously, lose some of the main components of the game as well. The most obvious one is the way the players will score points or goals. Replacing one goal with two small goals means that the players will not perform any shooting in the practice. Instead, they aim to pass the ball into one of the small goals or the practice may involve them just touching or nudging it in as they are positioned right next to it. Therefore, the element of shooting is lost in this game practice, along with a number of other components that might not be quite as obvious. For instance, the positioning and number of goals impacts the defensive principles of the game. One of the main principles of soccer is to protect the goal, which is situated centrally, therefore, having two goals positioned in wide areas that the teams have to defend removes this key component from the game. The fact that the goals now being used are smaller than the goals in a normal game helps to compensate for the increase in the number of places that a goal can be scored. The size of the goals makes it much easier for the defenders to block and more difficult for the attacking players to score from a distance.

Although you may lose some of these elements of the game in this particular game practice, you gain increased levels of other key principles of the game. For example, a key principle of the game when a team is in possession of the ball is width. A common request from a coach when the players have the ball is to make the pitch 'big', and part of achieving this is to make full use of the width of the pitch. Having the goals situated close to the corners of the pitch encourages the players to position themselves in wide areas as this puts them in a place where they have a good chance of scoring a point, should they receive the ball. In addition to this, because the defending team have to be mindful of defending two different areas on the pitch, they will be less compact and therefore there will be larger spaces for the attacking team to exploit. This, in turn, provides greater opportunities for the players to find space and to penetrate the opponent's defensive lines, which are two more key principles of soccer for when the team are in possession of the ball.

There are further benefits of having two small goals rather than one central goal as it helps to exaggerate other aspects of the game. Having two options where you can score a point helps to develop players' awareness when they are in possession of the ball.

As they have more than one option, players are more likely to scan larger areas of the pitch, compared with what they usually do in a normal game. The first place they usually look is the area of the pitch where the goal closest to them is situated as this provides them with the quickest route to score a point, and it is unlikely that it will actually require the player to scan as it will be directly in their eyeline. However, just because it might be the quickest route to scoring a point does not mean that it is the best option; it is possible that the opposition will have a number of players blocking this particular goal and, therefore, the player on the ball needs to look to see if the other goal is a better option. Similarly, when a player is situated further away from the opposition goals and are looking to play the ball forward, they are likely to have options either side of the pitch and need to scan both sides. Other components of the game that are usually exaggerated in this particular game include dribbling, which is often seen more due to the small goals that are used, because it will sometimes take a player on the ball to go past an opponent in order to create space, so they have an opportunity to score a point. Other aspects of the game will also be more noticeable in this particular game practice, and it is just a matter of understanding what we may lose from playing a game with this set-up, and also identifying what additional returns we will gain. Then once we do understand what we gain and lose from this practice, we can select when we should and should not use it.

One other aspect that should be considered with this particular practice is the number of players that we use in it. This game-based practice is geared towards low numbers and should ideally be used with approximately four players on each team; otherwise, we can lose a lot of the additional returns outlined earlier. In the set-up shown for the core practice, it shows a six versus six, and this is the absolute maximum number of players that we should have in one game. Once we get above these numbers, we should have two separate pitches, so instead of having a seven versus seven, we could have a four versus four and a three versus three. Therefore, the example shown could easily be split into two separate games, especially if we have the resources and/or room to do so. If we have high numbers in this practice, teams are likely to find it easier to cover the two goals and could, therefore, just 'sit-in' when they do not have possession of the ball, making it really difficult for their opponents, as this will likely mean that there is little space between the defensive line and the goals behind them. A small number of players in the game allows for all of the other benefits with small number games, such as more touches of the ball for the players, constant player involvement, less decision making (which helps younger and less experienced players) and many more.

Practice I: Original Set-Up

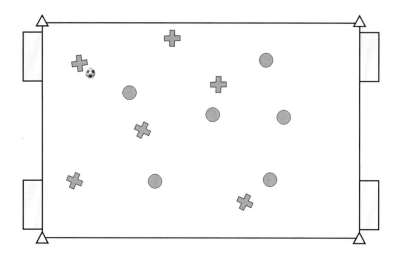

Set-Up

- An area or pitch relevant to the group of players.
- Players split into two teams.
- Two small goals situated at each end of the pitch.
- Teams win a point by scoring in either of the two goals at the end of the pitch that they are attacking.
- If the ball goes out, players restart by either passing or dribbling the ball back in.

Focus

- Can you create space on one side of the pitch by forcing the opposition to defend the goal on the other side?
- Aim to identify and then exploit the space that has been created.

Possible Progressions/Regressions

- Alter the size and/or shape of the pitch.
- Add a further goal at each end of the pitch.
- Alter the positioning of the goals.
- Use different size goals.
- Use a smaller ball.

Practice I: Forward Passing

Now that we have moved onto game practices, the environment becomes a lot more random. In the previous practices, the environment the players are placed in is more variable as they get to practise a specific element of the game in often different situations. So, for instance, if the topic is forward passing, each time the player performs the pass, it will be different from the previous time they did it. For example, the distance and/or the angle of the pass will be different, the positioning of the opposition player or players will also change, as will the amount of pressure they are applying. Therefore, they are getting lots of opportunities to practise the topic of the session in a wide range of different situations. Whereas in a random practice, the players get fewer opportunities to practise the topic of the session but the environment is a lot closer to the actual game of soccer. The important point is that they still perform the focus of the session, more often than they would in a normal game and in an even wider range of situations than they would in a variable practice. So, though the number of times the players practise the topic reduces in a game practice, the number of different ways they perform it and the decision-making process that goes with it significantly increases. So, in this particular practice, the players pass the ball forward across all sorts of distances and angles, not just when they are attempting to score a point but in all aspects of the game. The actions and positioning of their teammates and the opposition players also increase the unpredictability of the practice, and when you add in all of the other actions that the players have to complete within the game, such as dribbling, receiving, turning, defending etc., it adds up to a completely random environment.

One of the really effective progressions with this practice is only allowing the players to pass the ball forward. Obviously, this links in really well with the focus of the practice, and it also forces the players to do something they are not always comfortable doing: passing to a teammate in an advanced position. As discussed in chapter 1, players often look to pass the ball backwards or sideways as it is a safer and easier option than playing it forward where there are likely to be a lot more opposition players and a lot less space to be able to play the pass. Therefore, the pass is a lot more difficult and riskier when it is played forward, compared with a ball that is passed sideways or behind, so it is understandable that players are quite often reluctant to pass the ball forward. By making them play a forward pass, we help to ensure that they actually practice a key component of the game. We just need to be mindful that we do not use it too often or for too long as it could result in the players getting frustrated and losing some level of confidence.

Practice I: Forward Passing

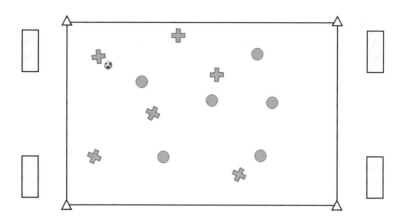

Alteration to Original Set-Up

- The four goals are moved away from the edge of the area. Players can now only score a point by passing it into a goal, the option of nudging it in will no longer be available.
- Players must remain inside the pitch at all times.

Focus

- Ensure there is a clear pathway between the ball and the small goal. If there is not, can you manipulate the ball so that there is?
- Weight and accuracy of pass.
- Selection of pass and the technique to perform it.

Possible Progressions/Regressions

- Alter the size and/or shape of the area.
- Players are only allowed to pass the ball forward. They can travel with the ball backwards, but any pass that they play must be played forward.
- Move the goals further away or closer to the area.
- Add a further goal at each end of the pitch.
- Alter the positioning of the goals.
- Use different size goals.
- Use a smaller ball.

Practice I: Finishing

This practice really encourages the players to shoot early and from all types of angles and distances. Because there are two goals and just one goalkeeper, the outfield players are, understandably, more confident in their play and more likely to attempt the shot on goal, compared with when they are playing in a normal game. And due to this increase in the number of shooting opportunities in the game and the number of shots that occur as a result, the players will find it an enjoyable and exciting game to play. The goalkeepers usually enjoy the practice as well, as they find the task of having to protect two goals really challenging and gain real satisfaction when they make a save. They particularly enjoy it when it involves having to move quickly across the area from one goal to make a save in the other one. We can also increase their involvement and make them feel just as important as the outfield players by including them in the point-scoring system. It could be that their team wins a point for each shot they save, which then also puts more emphasis on players scoring with their shot.

The difficulty of the practice will depend largely on the positioning of the goals. Not only in terms of how far away they are from the area but also their proximity to each other and the angle at which we position them. The further away from the area the goals are placed, the more power needed when striking the ball, which will have an impact on the accuracy of the shot. The amount of distance between the goal and the area will also alter the amount of time the goalkeeper has to react to the shot and get to the ball. Similarly, the distance between the two goals also affects the level of difficulty in the practice. The further apart that we place them, the greater the distance the goalkeeper has to cover to get from one goal to the other. This is another example where we can differentiate between the two groups of players in a practice – the goals at each end of the area do not have to be placed the exact same distances from the area or be equal in terms of how much of a gap there is between each pair. If we feel that one group of players needs to be challenged more than the other team, then the goals they are attempting to score in can be placed further away from the area and/or closer together, compared with the goals their opponents are attacking at the other end of the pitch. A final consideration for how or where the goals are positioned is the angle that they face in the area. Normally, and understandably, they would be positioned square-on to the area but angling them either inward to each other or away from each other affect not only the type of shot the players perform within the practice but also the level of difficulty. If they are angled to face slightly away from each other, it makes it harder for the goalkeeper to protect and therefore easier for the players to score in and vice versa.

Practice I: Finishing

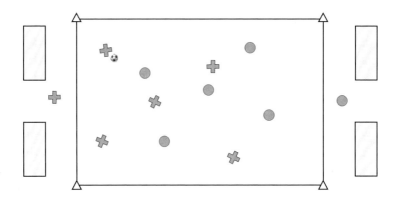

Alteration to Original Set-Up

- The four goals are moved away from the edge of the area.
- The small goals are now replaced by larger goals.
- Each team now has one goalkeeper positioned outside the area that has to protect both goals.
- Players now score a point by shooting into a goal rather than passing it in.

Focus

- Aim to have an attempt on goal at the earliest possible opportunity.
- Decision making: which goal to shoot at.
- Selection of shot: consider where you are in the area and the positioning of the goalkeeper.
- Ensure the shot is on target and struck with power or placement.

Possible Progressions/Regressions

- Alter the size and/or shape of the area.
- Move the goals further away or closer to the area.
- Alter the positioning of the goals.
- Split the area in half, players then earn extra points if they score in the goal that is in the opposite half to where they took the shot from.
- Teams lose a point if the shot is off target.
- After a goal has been scored, the team can no longer score in that particular goal until a goal has been scored in the other goal, that then becomes locked.

Practice I: One Versus One Attacking

Introducing an extra goal at each end of the area and placing them centrally brings the concepts and principles of the practice back towards the main game of soccer. The purpose of adding the extra goal in this central position is to give the players in the middle area something to attack when they have the ball and something to protect when they are out of possession. To give this principle of attacking centrally more emphasis, we can adjust the scoring system, so the teams earn more points if they score in this goal, compared with the two goals positioned at the end of the wide areas. We just need to ensure that if we do this, we do not completely discourage the players in the middle from passing the ball into a wide area. The main purpose of this adaption is for players to try to attack centrally but then also recognise that when it is congested centrally, there is space in wide areas where a teammate has an opportunity to exploit a one versus one situation.

Another decision that we need to make with the set-up of the practice is the ruling once the ball has entered a wide area. Once the ball has been passed into a player situated in one of the wide areas, we need to decide whether we allow this player to pass it back into the central area or whether it must remain in there until either a point is scored or it goes out of play. By not allowing the ball to be passed back into the central area, we force the two players to compete against each other in a one versus one, which is the focus of the practice. As highlighted earlier in the book, it is important that a practice allows the topic to occur regularly and more often than it would in a normal game of soccer. If we allow the player receiving the pass to play the ball back into the middle area rather than attempt to go past their opponent, there is a possibility that what we actually want the players to practise does not occur very often. However, there is also a chance that the players in the wide areas do not find much success and, if this happens, their teammates might be reluctant to share the ball with them. Therefore, whichever rule is selected needs to be monitored and altered when needed.

The positioning of the goals in the practice is also important; the ones at the end of the wide areas are positioned away from the area so the defender cannot choose to stay at the end of the area and block the goal. Moving the goal away from the area does not allow the defender to block it and it forces them to engage the player on the ball. Whereas the goal positioned centrally is just placed on the edge of the pitch so that it is more difficult to score a point in, which will, therefore, encourage teams to play into the wide areas.

Practice I: One Versus One Attacking

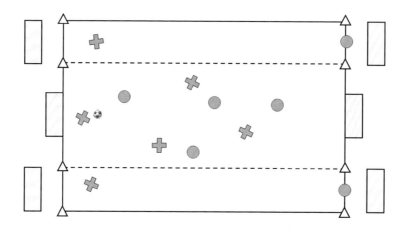

Alteration to Original Set-Up

- The four goals are moved away from the edge of the area.
- A further goal is added at each end of the area and positioned centrally.
- The area is split in three, with the central area wider than the two 'wide' channels.
- One player from each team is placed in each of the wide channels and locked in. All the other players are locked in the central area.
- When their team is not in possession of the ball, they must stand at their end of the area. If the ball enters the area (i.e. it is passed to their opponent), they are released and can attempt to tackle the opposition player.
- Players can only score in the goal that is positioned at the end of the area that they are locked in.

Focus

- Feint and disguise to shift the defender's body weight in a selected direction.
- Shift the ball quickly in the opposite direction.
- Decision making once the space has been created; accelerate to get closer to the goal or attempt to score the point immediately.

Possible Progressions/Regressions

- Alter the size and/or shape of the area/areas.
- Allow an extra defender to enter the wide area to make a one versus two.
- The defender in the wide area does not have to retreat to the end of their area.

Practice I: Shielding

The set-up of this particular adaption provides the players with a picture they will see during an actual game and a scenario where they can rehearse shielding the ball in a game-like situation. Positioning the target areas at each end of the pitch near the goals the teams are attacking produces a similar picture to when the ball is played into a centre forward during a game, and they are unable to play forward due to the positioning of a centre-back directly behind them. In this situation, the centre forward needs to shield the ball until they are able to lay the ball off to a supporting teammate, who is likely to come from a midfield position. This picture is almost completely replicated in this adaption; the ball is played forward into the target player who holds it up until they can identify a supporting player before passing to them. A key element of the set-up is not allowing the target player to pass the ball back to the teammate who played the initial pass to them. Because the target player will be aware of this player as this is where the ball came from, they will be able to play a pass back to them quite quickly, and there is a possibility that they will not need to actually shield the ball. Forcing the target player to pass to a different teammate means that they need to spend time scanning the pitch looking for a viable option to lay the ball off to and, while they are doing this, they need to 'shield' the ball.

The position of the defender from whom the target player has to shield the ball from, depends on the group of players participating within the game. In the initial set-up of the practice, the defender is positioned outside the target area. This allows the target player to get the ball under control before the defender can apply any pressure. However, we need to be mindful that during this time the target player might also identify the teammate they can pass the ball to and, therefore, they either need to spend only a small amount of time shielding the ball or they will not need to shield it at all. If this occurs in the game, we need to allow the defender to start inside the target area. As with other practices that have the same focus, we might need to add an additional rule that the defender cannot attempt to win the ball until the target player has had their first touch to ensure they get an actual opportunity to practise shielding the ball. A final key aspect of the practice is the size of the target area. If the area is too large, it is likely that the task turns into more individual possession rather than shielding the ball. We need to restrict the area that target player has to operate in so that they have limited room to manipulate the ball and instead their focus is to protect it from the defender who is attempting to win it off them.

Practice I: Shielding

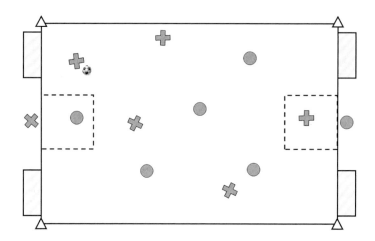

Alteration to Original Set-Up

- Two areas are added (target areas) to each end of the main area and positioned centrally between the two goals.
- One player (target player) from each team is added to the area situated near the goals the team is attacking.
- One player (defender) from each team is positioned just outside the area situated near the goals the team is defending.
- Before attempting to pass into one of the goals, the ball must be played into the teammate in the additional area, who then tries to play it back out again (they cannot play it back to the player who passed it to them).
- Once the pass has been played into the additional area, the defender just outside can enter and try to win the ball off the attacker.

Focus

- Body shape to receive the ball; wide stance and side-on.
- Knees bent and arm up against the defender.
- Control with the outside of the foot, using the foot closest to the player passing.
- Use your body to protect and shield the ball.

Possible Progressions/Regressions

- Allow the defender to start inside the target area.

Practice I: Receiving Under Pressure

This game has a similar set-up to the adaption from chapter 9, with the same focus of the players receiving the ball while under pressure from an opponent locked into the same zones as them. As with the other practice, one of the key components of this game is when the players position themselves in their zone, it is important that when they receive the ball, they position themselves so they have a number of options in terms of where they can go. This is important as it will make it more difficult for the defender in the zone to predict where their opponent will attempt to take the ball and then pass it on. This will be reduced in the final zones, as the main emphasis for the defender in these zones is to protect their goal and, therefore, they might put more priority on ensuring the attacker does not score rather than attempting to win the ball back. This will influence how the attacking player receives the pass and what they do once they are in possession of the ball. If the defender comes tight and tries to win the ball back as it is played into the zone, the attacker needs to recognise that the best opportunity to score a point is to make the most of the defender coming tight and, therefore, opening up the space close to the goal. Once the defender has been unable to win the ball in the initial moments in the zone, it is likely their focus will shift to protecting the goal. Therefore, the attacking player's first touch as they receive the ball while under pressure from the defender needs to give them an opportunity to make the most of the space the defender has vacated, so just 'collecting' the ball is now not enough. Because of this, it is also important that the zones that the players are allocated to, are rotated regularly.

If we have additional players for this particular practice, there are, of course, several options available to accommodate these extra numbers, including increasing the number of zones inside the pitch or just setting up two pitches. Another option, however, is to have a support player at each end of the pitch placed in between the two goals their team is defending. This allows the teams to have more control in their build-up. When the ball is in one of these first two zones, the player with possession is quite restricted in where they can play a pass, and the main focus for the attacker is to try and play forward. However, at times, it is just not possible to play forward, and we want the players to recognise this and understand that sometimes it is the right decision to retain possession rather than to attempt something likely to result in the ball being lost. Therefore, if we can provide an option where they can play backwards, it is definitely beneficial. It also allows the players to practise the topic more, as all restarts can go through the support player who will play into a teammate who will need to 'receive under pressure', plus when they receive it, they again will need to play it back in again.

Practice I: Receiving Under Pressure

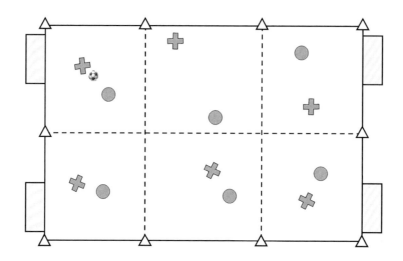

Alteration to Original Set-Up

- The pitch is split into zones, with a player from each team locked into each zone.
- The ball can only be passed between zones (i.e. players cannot dribble into it).
- Players can pass to the two teammates whose zones are attached to theirs.
- Only the players in the zones situated next to the goals can attempt to score a goal.

Focus

- Awareness of their partner's position.
- Body shape as they receive the ball.
- Which foot is used to receive the ball?
- Positioning of the teammate to support the player on the ball.

Possible Progressions/Regressions

- Alter the size and/or shape of the area and/or zones.
- Allow an attacker to join the zone next to them to support their teammate on the ball, but the defender from the same zone can follow them.
- Add an additional ball.
- Use a smaller ball.

Practice I: Team Possession

The set-up for this adaption provides the players with an opportunity to practise playing in a way that most teams enjoy playing, which is by playing out from the back. Forcing the teams to complete a set number of passes in their own half allows the build-up phase of an attack to be replicated. It is important that the teams only have to complete these passes in their own half of the pitch as once they enter their opponent's side, they need to be given the freedom to attack the goals in any way they choose and to try to score a point at the earliest opportunity. If the teams have to complete a number of passes in the attacking half of the pitch, there is a possibility that we will prevent them from playing the way we would want them to during a game. For instance, if, during a match, an opportunity came up to score a goal, we would want them to try and take it straight away. So, what we do not want to happen in this particular game is for the players not to take the opportunity to score a point because they had not completed the required number of passes. Therefore, we cannot restrict them in this part of the pitch, it needs to be part of the build-up phase only. Similarly, what we cannot do, is set the required number of passes needed before they can progress into the next half too high. We do not want to force the teams to keep the ball just for the sake of retaining possession. The number of passes that they must complete needs to help the players to build up the play with controlled possession before being more direct when the opportunity arises.

There are no constraints in the game in terms of where the players can and cannot go, but there is an option to lock players into specific halves of the pitch to help the teams retain possession in their defensive half. For instance, if three players are locked in the defensive half and two are locked in the attacking half of the pitch, it would create an overload in the half of the pitch where the team has to complete the set number of passes. However, because we have now moved into game practices, the decision-making element of the focus becomes more important. So, in this particular instance, the players need to recognise where they are needed on the pitch to help their team achieve their primary goal at that moment in the game. At the early stages of the pass count, most of the players are needed in the defensive half of the pitch to help the team achieve the required number of passes. Then as the team gets closer to achieving the number of passes that they need to complete, they need to start to think about progressing up the pitch. Therefore, some of the players need to decide whether they are needed to help the team complete the remaining passes or if they would be better positioning themselves further up the pitch to be in a position to help the team play forward once the required number of passes has been achieved.

Practice I: Team Possession

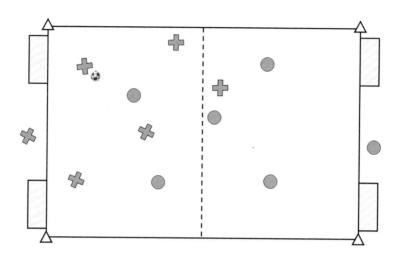

Alteration to Original Set-Up

- The pitch is split in half.
- One player from each team is positioned just outside of the area situated near to the goals that the team are defending.
- Restarts always begin with the player positioned outside the pitch.
- Teams must complete a set number of passes in their half before they can transfer the ball to the opponent's half, where they can attempt to score a point.
- If a team wins the ball in their own half, they must complete the set number of passes; if they win it in the opposition's half, they can go on and attempt to score a point.

Focus

- Identify where your teammate wants the ball to be played to them.
- Angle and distance of support.
- Recognise when to retain and when to pass the ball on.
- Once the set number of passes has been completed, identify the correct time to progress forward.

Possible Progressions/Regressions

- Alter the size and/or shape of the area.
- Change the number of passes that must be completed.

Practice I: Turning

This game provides the players with a range of situations where they need to execute a turn because of the positioning of the goals and also the different directions from which the two teams are attacking. When a team initially wins possession, the direction they need to travel will be different to that in a normal game of soccer. Instead of looking to play forward quickly, they will try to play to either the left or right, in other words, towards one of the two goals they can score in. This will quite often involve the players needing to complete some form of turn so they can travel away from the congestion and towards a goal. Players will also probably perform a turn throughout the game when they are travelling towards one goal and the space they are moving towards becomes crowded. Therefore, the likelihood of them scoring in it is reduced significantly. By turning quickly, they can exploit the space that will be available due to most of the opposition players defending the space in front of the other goal. Players will also perform turns throughout the course of the game because of the way that it is set up; much of the play will occur in the middle of the pitch, which means it will become crowded and tight. To escape this congestion, players need to manipulate the ball, and sometimes this will involve changing direction.

The initial set-up of this adaption does not involve changing the shape of the pitch, so it is played in a rectangle. Because of this, the distances between goals for the two teams will be different; the goals for one of the teams will be much greater compared with their opponent's. This does necessarily mean that one team has an advantage over the other; just because one team's goals are closer together does not mean that it is easier for them to score a point. Although they may need to travel less distance to be in a position where they can attempt to win a point, their opponents have more space when they are attacking, which makes it easier to retain the ball and create opportunities to score a goal. Therefore, using a normal shaped pitch will provide different experiences for the two teams playing the game in it. So, it is important that we swap which goals the teams attack and defend, not to make it fair but to ensure that each team gets to experience both the situations that the pitch produces. Alternatively, the shape can be changed to a square. By doing so, the two teams will experience the same challenges and there is no need to swap which goals the teams try to play the ball into. Using a square pitch will also reduce the size of the area that the game is played in, and it is likely this will increase the number of turns that occur in the game. There are good reasons to use either a square or rectangle for the pitch; it is just a matter of choosing which one we believe is best suited to meet the needs of the players at that particular moment in time.

Practice I: Turning

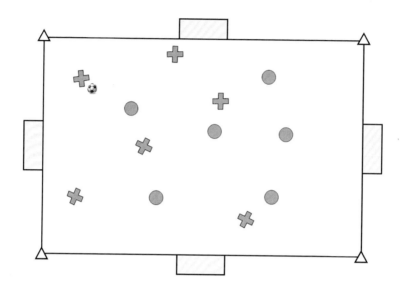

Alteration to Original Set-Up

- The four goals are repositioned. One goal is on each side of the pitch and they are positioned centrally.
- Teams still try to defend two goals and score in the other two. A goal is paired with the one facing it, so one team looks to score one way across the pitch, and their opponents try to score the other way.

Focus

- Identify when you should turn.
- Choice and execution of turn.
- Touches: use the smallest number of touches needed to execute the turn.
- Speed: sharpness of turn and acceleration away from the turn.
- Decision making after the turn: pass, drive with the ball, dribble, etc.
- Possible Progressions/Regressions
- Alter the size and/or shape of the area. Consider using a square.
- Alter the positioning of the goals.
- Use different size goals.

Practice I: Pass or Dribble?

Changing one of the small goals with a set of gates now alters the decision-making process for the players. Previously, practices with the same focus concentrated mainly on the decision-making process of the player on the ball and whether they should retain it themselves or pass it onto a teammate. Although this practice also incorporates this element of decision-making for the player with possession of the ball, it now also requires the same player to consider where their teammates who are available to receive a pass are positioned. For instance, before deciding whether to pass the ball to a teammate positioned on the side of the pitch with the gate, consideration needs to be made whether they are in a position where they have a chance to score a point. So, for instance, the amount of space available in that area of the pitch needs to be considered, as do the number of defenders and their positioning. The same also applies when a player is attempting to pass to a teammate on the opposite side of the pitch, but what they are specifically looking for is different. The requirements for a player to have the opportunity to complete a dribble successfully are not the same as when they are attempting to execute a pass. Therefore, we are asking the players to start to identify what their teammate could do if they pass them the ball. We are helping them develop their understanding of the game.

The decision-making process in the game can be transferred back to the player having to decide whether to pass or dribble by replacing all the goals with gates. Players can then score a point by either passing or dribbling the ball through a gate. Therefore, once they have received the ball in an area of the pitch where they have the opportunity to score a point, they need to choose how they will attempt to do it. First, the player needs to identify whether the pass is a viable option – is there a clear pathway between the player and the gate? If yes, they still have to decide if the pass is likely to be successful and a number of factors need to be considered, such as the distance the ball has to travel, the angle of the pass and the number of defenders potentially in a position to intercept the pass. If after this, the pass does not look like the best option, the player has to make a further decision: do they retain the ball and attempt to win a point by dribbling through the gates rather than passing it or do they pass it onto a teammate? Again, there are a large number of factors the player needs to think about during this decision-making process. Once more, which option we choose to go with when setting up the practice will depend upon what exactly we want the players to develop while they are playing the game.

Practice I: Pass or Dribble?

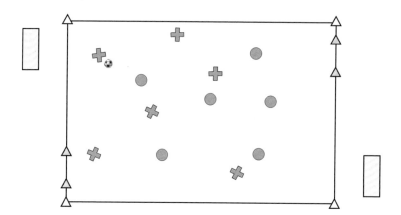

Alteration to Original Set-Up

- Two of the goals are replaced by gates so each team now attacks a small goal and a gate.
- The small goals are moved away from the edge of the area.
- To score a point, teams either need to pass the ball into the small goal or dribble through the gate.

Focus

- Decision making: when to retain the ball and when to pass it.
- Which is the best option to score a point? The gate or the small goal? Take into consideration what is in front of you.
- Do you need to go past a defender? Draw them in before releasing the ball.
- For the supporting players, what type of run could you make? Consider what the player on the ball is heading towards – the small goal or the gate?

Possible Progressions/Regressions

- Alter the size and/or shape of the area.
- Change the width of the gates.
- Move the goals further away or closer to the area.
- Alter the positioning of the small goals and/or the gates.
- Use a smaller ball.

Practice I: Recovery Runs

Not only does this adaption allow the players to practise their recovery runs, but it also allows the defenders to work on their positioning when their team has the ball and also when they are out of possession. For the recovering defender to have a chance of preventing the attacker from scoring, they must position themselves close to the other half of the channel, which is occupied by their teammate. By doing so, they can quickly get across to the attacker breaking through the channel and get themselves in a position between the goal and the ball. Not only will this prevent the attacker from scoring a point straight away but it will also provide the defender with an opportunity to win back the ball. Having two defenders identify that they need to position themselves close to each other installs good habits in the players as it encourages or reminds them to stay 'compact' when their team does not have the ball. Similarly, when the team is in possession of the ball, the two defenders allocated within the channel need to position themselves further apart to provide two options for their teammates. If they remain close together, they are essentially the same option. So again, we install key principles of the game into the players: in possession, they need to position themselves to help the team make the pitch as big as possible in terms of both width and depth. So, as the game is being played, their reaction to changes in possession is really important as they need to alter their position depending on which team has the ball, as they have to during a normal game of soccer.

In terms of the actual recovery run, it is essential the defender that needs to defend against the opponent breaking into the final third recovers quickly enough, as once the attacker has travelled through the channel, they will be in a position to try and score a point. They need to identify that an opponent is about to enter their teammate's half of the channel and adjust their body position to accelerate out of their own half as soon as the attacker breaks out of the central area. They also need to be on the move as soon as the player on the ball is close to entering the channel to get themselves goalside of the attacker as well as the ball. The need to anticipate the movement of an attacker also provides the players with a scenario they will come across when they play the actual game of soccer. Tracking the run of an opponent breaking the final defensive line, either with or without the ball, is a key requirement of both centre backs and full backs. To increase this realism, we can allow a player from the attacking team to break from the central area by dribbling (the original rule) and running onto a pass, with the channel acting as the offside line.

Practice I: Recovery Runs

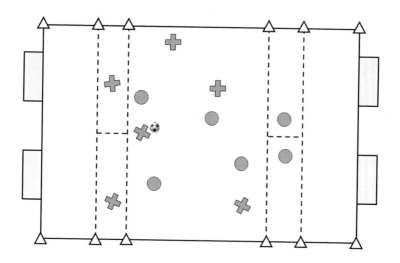

Alteration to Original Set-Up

- Two channels are added to split the pitch into thirds.
- The two goals are moved closer together.
- The channels are split in half with a defender allocated to each half of the channel.
- The remaining players are locked into the central area.
- Attacking players try to break out of the central area by dribbling in and through the opponent's channel.
- The defender in the half of the channel that the attacker enters cannot engage them. Instead, the other defender is unlocked and can recover into the final area, where they try to prevent the attacker from scoring.

Focus

- Do not wait for the danger; try to predict it.
- If time allows, head towards the furthest post of the goal the attacker is approaching.
- Do not engage the attacker; try not to win the ball from the behind, unless there is no other option.

Possible Progressions/Regressions

- Allow another attacker to break out and release the other defender (after the attacker has passed through their half of the channel) to create a two versus two.

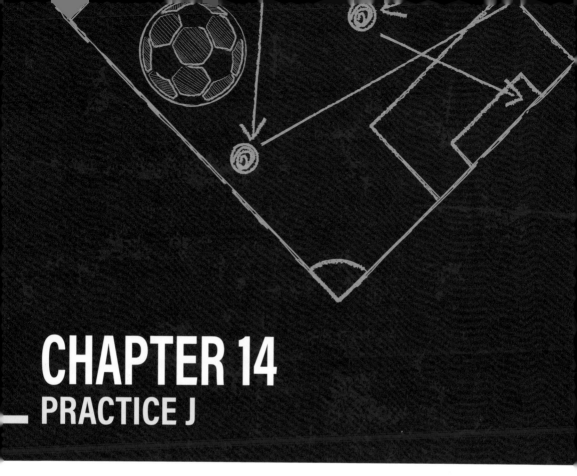

CHAPTER 14
PRACTICE J

Each time a core practice has been introduced in this book, the design and set-up of these practices has moved a step closer and closer to the actual game of soccer. And now that we have got to the final core practice, we have, more or less, reached the full version of the game, and all that makes it different from the game of soccer is that in the core practice the pitch is divided into thirds, and the players are allocated to a specific third. As outlined in the introduction, we need to provide the players with an opportunity to practise everything they have learnt previously in the session in a game situation. This natural progression within the session gives the players a chance to develop and practice the topic before the final challenge of applying it in a game. However, before they reach this final challenge, they have the opportunity to practise the topic in this conditioned game. In this game practice, the challenge is reduced slightly because of the three different areas the pitch is divided into, which helps to reduce the level of randomness the players have to deal with. Then once we head into the final stages of the session, the conditions can be removed from the game. This allows the players to move into a normal game of soccer, where they have the opportunity to apply all the coaching points they were introduced to and learned, while taking part in the previous practices within the session.

The key to this particular practice is the way the thirds are used and how the players are allocated within them. In the diagram that shows how the game is organised, the teams are set up with two defenders, two midfielders and one attacker to replicate similar pictures that will be found within the actual game of soccer. Therefore, in the likelihood there is a different number of players at the training session, we need to try to reproduce similar pictures that are seen within this original set-up. If we take the middle third first, or the midfield area, it is not necessarily the number of players allocated to this particular area of the pitch that is key, it is the fact that the teams have the same number of players. If we consider the midfield area in the full format of the game, it is often characterised as congested with teams attempting to gain an advantage over their opponent. This is usually achieved by creating overloads, which helps the team either retain or win possession of the ball and progress towards the opposition's goal. Ensuring that the teams have the same number of players in this middle third helps create an environment that is crowded and competitive and pushes the players to take ownership and responsibility for their play, in other words, getting on the ball and staying on the ball. It also encourages players from the defensive third to join in and produce an overload. A key element of all the practices in this book is that they help to promote and develop players that are positive and confident when they are in possession of the ball themselves or when a teammate has it. Therefore, when players are allocated to a defensive position, we do not want them to think that they are there just to prevent their opponents from scoring; they need to be encouraged to progress forward and be a continuous part of the team's attacking play. So, when the ball is located in the central third of the pitch, the rule allows one defender to leave their area and progress forward to support their midfielders, creating the overload.

In the two end thirds, there are more defensive players than there are attackers. This is important for both attacking play and also the defensive work that takes place within these areas. When the defenders have possession of the ball, it is normal for them to have an overload as though the opposition may try to win the ball high up the pitch, they will still ensure that they have a number of players holding back, protecting their own goal. A simple equation we can give to young players to help to remind them how many defenders should remain and protect the goal is the number of attackers plus one. No matter how many attackers there are close to the opponent's goal, the team protecting the goal should always have at least one more. This also means that when the defenders have the ball, they will have an overload that makes it more achievable for them to retain possession and progress forward. Within this practice, not only are we providing the players with a realistic situation but we are also encouraging and helping them to begin the team's attack from the back and play controlled progressive soccer, rather than favouring a more direct route, which increases the risk of the team losing possession of the ball. Allowing one defender to enter the midfielder area when their team has possession of the ball goes against the principle of always having one more than defender than there are attacking players. We need to support the players in their decision making and help them identify or even predict when their teammates need support, and also to recognise when they are no longer needed, and it is time to return back to their designated area.

If we then flip it around and look it at the from the attacker's perspective, they will, of course, see things from the opposite viewpoint as, in most situations, their opponents will outnumber them. Therefore, there is a need for them to be creative and positive on the ball if they are going to produce goal-scoring opportunities. To support this, they also need some form of help from their teammates designated to the midfield area. Once the ball has been played into the final third, a midfielder needs to make a supporting run so the attacker has, at least, got the option of passing the ball if they want to. Providing this additional option for the attacker also increases the decision-making process for the defenders, as they will no longer know what the player on the ball will do. If they have no support, they have no choice but to retain the ball themselves, but if a teammate supports them, they have the additional option of passing it on. Introducing these options for the attacker not only increases the number of decisions the defenders have to make but also increases the likelihood they will make a mistake. In addition to this, runs from behind the ball are often harder for the defenders to track and deal with. Therefore, the importance of these midfielders making these supporting runs cannot be understated, and it is a key element of this practice.

Although this allocation of players is the recommended way to set up the practice as it allows key principles of soccer to take place and for game-like scenarios to occur, it does not have to always be played in this exact format. For instance, if we want to make it more difficult for the players to play out from the back, we can change the allocation of players so they are equally matched in the final thirds, the same way that they are in the middle area, or we could even overload it in favour of the attackers. Or we could allocate the players in each of the teams differently, so even though they have the same number of players, they have different formations. So, for example, one team could play in a one, two, two, one formation, as shown in the set-up for this core practice, while the players for the opposition are set up as one, two, one, two. We just need to consider what will occur in the game by doing this and whether it will relate to the topic of the session.

Practice J: Original Set-Up

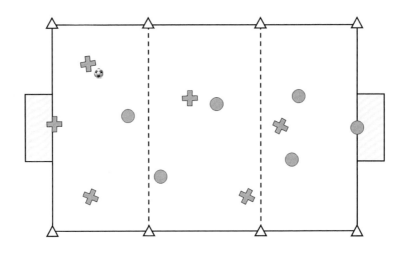

Set-Up

- An area or pitch relevant for the group of players, which is split into thirds.
- Players split into two teams.
- Players are locked into their designated third.
- The ball can only be transferred from one third to another through a pass.
- Once the ball has been passed to the next third, one player from the third it was passed from can follow it.
- When a team loses possession or the ball goes out of play, any players not in their designated third must return to it straight away.

Focus

- How can you exploit the overload?
- Look to play forward. If you cannot play forward, can you play a pass to a teammate who can?
- How can you support the player on the ball when it is in the same third as you and also when it is in the adjoining third?

Possible Progressions/Regressions

- Alter the size and/or shape of the area.
- Players can move into the next third before the ball.
- Release all players (i.e. it just becomes a normal game).

Practice J: Team Possession

As with a number of the adaptions for this game practice, this particular adaption does not require many alterations to be made. Making just a small number of changes to the rules of the game allows the players to play in an environment where there is a clear focus on the team working together to retain possession of the ball. Like the game practice in the previous chapter that also focuses on team possession, it is important the teams only have to complete the set amount of passes in specific areas of the pitch. In this particular instance, it is in their defensive third and the central third. Therefore, just as before, once they get close to their opponent's goal, they are given the freedom to attack the goal in any way they choose, and they can attempt to score a goal whenever they have the opportunity to do so. The only slight difference between this and the practice in the previous chapter is that they need to complete the set number of passes within the first two thirds rather than their own half. This means that the build-up play takes place in a larger area of the pitch. Looking at these two pictures in a game context, the practice from the previous chapter where the passes must be completed in their own half is similar to the situation a team will find themselves in when the opposition set up with a mid-block. And in this particular game, the picture is similar to when the team out of possession and defends in a 'low-block'. In both circumstances, the team with the ball needs to remain patient and retain possession of the ball until the right opportunity arises and they can penetrate the defensive lines and progress forward.

Again, a key element of this practice is allowing the players from the team with possession of the ball, to go anywhere they want in the pitch. Just as with the previous practice, allowing the players to go where they want means they can identify where in the pitch they are needed, and they can also make the decision when they need to start to provide support further up the pitch for their team can progress towards the opposition's goal. We should be mindful however that teams try to complete the required number of passes in their own defensive third. Although there is some risk in this as they are doing it close to their own goal, what they have probably recognised is that there is only one opposition player in this third and it will be extremely difficult for them to win the ball, so it should be relatively easy to achieve the set number of passes. If this happens, we will see scenarios we will not see in a game of soccer. Therefore, changes need to be made to ensure we are providing a realistic environment, and the most effective one would be to unlock the defenders as well, so the safety net of completing the passes in the defensive third is removed.

Practice J: Team Possession

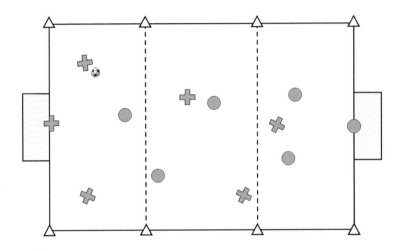

Alteration to Original Set-Up

- A set number of passes needs to be completed before the ball can be transferred into the final third.
- If the defending team wins the ball, they need to complete the set number of passes unless they win the ball back in the opposition's defensive third.
- When the team has the ball, all the players become unlocked.

Focus

- Identify where your teammate wants the ball to be played to them.
- Angle and distance of support.
- Recognise when to retain and when to pass the ball on.
- Once the set number of passes has been completed, identify the correct time to progress into the final third.

Possible Progressions/Regressions

- Alter the size and/or shape of the area.
- Change the number of passes that have to be completed.
- If the numbers allow (there is an odd number of players), use a support player to help the team in possession achieve the set number of passes (they can go anywhere on the pitch).
- Use a smaller ball.

Practice J: Pass or Dribble?

Restricting the number of passes available in specific thirds of the pitch puts a real emphasis on the importance of whether the players retain possession of the ball themselves or pass it onto a teammate. Allowing them only one pass in both the central third and attacking third means that once a player decides to pass the ball, they force their teammate to have it without having the option to share it with anyone else. Therefore, if they are in the central third, they need to get into the attacking third on their own without any support. Or, if they are already in the final third, they will be the only player that can have the shot on goal. The other factor that needs to be considered when these players receive the ball is that their opponents will also be aware they are not able to pass it onto anyone else. Because of this, there is no need for one of them to provide cover and support, and all the defenders can close down the attacker and attempt to win the ball, which further increases the challenge for the player who receives the pass. Therefore, before they pass to a teammate, the player on the ball needs to ensure there is little choice but to release it to the other player and that it is definitely the correct decision. The teammate must be in a better position; otherwise, the player on the ball must keep hold of it until either the situation changes and the pass is now the correct choice or they have been able to move into the next third or have an attempt on goal.

Similarly, how the ball is progressed from one third of the pitch to another is just as important and provides another opportunity for the focus of the session to be practised. It also has a significant impact on the decision-making process in the next third once the ball has been transferred there. By entering the next third of the pitch while in possession of the ball, the attacking player is likely to have some amount of space before they are closed down by a defender. They will be travelling with the ball as they are approached by the defender, which usually makes it easier to dribble and go past a player. Whereas if the ball is passed into a player already in the next third, they are likely to have less space, which can have an impact on the attacker's ability to beat the defender. This does not mean, however, that the better option is always to move into the next third by travelling with the ball; there are, of course, advantages to advancing by passing it as well. Passing the ball into the next third is usually the quicker option, meaning that there is less chance of the team losing possession of the ball and allowing them to get to a position where they can have an attempt on goal quicker. Passing to a player already in the next third means they will be further up the pitch placing them closer to the opposition's goal. As with every scenario in which the player has to decide to dribble or pass the ball, it is a matter of selecting the right option.

Practice J: Pass or Dribble?

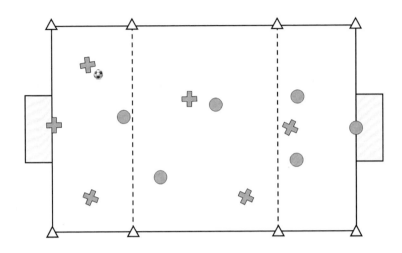

Alteration to Original Set-Up

- The central third is increased in size, which reduces the size of the two end thirds.
- The ball can now be transferred into the next third by a player either passing it or by them travelling with it (i.e. dribbling or running with the ball).
- Once the ball has been transferred into the central third and attacking third, the team can only pass the ball once.

Focus

- Decision making: when to pass the ball into the next third and when to travel with it.
- Decision making: when to retain the ball and when to pass it.
- Can you use the supporting players to help keep the ball individually?
- Do you need to go past the defender? Draw them in before releasing the ball.
- For the supporting player, what type of run could you make? Player in the same third as the teammate on the ball and also the players in the next third.

Possible Progressions/Regressions

- Alter the size and/or shape of the area/areas.
- Allow the players an additional pass in one of or both of the thirds.
- Unlock the players, but the rules around the number of passes permitted in the central and the attacking thirds remain.

Practice J: Cover and Support

As players are now only allowed to enter the final third of the pitch by moving into it with the ball, it provides the perfect environment for them to work on defending in a two versus two situation. One of the defending players needs to close down the player on the ball, while the other provides their teammate with cover and support. The first decision that needs to be made is which player closes down the opponent entering the final third with the ball. This decision should be quite an easy one to make, providing they are positioned correctly when the attacking player heads towards the final third. If they are in the correct position, close together and central, then it is just a matter of which player is closest to the player about to enter their third engaging that attacker, while the other defender provides the cover and support. The positioning and the decision making of the defender who is not closing down the player on the ball will be crucial in whether they will be successful in preventing the other team from scoring. As the first defender approaches the player on the ball, their teammate needs to reposition themselves to ensure they are providing cover and support, as well as protecting the goal and being aware of the second attacker. As the player on the ball alters where the ball is situated on the pitch, whether through dribbling, turning or even passing, it will affect not only the defender closest to them but it will require the second defender to adjust their position as well. In addition, the movement of the other attacker also needs to be monitored, and the defender providing the cover and support will constantly need to monitor and adjust their body position and where they are situated on the pitch.

Restricting the attacking team to only being able to progress into the final third by a player entering it while in possession of the ball makes it easier for the defenders to identify and prepare for who will close down the attacker and who will provide the cover and support. Introducing the progression of allowing teams to enter the final third by a midfielder running onto a 'through ball' significantly increases the level of difficulty for the two defenders. In the original set-up, a team can only enter the final third by a player entering it while in possession of the ball, which makes it quite clear to the defenders how and where the ball would enter. This changes significantly when a pass can be played into this part of the pitch as the defenders need to make more decisions, which also become increasingly complex. For example, the defenders may think they know where the ball will enter because a player with possession of the ball is travelling towards the final third, but if just before they cross the line that separates the two areas they play a forward pass so that a teammate can run onto it, the dynamics of the situation are completely changed. The defenders now have to reassess the situation and make quick decisions to ensure they can prevent the other team from scoring.

Practice J: Cover and Support

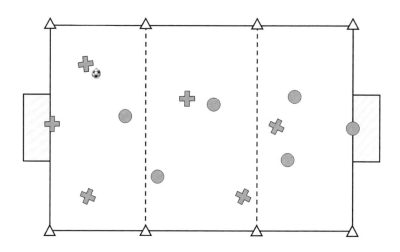

Alteration to Original Set-Up

- To progress into the final third of the pitch, a player must travel into it with the ball (i.e. players cannot pass into the final third).

Focus

- Who closes down the player entering the third with the ball, and who provides the cover and support?
- The second defender should be situated further back than the first defender, so they are in a position to provide cover and support.
- If the player on the ball goes past the first defender or if they pass the ball onto their teammate, the second defender needs to engage the player on the ball (i.e. they become the first defender). The other defender needs to recover and get back to goalside to provide their partner with cover and support.
- Communication between the two defenders: where does the first defender want to show the attacker on the ball? Who is going to the ball, who is providing cover and support?

Possible Progressions/Regressions

- Alter the size and/or shape of the area/areas.
- A player can enter the final third by running onto a through ball. The line separating the final third and the central third acts as an offside line.

Practice J: Individual Possession

The example provided for this particular adaption shows the middle third split in half and the focus of the session taking place within a specific part of the pitch. This particular area of the pitch has been selected as it is likely this is where this part of the players' performance will take place more often than anywhere else. The nature of the midfield area means the spaces within it are often tight and congested, so players need to retain possession of the ball while they look for a route out, whether this is through a pass or travelling with the ball. However, this does not mean that the players will not perform this part of the game in any area of the pitch. Earlier in the book, the need for defenders to be able to retain possession of the ball individually due to the common tactic of the high press was discussed. Therefore, if we wanted to, we could leave the central third alone and section off the end thirds instead to create an environment where the defenders must retain the ball individually (this will require an alteration to how/where the players are allocated). If this option is used, it is recommended that the goalkeeper does all the restarts to ensure there is plenty of repetition. And when the ball is played into the attackers, we can either keep the players locked in so they get to practise the topic or we can unlock them and the defenders, so the focus is solely on the defenders. We can, of course, also flip this around so the attackers become the focus of the game or implement the rule for both defenders and attackers, so more players get to work on the focus of the session.

In the set-up shown for the practice, the main emphasis should be on the midfielders keeping possession while they find a way to either pass forward into the final third or travel there themselves while still retaining the ball. Once a pass has been made into the midfield, the priority should be to keep making progress up the pitch and towards the opposition's goal. The players should be encouraged to keep hold of the ball while they assess the situation and look for a way to get the ball safely into the final third. The key element of this is transferring the ball into the final third 'safely'. As always, we want the players to take risks so that they develop into creative and confident players and, quite often, to create goal-scoring opportunities, they need to take risks with the ball. However, we cannot expect them to constantly take risks, and we need to help them recognise when it is the correct time to take a risk and when they should try to ensure their team keeps possession of the ball. So, in this game, when a midfielder has the ball, they should try to play forward, but the longer it takes them to do this, the greater the possibility that they will lose possession. Therefore, they need to recognise when the safe option of playing to the other midfielder or back to a defender is needed.

Practice J: Individual Possession

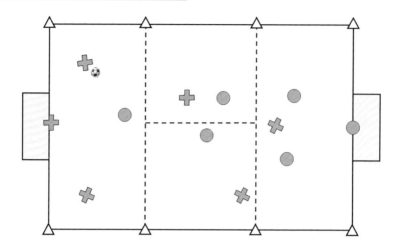

Alteration to Original Set-Up

- The central third is split in half.
- One player from each team is locked into each half of the central third.
- The ball can only be transferred from the defensive third to the central third through a defender or the goalkeeper playing a pass.
- Once in the central third, the midfielders can pass the ball between themselves back to a defender into the striker, or they can travel with the ball into the attacking third.
- The defenders cannot attempt to win the ball until the attacker they are paired up with takes their first touch.

Focus

- Protect the ball, keep your body between the defender and the ball.
- Use the foot furthest away from the defender.
- Use feints/disguise to create space.
- Look to play forward if you can. But prioritise retaining possession of the ball.

Possible Progressions/Regressions

- Alter the size and/or shape of the area/areas.
- An additional player from the team who is out of possession can enter the half of the middle third where the ball is to create a one versus two.

Practice J: Receiving to Play Forward

This adaption provides a good progression for the practice with the same focus as chapter 10, with both practices having a strong focus on the movement needed by the player to receive the pass so they can play forward. To begin with, the defending players are not allowed to enter a channel until the receiving player has had their first touch; the attacking player still needs to collect the ball in some element of space. This is not only because they need to do this in a normal game of soccer, but if they want to receive a pass so they can play forward, they will need to be in space to be able to do this. In addition, in this game, even though defenders cannot enter the channel until the attacking player has had their first touch, they can still close down the area just in front of the channel preventing the attacker from progressing forward. How much emphasis we place on the movement needed to receive to play forward can be controlled by the width of the channels. The narrower the channel, the more difficult it will be for the attacking player as the gap between them and the position where their opponent can position themselves will only be a small one, allowing the defender to close down quickly. Making the channel wider makes it easier for the player receiving the ball as they will have more time and space before the defender has an opportunity to get to them.

Because the players are evenly matched in the central third, and the defenders have an overload in the final third, it will be difficult for the attackers to lose their markers sufficiently to create the space needed to receive the ball and advance forward. In chapter 10, we discussed the importance of the timing of the players' movement to ensure they do not arrive in the area where they want to receive the pass too early, as it will provide the defender with the opportunity to catch up and close down the space. To supplement the timing of this movement, we can now look at what the initial movement looks like, which will help increase the advantage the attacker can gain over the defender. If a midfielder or an attacker wants to receive a pass from the previous area, they need to make a movement towards the ball if they are going to enter the channel that separates the two thirds. If they want to receive it in this area of the pitch, their initial movement should be in the opposite direction to move the opponent far away from it before moving quickly towards it. This change in direction should be executed as soon as the attacker has identified that their teammate on the ball is in a position to play the pass. To make this movement even more effective, just before they change direction, the attacker should give their opponent a slight nudge, again in the opposite direction of where they want to go, shifting the defender's body weight, slowing them down further.

Practice J: Receiving to Play Forward

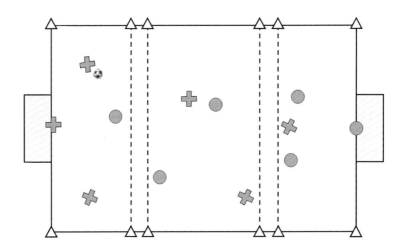

Alteration to Original Set-Up

- The thirds are now separated by channels rather than just lines.
- To transfer the ball from a third into the next one, a player must receive a pass in the channel. This can either be a player from the third where the pass is coming from or from the third that it is being transferred into.
- Defenders cannot enter a channel until the attacking player has had their first touch.
- If a player chooses to play a pass backwards into the third behind them, it does not need to be played into the channel.

Focus

- Identifying when there is an opportunity to receive the ball within the channel; is the teammate on the ball able to play the forward pass?
- Angle of approach and body shape to receive the pass.
- Timing of movement to receive the pass in the channel.
- Pass from the player on the ball needs to be early and onto the furthest foot of the receiving teammate.
- First touch from the receiving player, positive and forward.

Possible Progressions/Regressions

- Alter the size and/or shape of the area/areas.
- Allow one defender to enter the channel.

Practice J: One Versus One Defending

Once the attacking player enters one of the halves of the final third, they will be in a position where they can have an attempt on goal. Unlike some of the previous practices, which focus on this topic, the defender needs to ensure they close down the attacker immediately; otherwise, the opportunity to actually win the ball could be gone before they had a chance to get close enough. At the same time, they need to be mindful that the attacker will be travelling with the ball, and it is likely that they will be doing so with pace and purpose as they will know they will not have any support and, therefore, need to complete the task on their own. So, though the defenders may need to position themselves close to the central third so they can engage the attacker as far away from the goal as possible, they need to be aware that by doing so, they may actually make it easier for their opponent to go past them. By allowing the attacker to enter the final third, the defender is inviting them either to get closer to the goal by beating them in a one versus one or to take the shot immediately. However, once the attacker has entered the final third, the defender will be in a position to take control of the situation and they can dictate which direction they want their opponent to go.

In terms of the direction the defender chooses to try and force the attacker, they have two choices; they can either try and move them away from the goal, making the angle harder to execute the shot and actually score. Or, they can force them inside where they will get closer to the goal and be in a position with more options regarding the type of shot they use and where they try to place it, but they will also be moving towards the other half of the third where the other defender is waiting. The key to the game is the choice the defender makes about which direction they try to force the attacker and the technique they use to achieve this. When which direction to force the attacker, the defender needs to consider a number of factors, such as the attacking player's preferred foot, where they are in the area and the positioning of the defender in relationship to the attacker and the goal. Once the decision has been made about where they want to try and force the attacker, it is then a matter of positioning themselves correctly to give themselves the best possible opportunity to direct the player on the ball into the area that they want them to go. While they are doing this, they also need to look for the right opportunity to try to win the ball. Even though they are trying to make the task harder for the attacker to complete (i.e. to have a shot at goal), forcing them into a chosen part of the pitch does not fully prevent them from doing this. Therefore, if the defender is to actually stop them from shooting, it is likely that they will need to win the ball.

Practice J: One Versus One Defending

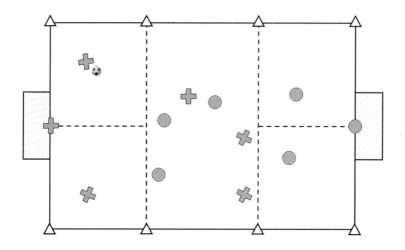

Alteration to Original Set-Up

- The two end thirds are split in half.
- One defender is locked into each half of the defensive third.
- The attacker from both teams is now located in the central third, creating a three versus three.
- The ball can only be transferred from the central third to the attacking third through an attacking player travelling into it with the ball (i.e. players cannot pass into the final third).
- Once they have entered one of the halves of the final third, the attacker can transfer between the two different areas of the third. The defenders remain locked in.

Focus

- Angle and line of approach.
- Body position to be side-on and knees bent.
- Aggressive in trying to win the ball back, take control of the situation.
- How early can you win the ball back?

Possible Progressions/Regressions

- Alter the size and/or shape of the area/areas.
- A player can enter the final third by running onto a through ball. The line separating the final third and the central third acts as an offside line.

Practice J: Finishing

As with the practice in chapter 7, the end thirds of the pitch are channelled towards each of the goals, which, again, encourages the attackers to travel towards the goal, which, in turn, helps persuade the player on the ball to have a shot on goal themselves, rather than share it with a teammate. On a side note, this pitch shape also helps players practise playing out from the back as it encourages some of the players to take up wide positions higher up the pitch. This provides the defenders with the type of passing options they will have during a game.

The proportion of the different thirds and the overall size of the pitch are essential to the success of the practice. We need to ensure that players get the opportunity to have lots of shots on goal; we do not want them spending too much time trying to get to a position where they are within range. We almost want to replicate a game of basketball where the teams are in a position to try and score almost immediately, and nearly every attack results in a player attempting to win a point. Therefore, the pitch size needs to allow the teams to get to the opposition's goal quickly while also ensuring there is enough space to help them retain the ball and progress forward.

The game encourages all types of finishing, and the aim for the players, once the teams have entered into the final third, is just to try and score. The game can easily be adapted so it has more of a focus on a particular type of finish. So, for instance, if we want the game to focus more on close range finishing, we could reduce the size of the final thirds so that once the ball enters these areas on the pitch, it is 'close' to the goal. However, we do not want to make it a rule that a goal can only be scored in the final third as it will create two issues. First of all, the defending team will be aware that their opponents can only score from this particular part of the pitch, and so they will change the way they defend, which produces unrealistic pictures. Secondly, it will prevent the attacking players from having an attempt on goal when they are in a position where they should be shooting. Therefore, instead of restricting them to only being allowed to score from within the final third, we should encourage them instead, which can be achieved through the points scoring system. So, for example, if they score from inside the final third, they are rewarded with two points instead of the normal one point. By doing so, players are still given the freedom to try and score from anywhere on the pitch, which allows them to choose whether or not they should try to score. And this can be the same for any particular type of finish that we want the players to concentrate on – long range finishing, first time finish, etc. We can encourage and reward rather than restrict, which takes away elements of decision making from the players.

Practice J: Finishing

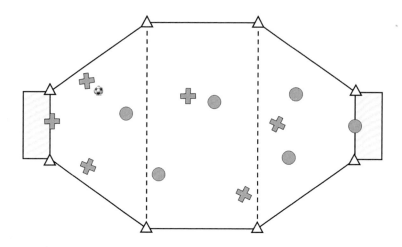

Alteration to Original Set-Up

- The sides of the two end thirds are angled in towards the goals, as shown in the diagram.
- Players are not locked in and can go anywhere on the pitch.
- Players can only attempt to score from the final third.
- If the ball goes out of play, players dribble the ball back in to restart the game.

Focus

- Try to have an attempt on goal at the earliest possible opportunity.
- Selection of shot: consider where you are in the area and the positioning of the goalkeeper.
- Ensure that the shot is on target and struck with power or placement.

Possible Progressions/Regressions

- Alter the size and/or shape of the area/areas.
- Position the goals further away from the pitch.
- Teams lose a point if a player has a shot on goal and it is off target.
- Players can shoot from the central third and win extra points if they score from inside this part of the pitch.
- Extra points are earned through specific type of goals (e.g. header, one-touch finish, etc.).

Practice J: Driving With the Ball

The key focus of this particular adaption is the decision-making process of the player who enters the final third by driving into it with the ball. Not allowing any other players to enter this third until the ball has entered it provides a similar picture to a player breaking the final defensive line in a normal game of soccer. In this situation in a game, it is very unlikely that if a player were to do this, it would be in the central area of the pitch, that is directly in front of the goal, as this will be where the defending team will provide the most protection. Any attacking player breaking the final line in a game of soccer is likely to do so within a wide area of the pitch, and this will be the same within this adaption; the defenders will block the central part of the area, making it easier for an attacker to drive into the final third through a wide area.

Because the players will mainly enter the final third in a wide position, they have a number of options and decisions to make once they have entered it. The best possible outcome for an attacking player breaking into the final third is to drive towards the goal and have an actual shot. To attempt this, the attacker needs to use elements of what they have learnt in the previous practices with the same topic, for example, to get their body between the recovering defenders and the ball and drive towards the goal. However, quite often this is not always possible due to where the attacker breaks into the area, so they have to choose from a number of different options, such as crossing the ball, combining with a teammate or playing a forward pass for another player to run onto. The important part is that they continue to drive forward with the ball, which ensures that the defenders must keep running towards their own goal. As soon as the player on the ball slows down or hesitates, the defenders have the opportunity to get in a position to get organised and face the ball rather than their own goal. To ensure their opponents do not have the opportunity to get into shape and protect the goal, the player driving with the ball needs to keep moving forward while assessing the situation before selecting what they believe is the correct decision. Once they have done this, they need to execute the necessary technique to complete whichever option they chose, for instance, cross, pass, etc. To achieve this, they need the immediate support of their teammates, so they have the required options while driving with the ball. Any delay in this support from their teammates will result in the player on the ball having to slow down or even stopping and possibly turning back. Again, this allows the opposition players to get organised and in a position to protect their goal more effectively. So, while the player on the ball needs to be positive and direct, their teammates need to predict that they are going to break out, so that they can start their supporting runs early.

Practice J: Driving With the Ball

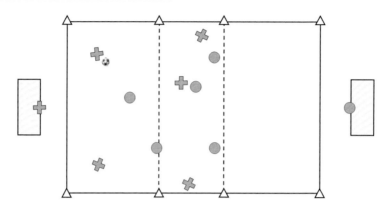

Alteration to Original Set-Up

- The goals are situated a small distance from the pitch.
- The central third is reduced in size, which increases the size of the two end thirds.
- The game always restarts with a goalkeeper who plays into the first third.
- Teams are restricted to the first third and the central third.
- Teams can only enter the attacking third by a player driving into it with the ball.
- Once an attacker player has entered the final third, all the other players are also allowed to enter it.

Focus

- Identify when there is an opportunity to drive with the ball.
- First touch: strong touch out of your feet and forward.
- Identify whether or not you need to get your body between the ball and the defender.
- Strong controlled touches to allow long strides while running.
- Shift the ball off the initial line when needed.
- Decision making once you have entered the final third.
- Technique to execute the next task: pass, shot, etc.

Possible Progressions/Regressions

- Alter the size and/or shape of the area/areas.
- Limit the number of players that can enter the final third.
- Maximum number of passes before the ball has to go into the final third.
- Restrict the number of passes that can be made once the ball has entered the last third.

Practice J: Counter-Press

As with the other practices that focus on counter-pressing, we need to ensure that the player or team lose possession of the ball, so a situation is created where they need to win it back. In this particular game, this need to win the ball back quickly is increased by encouraging the teams to have all their players in either the central or attacking third when in possession of the ball. Because the defending team are restricted to these two areas of the pitch, and the attacking team are not allowed to play back from the central third, we make it difficult for the set number of passes to be completed. Therefore, it is likely that the team in possession of the ball will need all their players in these two thirds of the pitch to give them a chance of completing the required number of passes. With all their players high up the pitch, they are exposed to a counter-attack should they lose the ball, and with the team winning the ball allowed only a small number of passes, this encourages them to play direct and forward quickly. All of this creates an environment where the team that loses the ball needs to win it back in the area that they lost it quickly.

Because of the situation we created with all the players positioned in the final two thirds of the pitch, the space where the majority of the game will take place will be quite restricted. So, when a team does lose the ball, the spaces between their players are likely to be smaller than they would be in a normal game of soccer. This provides an opportunity to concentrate on winning back possession immediately, by more than one player closing down the opponent with the ball. It is important that the players aiming to win back possession do not all try to win the ball off their opponent. If we want more than one player to press a player on the ball, we need to ensure they understand what is needed; otherwise, there could be a number of different opportunities to get through the press. Before they decide whether to press in numbers, the players need to calculate whether they are likely to arrive in time to help stop the opponent from getting out of the area that they are in. To do this, a number of factors need to be considered, such as the distance they need to travel and the positioning of their teammates. In addition, a key factor to consider is the type of possession the player on the ball has – do they have good possession? If the opposition player has good control of the ball, it will be much easier for them to move it on and avoid the counter-press. If the player does not have the ball under control because of their touch, the pass that was played into them or because they have only just won the ball, this can be a trigger that the opposing players can use to identify that it is an opportunity to press in numbers.

Practice J: Counter-Press

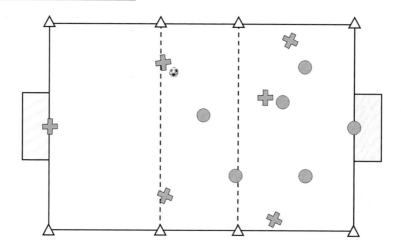

Alteration to Original Set-Up

- The central third is reduced in size, which increases the size of the two end thirds.
- The game always restarts with a goalkeeper who plays into the first third.
- When this happens, the defending team are not allowed into their attacking third.
- The team starting with the ball must then complete a set number of passes in the central third and the attacking third.
- Once they enter the central third, they cannot go back into their own defensive third.
- If the other team wins the ball, they can attack immediately and become unlocked, but they only have a set number of passes before they have to try and score.

Focus

- Immediate reaction to win back the ball: determination and aggression.
- Awareness of where in the pitch your team has lost the ball.
- Recognising where your teammates are situated and what they are attempting to do.
- Counter-press or move into a block?

Possible Progressions/Regressions

- Alter the size and/or shape of the area/areas.
- Increase the number of passes that need to be completed.
- Restrict the team that starts with possession of the ball to a set number of touches.

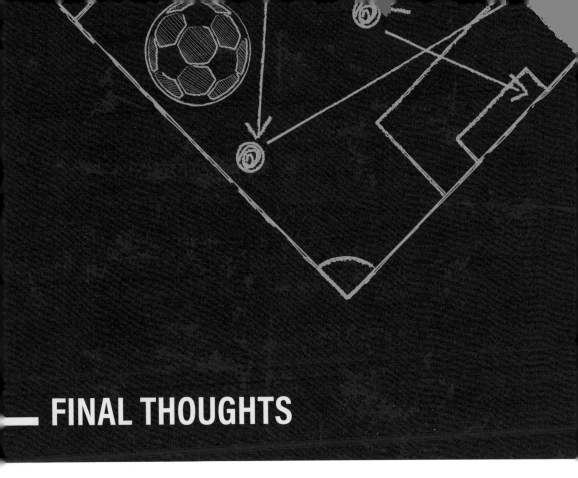

FINAL THOUGHTS

Whether you use all 100 practices to form a curriculum for a full season of training, or if you choose to use only a small number of the practices alongside a number of your own, the purpose of the book remains the same. The game of soccer is quite simplistic in terms of how it is played and what is needed to be successful. As an invasion game, the main principle is to protect your own goal while also trying to progress forward towards your opponent's goal, with the overall aim of scoring a point or goal. The complexity of soccer comes in the form of the different challenges within it and the unpredictable and random actions of those playing the game. It makes sense that when the players are training, they are placed in an environment that replicates the game of soccer and allows them to develop their decision-making skills through solving similar problems that they will come across when playing a match. They do not want to spend time working out what they have to do within the practice when, instead, they could be active and learning the topic of the session. The practices need to be simplistic in their design and easy for the players to understand, so they can concentrate on playing and learning. Making the practices straightforward in terms of the set-up and the rules helps ensure it replicates the environment in which the game of soccer is played.

We need to consider what it is we want young soccer players to learn from these practices, and what they need to develop. We need to understand that we have a significant number of years to work with the players, and their development should be seen as a long-term process, in which they take small steps to reach the endpoint: the full version of the game. Understanding and recognising this allows us to identify and concentrate on what we see as the key aspects of the game that are crucial to the players' development. Concentrating on these important areas of the players' performance provides the essential foundations for everything they need to succeed when they come to the end of their developmental journey.

Making sure every practice is both fun and competitive helps ensure the players enjoy them. In turn, this will ensure they do not get bored taking part in the same practices, and that they are happy to keep playing them each time they turn up for training. This is important, not just because we want to use the practices regularly throughout the season but also because placing the players in an environment that is fun, challenging and competitive is usually the most effective way for children to learn. If the players are having fun being challenged and solving problems, it is likely they will not even consider it as training or something they have to learn; they will see it as playing a game with their friends. In addition, if the players enjoy taking part in a particular practice, they will not only be happy to see it when they come to training, they will probably even ask to play it again, the same way they will always ask: when are we going to play a game?

Using the same practices to create a training curriculum for the full season not only benefits the players in terms of providing them with more ball rolling time and giving them the opportunity to concentrate on playing and developing, but it also helps the coach. As well as removing the pressure of having to produce a number of practices each week, it also allows the coach to concentrate solely on the players' performance in the session. If different practices are used every week, a significant amount of the coach's time is spent observing the practice rather than the players to ensure it is appropriate and relevant for the players and the session topic and whether any changes are required. There is, of course, also the possibility that when we use a practice for the first time, it does not work in terms of allowing the players to practise and develop around the session focus. Or maybe it just does not work as an actual practice; for instance, the players are not active enough or what we ask them to do is far too difficult or impossible. Therefore, rather than observing and analysing the players and identifying who needs help, we can end up focusing on the practice design and set-up. However, if we use a practice that we know works because we have used it many times before, we do not need to spend much time, if any at all, checking to see if any adjustments are needed. This lets the coach fully focus on the performance of the players and identify their individual needs.

Having a training programme for the full season in place and using practice designs we know are suitable for the different topics that form our training curriculum allows us to focus completely on the performance of the players. But if we are going to support them completely in their developmental journey, we need to fully understand the different elements of the performance. For instance, we need to know what the different components are that make a successful pass or what we need specifically to ensure that a dribble is effective, in other words, we need to know the coaching points of each individual element of the training curriculum. And then, once we know this information, we also need to understand the different strategies that we can use to share this knowledge with the players. We can then help the players develop around each coaching point for all the different parts of the training curriculum. How and when we do this is a key ingredient in the development of the players. This includes recognising when the full group of players will benefit from a stoppage and support from the coach and when it would be more suitable and beneficial to work with an individual player while the rest of the group continues to play, allowing them to take full advantage of more ball rolling time.

Getting all these key components of a training session right will go a long way towards creating the perfect environment for the players to develop all aspects of their performance and get as close as possible to reaching their full potential. And though this may sound reasonably simple, it is, of course, far from it. Therefore, where possible, we need to make the process as easy and simple for both ourselves and the players. Using the practices provided throughout this book allows you to focus fully on supporting the players while they are performing rather than worrying about whether the practice you have designed or borrowed is working. At the same time, the players can concentrate on just playing instead of spending time working out what they are meant to be doing in a practice not relevant for their development. Consequently, these 100 practices allow the players to maximise their playing time and work on their development, as well as provide the coach with the opportunity to coach.

PRAISE FOR *THE INTELLIGENT SOCCER COACH*

Superb book for all football coaches

A superb read, full of thought-provoking principles and ideas. Aimed at youth team coaches, there's a lot you can take into coaching adults as well. Sure, this includes some crisply laid out session plans with ideas for adaptations and progressions to use directly when working on different topics. But the genius of this book is the questions it encourages you to ask yourself about your own coaching process and about yourself as a coach. Could not recommend more highly.

–Tony Allen

Something for everyone

This is a very well thought through and carefully put together book. Very easy to read and digest, and I have taken lots of carefully considered points into my coaching sessions, little tweaks here and there that have made sessions even better for the players. I would highly recommend this book.

–Damian Mills

Essential reading for all grassroots coaches

The best Christmas present a coach could get; it's a brilliant read, full of thought-provoking ideas, lots of valuable insight on understanding your players and how to get the best from them. The sessions are great, easy to adopt and adapt to your level of player. Your team will only benefit from these ideas. I will go back to this book over and over again.

–Robert Short

Essential reading

I think all grassroots clubs should keep a copy of this book for all new and current coaches to read. It breaks down the fundamental elements of the game, but also emphasises the reason we get into coaching, i.e. for the kids. Football is about enjoyment; kids love competing but most of all they love playing the beautiful game. Any child who gets coached by adults who embrace the ideas in this book will love football as much as we coaches do.

–Dave Parsons

A must read/must keep coaching resource

This book is a must read for any coach. As the owner of around 20 coaching books, I can honestly say that this book added something valuable that no other book has to date– guidance that is akin to a framework and provides real clarity for my coaching methods going forward. I will certainly refer back to this book at regular intervals.

Credits

Cover and interior design: Anja Elsen

Layout: DiTech Publishing Services, www.ditechpubs.com

Cover and interior graphics: © AdobeStock

Interior figures: Courtesy of Carl Wild

Managing editor: Elizabeth Evans

Copy editor: Sarah Tomblin, www.sarahtomblinediting.com

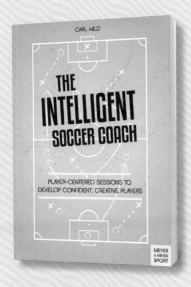